Trade in Zimbabwe

DIRECTIONS IN DEVELOPMENT
Trade

Trade in Zimbabwe

Changing Incentives to Enhance Competitiveness

Richard Newfarmer and Martha Denisse Pierola

1818 H Street NW, Washington, DC 20433
Telephone: 202-473-1000; Internet: www.worldbank.org

1 2 3 4 18 17 16 15

ISBN (paper): 978-1-4648-0446-5
ISBN (electronic): 978-1-4648-0447-2
DOI: 10.1596/978-1-4648-0446-5

Cover photo: ©Nadia Piffaretti. Used with permission. Further permission required for reuse.
Cover design: Debra Naylor, Naylor Design

Library of Congress Cataloging-in-Publication Data

Newfarmer, Richard S.

Trade in Zimbabwe : changing incentives to enhance competitiveness / Richard Newfarmer and Martha Denisse Pierola.
pages cm. — (Directions in development)
Includes bibliographical references.
ISBN 978-1-4648-0446-5 (alk. paper) — ISBN 978-1-4648-0447-2 (eISBN)
1. Zimbabwe—Commerce. 2. Industrial policy—Zimbabwe. 3. Zimbabwe—Foreign economic relations. I. Pierola, Martha Denisse. II. Title.
HF3902.N494 2015
381.096891—dc23 2015012226

Contents

Boxes

Figures

Tables

Acknowledgments

This work was produced by a team led by Martha Denisse Pierola and under the overall guidance of Nadia Piffaretti. The team members were Robert Davies, Lawrence Edwards, Ana Fernandes, Seedwell Hove, Robert Kirk, Aaditya Mattoo, Crispen Mawadza, Richard Newfarmer, Dirk van Seventer, and Reza Vaez-Zadeh. Martha Denisse Pierola and Richard Newfarmer prepared this report based on the following analytical papers:[1]

Ana Fernandes and Robert Kirk, 2013, "Creating Incentives for New Dynamism in Zimbabwe's Merchandise Exports: The Role of Trade and Industrial Policies"

Lawrence Edwards and Robert Kirk, 2013, "The Opportunities and Constraints for Stronger Regional and Global Integration of Zimbabwe"

Aaditya Mattoo and Eshrat Waris, 2013, "Zimbabwe: Empowerment through Services Trade Reform"

Seedwell Hove, Crispen Mawadza, and Reza Vaez-Zadeh, 2013, "Zimbabwe—Trade Finance as an Instrument of Trade Openness: Issues and Challenges in a Dollarized Economy"

The authors of this report also benefited from the active comments of these contributors on earlier drafts. The analysis also drew from several papers from World Bank staff, including the series of notes prepared for the discussion with the Government on Economic Growth (2012)[2] and the Trade and Transport Facilitation Assessment—Zimbabwe.[3] Other contributions were also important. Brian Mureverwi contributed to the preparation of the note on trade and industrial policies (Fernandes and Kirk). Seedwell Hove and Mark Oxley conducted interviews of exporters for the notes on trade policy (Fernandes and Kirk) and regional integration (Edwards and Kirk).

The report has also benefited from comments by Enrique Aldaz-Carroll, Paul Brenton, Phillip English, Michael Ferrantino, Nadia Piffaretti, Gael Raballand, Jose Guilherme Reis, Markus Scheuermaier, and Charles Schlumberger and the generous support and feedback provided by staff of Zimbabwe's Ministry of Finance, Ministry of Industry and Commerce, and the Reserve Bank.

This report was presented at a high-level seminar ("Zimbabwe in the World Economy") in Harare in March 2014 to an audience of representatives from the public and private sectors and reflects the state of policy through mid-2015 when this book went to press.

The authors offer special thanks to Nadia Piffaretti and Paul Brenton for their helpful suggestions on all sections of the report, to John Panzer for his generous managerial support, and to Ehui Adovor for her assistance coordinating the editing of this report.

The authors gratefully acknowledge the support of the Zimbabwe Analytical Multi-Donors Trust Fund, Grant No. 013434. The findings, interpretations, and conclusions expressed in this study are entirely those of the authors. They do not necessarily represent the views of the World Bank, its executive directors, or the countries they represent.

Notes

1. http://go.worldbank.org/VUUHNGHSI0.
2. "From Economic Rebound to Sustained Growth," 2012. Team led by Nadia Piffaretti.
3. "Trade and Transport Facilitation Assessment in Zimbabwe," 2012, by M. Masiwa and B. Giersing, World Bank, Washington, DC.

About the Authors

Richard Newfarmer is a country program adviser with the International Growth Centre (IGC) and the IGC's country director for Rwanda, Uganda, and South Sudan. The IGC is a joint venture of Oxford University and the London School of Economics and provides independent, research-based policy analysis at the request of governments of selected low-income countries in Africa and Asia. He is also on the Advisory Board of the World Trade Organization (WTO) Chairs Program and a senior fellow (nonresident) at the World Trade Institute in Bern, Switzerland, and consults with international organizations, including the World Bank, the Organisation for Economic Co-operation and Development (OECD), and the International Trade Centre. Recently, he coauthored *Trade and Employment in a Fast Changing World* for the OECD (2012) and *Managing Aid for Trade and Development Results: The Case of Rwanda* (OECD, 2013) and has been a principal author of World Bank reports on trade and competitiveness in Botswana (2012) and Malawi (2014).

Before this, Mr. Newfarmer was the World Bank's special representative to the United Nations and WTO, based in Geneva, Switzerland, after serving in several posts at the Bank, including in the International Trade Department, the Prospects Group, and the East Asia and Latin American regions. Besides leading numerous country studies at the World Bank on trade, macroeconomics, and public finance, Mr. Newfarmer has written on foreign direct investment, with publications in the *Journal of World Trade, Cambridge Journal of Economics, Journal of Development Economics,* and *Foreign Policy*, among others. Before joining the World Bank, Mr. Newfarmer was a senior fellow at the Overseas Development Council and was on the economics faculty at the University of Notre Dame. Mr. Newfarmer holds a PhD and two MAs from the University of Wisconsin and a BA (highest honors) from the University of California at Santa Cruz.

Martha Denisse Pierola is an economist in the Trade and International Integration Unit of the Development Research Group of the World Bank. She has published several papers on export growth and exporter dynamics and cocreated the Exporter Dynamics Database—the first-ever global database on exporter growth and dynamics, based on firm-level export data. Her research studies the role of large exporters in driving trade patterns and export growth, and examines how exporter behavior varies with the stage of development. She was the leader of the team conducting the World Bank study on trade, competitiveness, and regional integration in Zimbabwe.

Ms. Pierola has worked on issues related to regionalism, trade costs, and trade and productivity. Before joining the World Bank, she worked as an economist for the Peruvian government (INDECOPI) and also consulted for the private sector and other international organizations. She has a PhD in economics from the Graduate Institute of International Studies in Geneva, Switzerland, and a master of international law and economics from the World Trade Institute in Bern, Switzerland.

Abbreviations

AEB	anti-export bias
AGOA	African Growth and Opportunity Act
BASA	bilateral air services agreement
BAZ	Broadcasting Authority of Zimbabwe
BPO	business process outsourcing
BRTA	bilateral road transport agreement
COMESA	Common Market for Eastern and Southern Africa
DIMAF	Distressed and Marginalized Areas Fund
EAC	East African Community
ERP	effective rate of protection
EU	European Union
FDI	foreign direct investment
GVC	global value chain
HS	Harmonized System
IBM	Integrated Border Management
IEE	Indigenization and Economic Empowerment
IEEA	Indigenization and Economic Empowerment Act
IT	information technology
MB	megabyte
MFN	most favored nation
MIC	Media and Information Commission
MTP	Medium-Term Plan
NRZ	National Railways of Zimbabwe
NTB	nontariff barrier
NTM	nontariff measure
NTP	National Trade Policy
OSBP	One Stop Border Posts
PGM	Platinum Group Metals
POTRAZ	Postal and Telecommunications Authority

QUASAR	Quantitative Air Service Agreements Review
RBZ	Reserve Bank of Zimbabwe
SADC	Southern African Development Community
STRI	Services Trade Restrictiveness Index
UAF	Universal Access Fund
USF	Universal Services Fund
VAT	value added tax
VoIP	Voice over Internet Protocol
WEF	World Economic Forum
WTO	World Trade Organization
ZETREF	Zimbabwe Economic and Trade Revival Fund
ZIMRA	Zimbabwe Revenue Authority

Overview and Summary of Major Conclusions

Introduction

Since the country's earliest days, trade has been integral to Zimbabwean civilization. In modern times, trade has been a driver of economic growth, rising incomes, and increasing employment. Since 1980, increases in exports have been positively associated with increases in national income. However, despite Zimbabwe's regional location, resource base, and relatively well-educated labor force, since 2005 export performance has fallen well short of its potential to power the Zimbabwean economy to high rates of growth.

The world economy today presents Zimbabwe with new opportunities that are more conducive to using trade to grow now than two decades ago. Falling communications and transportation costs have created new trading opportunities and new sources of investment—especially for landlocked economies. The emergence of global value chains has allowed developing countries to carve out whole segments of production, industrialize more quickly, and develop new sources of comparative advantage. This process has created opportunities for trade specialization and economic diversification that were unheard of at the time of Zimbabwe's independence in 1980. Moreover, better communication and transportation—more connectivity—have also opened up whole new sectors to international trade, most important among them services, which in itself provides new growth opportunities. Finally, China's presence in the global market has grown since the 1990s and, together with a more open India and Asia, China provides a vast and dynamic new market as well as a source of investment and low-cost imports, both consumer goods and inputs that can be further fabricated in global and regional value chains.

However, this new world also entails challenges. Many countries, both rich and poor, are already seizing these opportunities, so competitiveness in policy is as important as traditional comparative advantage. Many developing countries, including in Africa, are working hard to reform their business environments to encourage their own citizens to invest at home rather than abroad, and to attract prospective foreign investors, including from their respective diasporas. Even countries with abundant natural resources face competition in policy.

It is against this backdrop of changing international opportunities and changing sources of policy competitiveness that this report reviews ways Zimbabwe might use trade to elevate growth to a higher and sustainable level.

Trade Performance: A Retrospective

Trade Is a Sputtering Growth Engine

For the last decade or more, export performance has been insufficient to power the Zimbabwean economy to reach its high growth and job-creating potential. From the mid-1990s to 2009, export values actually declined in nominal terms (figure O.1). Since the economic rebound beginning in 2009, and with the support of record international price levels, exports of minerals—notably diamonds, platinum, gold, and other products—have injected new life into the economy. However, comparator countries have outperformed Zimbabwe, even taking into account new exports (figure O.2). In 2000, Zimbabwe exported roughly three times what Zambia exported in nominal terms. Since the crisis, Zambia's total exports are, on average, twice the size of Zimbabwe's.

In Zimbabwe, Trade Is Firing on Only One Cylinder

When measured in nominal values, agriculture and manufacturing show some signs of recovery (figure O.3, panel a). However, adjusting for the effects of changes in world prices and looking at volumes, the underlying picture is much

Figure O.1 Zimbabwe's Total Exports, 1990–2012

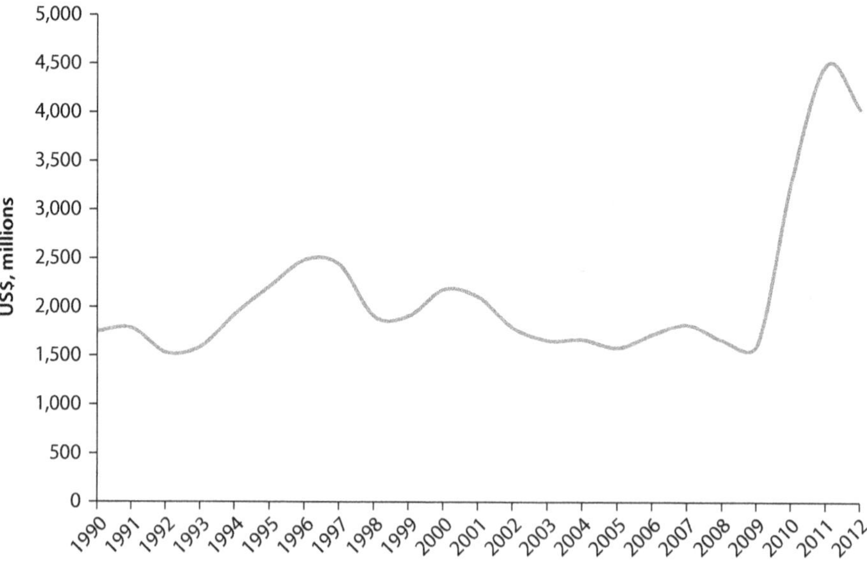

Sources: Edwards and Kirk 2013; Reserve Bank of Zimbabwe data at http://www.rbz.co.zw/.

Figure O.2 Zimbabwean Exports Compared with the Best Performers in the Region, 1990–2012

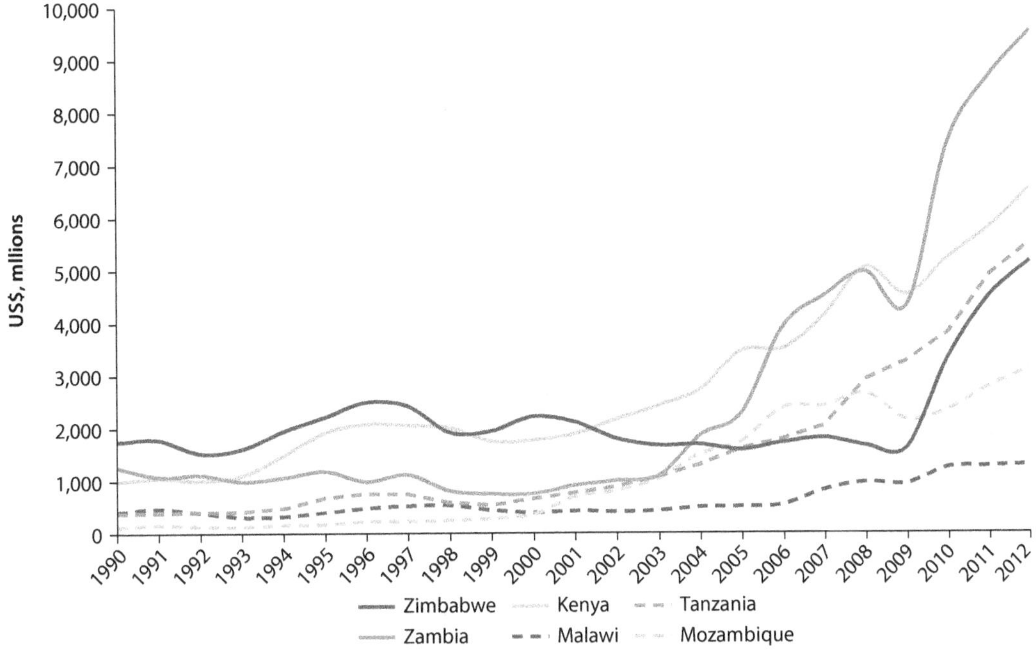

Sources: Edwards and Kirk 2013; Reserve Bank of Zimbabwe data at http://www.rbz.co.zw/.

bleaker—volumes in agriculture and manufacturing remain well below their peaks of 2000–01 (figure O.3, panel b). Agricultural exports, other than tobacco and cotton, have lost their once dominant role in the region, and have made only marginal contributions to the post-2009 recovery. They are no longer a source of diversification. Manufacturing has continued to wither in secular decline, and even though many firms are operating at less than 60 percent capacity, manufacturing firms seem unwilling or unable to sell their wares abroad. Services exports also have grown slowly.

A careful decomposition of export growth underscores this point (figure O.4). During the 1990s, agriculture was by far the main contributor to export growth; however, the contributions of the other sectoral drivers of export growth—mining, manufacturing, and services—although much lower, were relatively balanced. But by the start of the new century, a new pattern emerged. Only minerals contributed significantly and positively to export growth until the post-stabilization period. The trade engine was firing on only one of four cylinders

Diversification, a National Objective, Is Not Occurring

In its 2011 National Trade Strategy, the government rightly sought to diversify the export base, increase the technological content of exports, and leverage trade into better jobs. This objective was confirmed in the October 2013 Zimbabwe Action Plan for Sustainable Socio-Economic Transformation. One way to view the diversification process is through the lens of "product varieties." This method

Figure O.3 Export Values and Volumes since Dollarization, 1993–2012

a. Export values since dollarization

US$, millions

2,500
2,000
1,500
1,000
500
0

1993 1994 1995 1996 1997 1998 1999 2000 2001 2002 2003 2004 2005 2006 2007 2008 2009 2010 2011 2012

Manufacturing Agriculture Mining Services

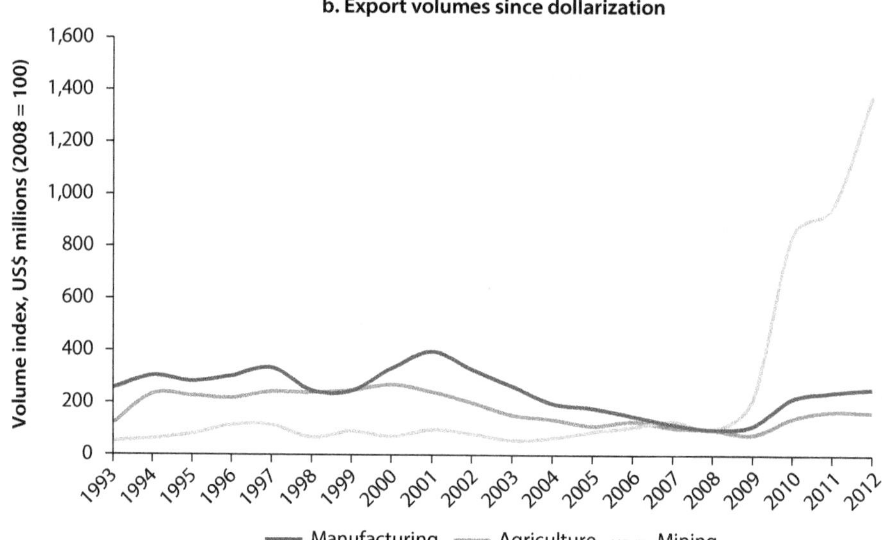

Source: Reserve Bank of Zimbabwe data at http://www.rbz.co.zw/.

simply counts the number of products sold to each national market around the world, thereby capturing efforts to introduce new products to new markets. Whereas most countries in the region have expanded the number of varieties they export, since 2000 Zimbabwean trade has gone in the opposite direction—selling fewer products to fewer markets (figure O.5). Most of this decline is associated not with a reduction in national markets served but with a reduction in the number of products exported.

Figure O.4 Export Growth Decomposition, 1993–2012

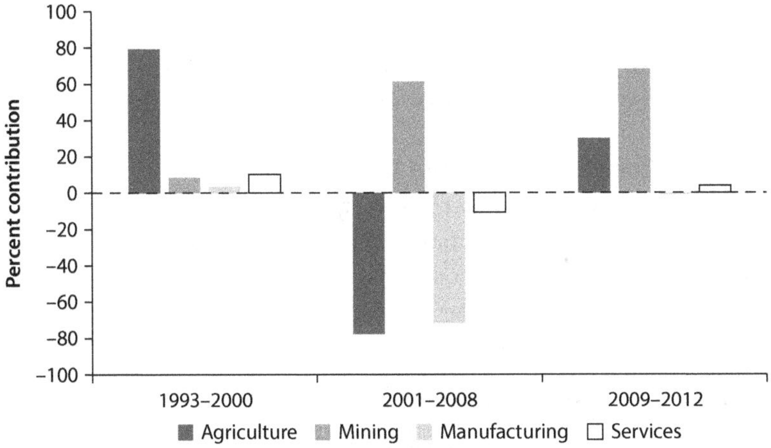

Source: Based on Reserve Bank of Zimbabwe data at http://www.rbz.co.zw/.

Figure O.5 Zimbabwe's Diversification in Contrast with Other African Countries

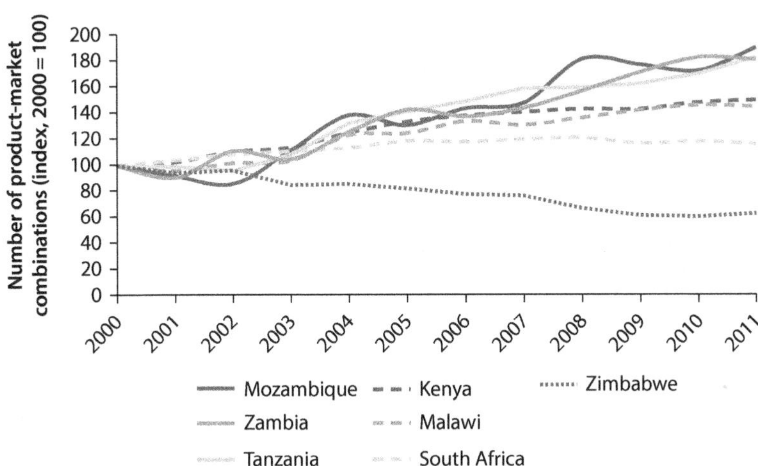

Source: Edwards and Kirk 2013.

Services exports are a logical source of new growth and diversification for landlocked Zimbabwe. The country has a relatively well-educated and English-speaking labor force and numerous tourist attractions, and services are a rapidly growing segment of the global market. However, while other countries in the region have harnessed their growth to services exports, services have largely stagnated in Zimbabwe. Zimbabwe has underperformed in services exports and in widening access to services for its firms, farms, and households. Zimbabwe's tourism earnings were traditionally greater than Tanzania's though that has not been the case through the 2000s and 2011. Exports of other commercial services—mostly business process outsourcing (BPO)—could be a source of high-skill employment for its English-speaking populations, much as in Kenya, but Zimbabwean exports in that sector are virtually nonexistent (figure O.6, panel b).

Creating Too Little Value Added and Too Few Jobs

A corollary to this growth pattern is that, contrary to the aspirations of the National Trade Strategy, the technological content of Zimbabwe's exports has not improved. Regrouping exports into resource-based (including precious stones, minerals, and processed raw minerals), labor-intensive (including tobacco

Figure O.6 Zimbabwe's Services Exports versus Comparator Countries, 2000–12

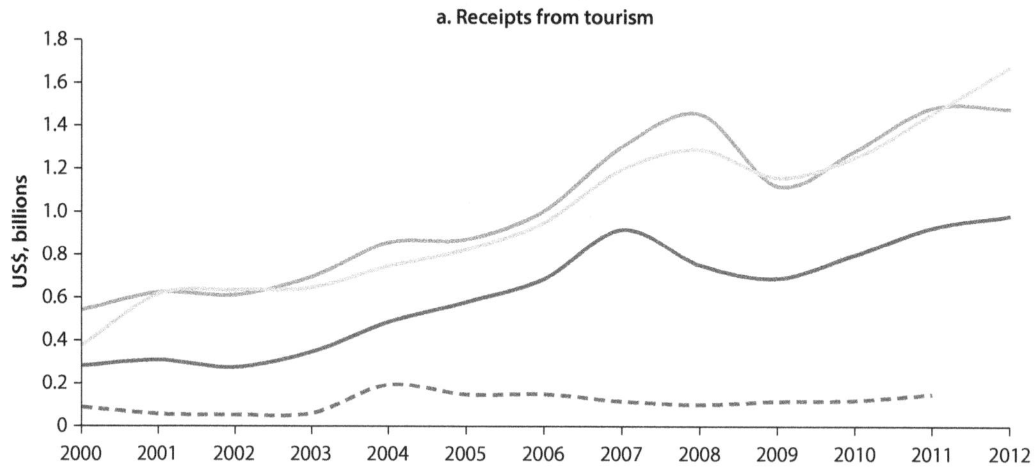

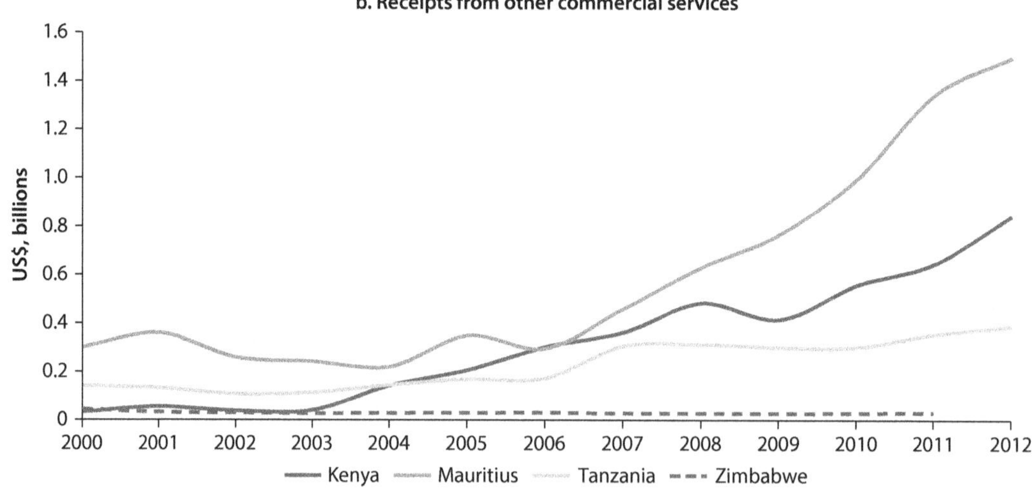

Source: Mattoo and Waris 2013.

and cotton lint), and medium- to high-technology (auto parts, electrical equipment, and the like) illuminates the retreat from technology. While resource-based exports have grown, labor-intensive products (including agriculture) have languished, and medium- and high-technology products have stagnated.

As a result of these trends, exports have become less diversified, less technologically sophisticated, and less labor intensive—and ever more dependent on a few large mining activities to provide foreign exchange and employment (figure O.7). Relative to the 1980s when manufacturing was the backbone of growth, job creation in the resource-driven economy is becoming more skewed toward a few high-paying jobs in mining and low-paying jobs in ancillary services and agriculture. It takes far fewer workers and a lot more capital to extract mining resources, so the returns accrue less to labor and more to capital. The implication is that an income distribution that relies mainly on minerals, rather than on the more diversified growth path that had been characteristic of Zimbabwe's earlier history, is likely to become more unequal over time.

Relying principally on mining as a source of growth is likely to mute the poverty-reducing effects of growth if no offsetting measures are put in place. Studies have shown that growth in resource-rich countries has a lower poverty-reducing effect than growth in resource-poor countries.[1] This effect occurs principally because resources—oil and minerals—are less labor intensive, and rents accrue in the first instance to mine owners and to the state through taxation as well as to the skilled labor that mines employ. Only if governments consciously adopt macroeconomic policies to avoid the effects of potential Dutch disease, design programs to channel these rents into the development of a more diversified economy, and create programs that enhance skills among low-income groups can

Figure O.7 Increasing Dominance of Resource-Intensive Exports

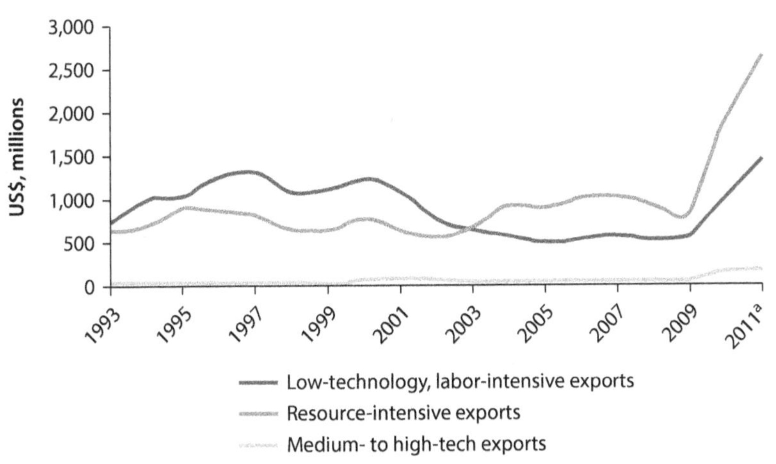

Source: Based on Reserve Bank of Zimbabwe data at http://www.rbz.co.zw/.
a. Projected.

Box O.1 A Note on Trade Data in Zimbabwe

To account for the evolution of export performance in Zimbabwe, different sources of available trade data were consulted in the preparation of this report. Given the availability of information on trade flows at a very high level of disaggregation—Harmonized System (HS) six-digit and market levels—for most countries around the globe, the first, and by now, the most standard source of trade data consulted for trade analyses, was United Nations Comtrade.

UN Comtrade allows two alternative ways to account for exports in a given country and year: (1) exports are reported directly by the corresponding authority in each country ("Exports, directly reported" in figure BO.1.1) and (2) exports can be constructed by adding up the annual amounts reported as imports from that given country by all existing trading partners in the database—so-called mirror data, or "Exports, mirror data" in figure BO.1.1.

Figure BO.1.1 Comparison of Directly Reported and Mirror Exports

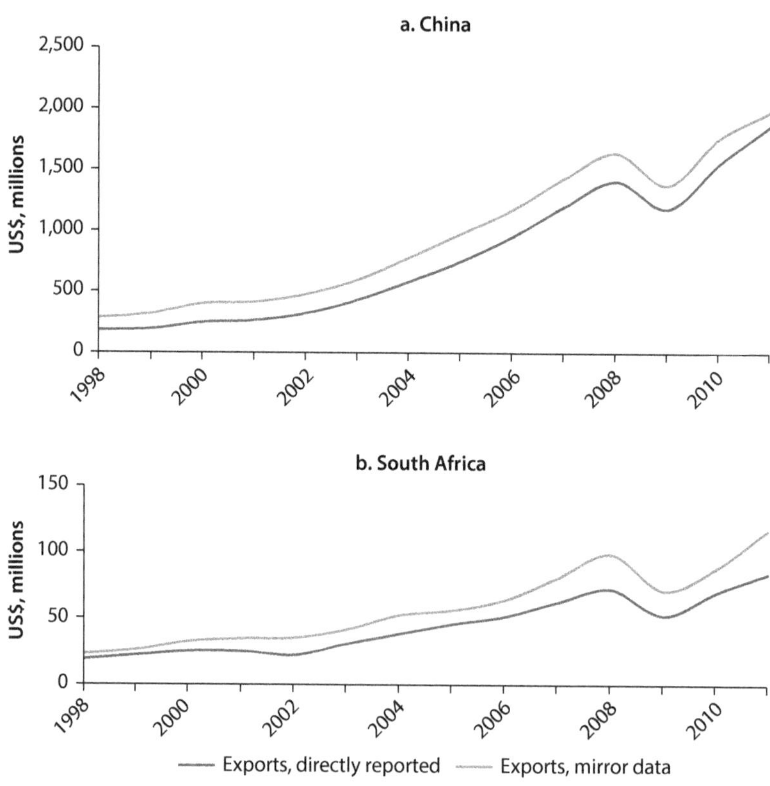

box continues next page

Box O.1 A Note on Trade Data in Zimbabwe *(continued)*

Figure BO.1.1 Comparison of Directly Reported and Mirror Exports *(continued)*

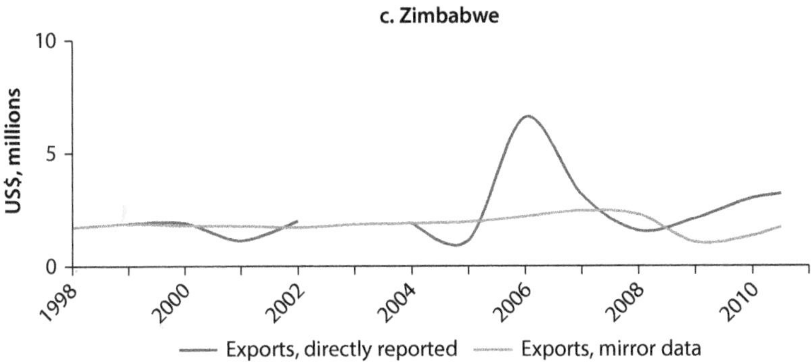

Source: UN Comtrade at http://comtrade.un.org/.
Note: Data for 2003 exports, directly reported, are missing.

Although discrepancies between the two sources of information are to be expected—import accounts consider other costs after shipment from the exporting country—normally these discrepancies are constant and follow a similar trend for most countries (see China and South Africa in figure BO.1.1). For Zimbabwe, these differences are erratic and follow no trend (see Zimbabwe in figure BO.1.1).

Given the economic crisis of the past decade and the distortions that may have been picked up in the data reported by Zimbabwe with the use of different exchange rates, and given the need to rely on highly disaggregated product- and market-specific trade data to analyze trade policies, the first decision made in preparation for this report was to consider mirror data.

However, the use of mirror data is not free of potential errors. In fact, although mirror data allow Zimbabwe's trade story to be told looking at specific products and markets from a long time series perspective, mirror data do not accurately reflect the sectoral composition of the recent export rebound. In particular, while domestic sources of trade data (Reserve Bank of Zimbabwe [RBZ], Zimbabwe Revenue Authority [ZIMRA], and the Zimbabwe National Statistics Agency [ZIMSTAT]) document the outstanding performance of the mining sector in recent years in Zimbabwe, this widely known surge only appears as a modest increase in mineral exports according to mirror data (figure BO.1.2, panel a). See annex OA for a complete account of Zimbabwe's trade story according to mirror data.

Available domestic sources of trade data show differences, but they are not as pronounced as UN Comtrade mirror data (figure BO.1.2, panel b). Considering that longer time series are needed to conduct a more comprehensive analysis of trade performance in a country, and

box continues next page

Box O.1 A Note on Trade Data in Zimbabwe *(continued)*

Figure BO.1.2 Comparison of Various Sources of Trade Data

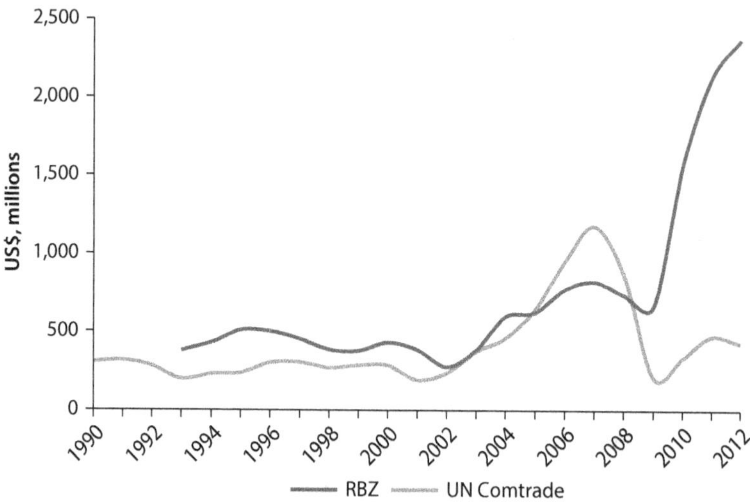

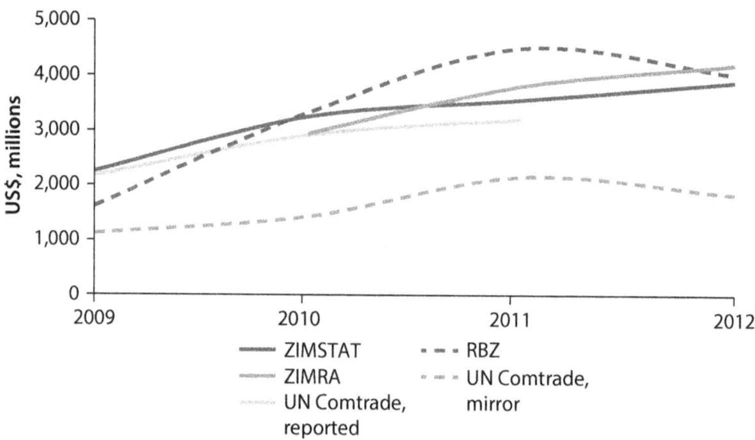

Sources: UN Comtrade, http://comtrade.un.org/; Reserve Bank of Zimbabwe (RBZ), http://www.rbz.co.zw/; Zimbabwe Revenue Authority (ZIMRA), http://www.zimra.co.zw/; Zimbabwe National Statistics Agency (ZIMSTAT), http://www.zimstat.co.zw/.

given that only RBZ data provide that possibility—with a reasonable, although broader, level of disaggregation by products—the approach taken in this report is to use RBZ data for the longer-term sectoral analysis of trade (in chapter 1). The use of UN Comtrade mirror data was limited to the empirical analysis of the impact of trade policy and integration on specific products and markets (as in chapter 2).

the growth path be made more inclusive. Botswana and Chile are examples of countries that have successfully implemented such strategies over several decades.

Policies Affecting Trade: Incentives and Connectivity

The underlying causes of these patterns, while diverse and complex, are firmly rooted in Zimbabwe's policy framework. Policies in four domains have inadvertently undermined export performance.

Poor Predictability of Macroeconomic Policy and Economic Governance Create an Unfavorable Investment and Trade Climate

Policy was at the center of the perfect storm in 2007–08: ill-conceived macroeconomic policies superimposed on counterproductive trade and industrial policies joined with a crisis and the worst global recession since the 1930s to hurl Zimbabwe into the recessionary jaws of hyperinflation. The lack of sound economic policies and the failure to service past debt meant that access to foreign borrowing was lost.

The government's decision in 2009 to allow full-scale dollarization ended recourse to the printing press and led to reactivation of the pricing and payments systems, with immediate positive effects on economic incentives. High inflation ended, exports and imports surged, and consumption and investment were reinvigorated. Government revenues improved and the cash deficit in the fiscal and quasi-fiscal accounts fell to 1.6 percent of GDP (IMF 2012). However, price stabilization is a necessary but not a sufficient condition for providing the macroeconomic incentives for a new and sustained period of export-led growth. Policy makers confront four related legacies.

First, the country has accumulated debt in excess of 80 percent of GDP (IMF 2012). Roughly half of this is arrears accumulated to the international financial institutions, Paris Club donors, private commercial banks, and others. At these debt levels, the country is vulnerable to capital volatility and capital flight. Although this vulnerability has subsided considerably since dollarization—debt levels were in excess of 125 percent of GDP in 2009—these high debt levels could still choke off imports, domestic investment, and growth.

At the same time, a second constraint looms. The government has little headroom in its fiscal accounts to begin making investments in badly needed infrastructure. Wages and other current expenditures already comprise such a large share of total expenditures that little room is left to invest in productivity-increasing infrastructure. Even though government spending, at 37 percent of GDP, is at one of the highest levels among developing countries at per capita incomes similar to that of Zimbabwe, public investment was projected to reach only 6 percent of GDP (IMF 2012), among the lowest figures in Africa. Yet high-cost electric power punctuated with frequent blackouts means machines in factories cannot operate competitively; pothole-peppered roads slow transport times and tear up trucks, driving up transport costs; inadequately maintained railways are forced to run at slow speeds to prevent derailments; the costs of connecting to the Internet are well above those in neighboring countries. Deteriorating infrastructure—critical to increasing exports—is already hampering growth.

There is also a long-term budget corollary associated with the shift to a resource-driven economy. Wealth generated by the mining economy accrues mainly to the firm in the form of profit and to the government in the form of taxes, royalties, fees, and any profits from state-owned mining companies. Unless these state resources are invested productively in lowering the cost of doing business, in infrastructure, and in the human capital of the populace—or rebated directly to the populace through dividends—experience in other countries suggests that low-income people will be left behind and become progressively disempowered.

A third immediate pressure point affecting nonmineral export prospects is the exchange rate. The U.S. dollar has appreciated more than 24 percent relative to the South African rand since early 2012 and is forecast to rise further in 2014 (Buiter 2013), though recent political gridlock in the United States widens the bounds of uncertainty around any forecast. Because such a large share of Zimbabwe's trade is with South Africa, this appreciation undermines the competitiveness of Zimbabwe's exports given that dollarized exports are now priced higher in the regional market. These international headwinds imply that Zimbabwe will have to make substantial efforts to increase productivity to maintain the hard-won macroeconomic stability that propelled the 2010–12 exports momentum and economic recovery. In the absence of a monetary instrument that would permit currency depreciation and economy-wide adjustment of wages to improve competitiveness, the government will have to ensure that increases in wages, particularly in the nontradables sector, increase only in tandem with productivity gains.

Finally, investor perceptions of consistency in economic governance remain a nettlesome issue that has depressed investment for most of the past decade. Policy changes, with first steps toward establishing a new regime that will tackle the problems of corruption head-on; replace discretionary and opaque regulations with transparency and political accountability; and reestablish the reputation of the country for sanctity of contracts, rule of law, and property, would greatly improve perceptions held by both domestic and international investors. Among the 139 countries that the World Economic Forum's Competitiveness Index tracks, Zimbabwe ranked 118 in overall score in 2013, and near the bottom in matters affecting investor confidence: 135 in property rights, 138 in policies and regulations, and 139 in policies affecting foreign investors (WEF 2013). These results mark a considerable deterioration since the mid-1990s. Similarly, according to the World Bank's World Governance Index, Zimbabwe had fallen to the 7th percentile of all countries in 2011, down from the 37th percentile in 1996, the first year of the index; and ranked at the lowest levels in various governance indicators that affect investors' perceptions and confidence in the economy (figure O.8). As investor confidence has fallen to new lows, investment rates, despite the economic rebound, continue to hover at levels

Figure O.8 Zimbabwe's Rankings in Matters Affecting Investor Confidence, 1996–2011

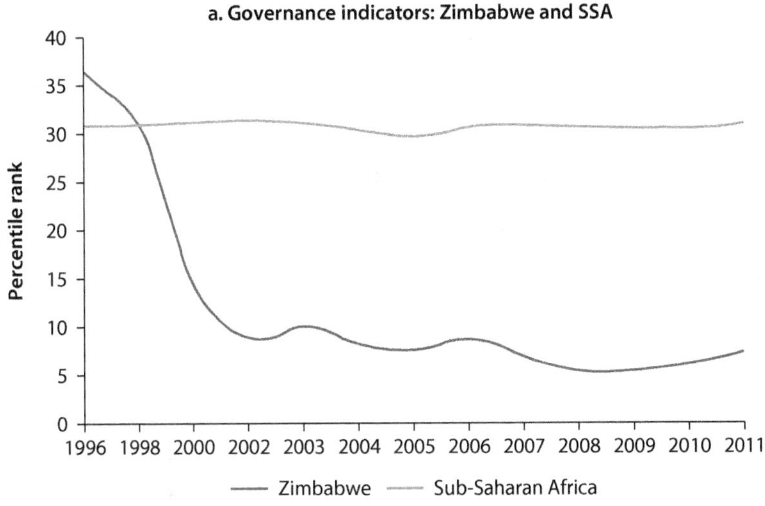

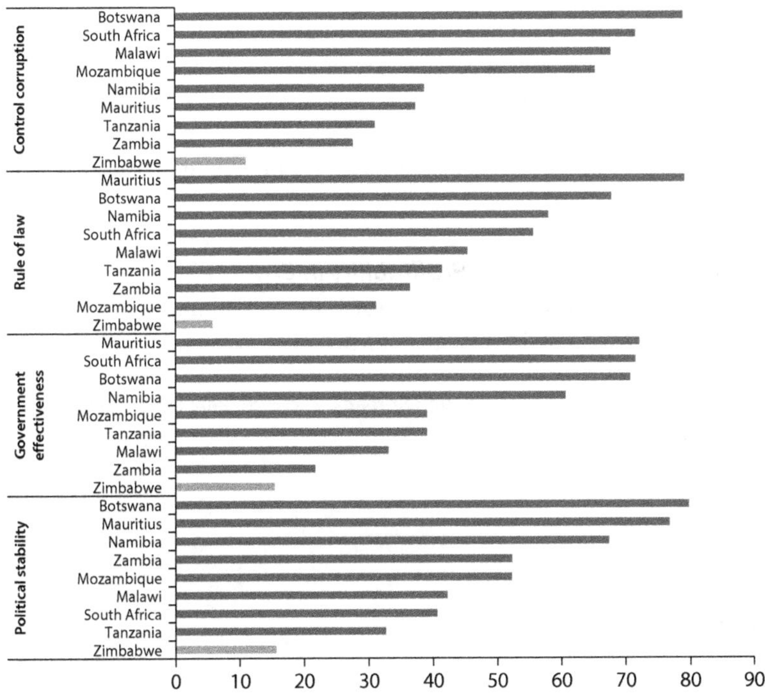

Source: World Bank 2013a.
Note: Average percentile rank values, 1996–2011; higher number reflects better governance. Data available at two-year intervals prior to 2002; annually thereafter.

insufficient to propel growth in every sector, save possibly mining. Real interest rates remain high. Substantial additional effort will be required to rebuild the confidence among both domestic and foreign investors that is necessary to improve trade performance. Political commitment together with massive public support will be necessary, and the jury of domestic and foreign investors is still out on these questions.

Country risk translates into financial sector risk that keeps real interest rates high. Limited investor confidence constrains the ability of the financial system to mobilize savings that could be used for investment in domestic productive capacity that could substitute for imports or produce for export. With nominal lending rates running between 20 percent and 25 percent and inflation hovering around 2.0–2.5 percent, real interest rates are typically 18 percent or more (World Bank 2013b). Bank spreads are enormous (figure O.9). These rates reflect a combination of factors, including rising nonperforming loans, but paramount among them is the perception of risk. A widespread perception of high risk has led to a low-level equilibrium in which both the public's desire to place funds at the banks is limited and the willingness of the banks to raise deposit rates sufficiently to entice the public to deposit is limited because of uncertainty. This risk perception, together with the dead weight of nonperforming loans, serves to keep real interest rates stiflingly high. These high interest rates limit Zimbabwe producers' access to trade finance as well as to working capital, to say nothing of long-term finance for investment in plant and equipment. Only large exporters that are part of global value chains can get access to trade credit from large foreign buyers or related parties, mainly the multinational mining companies.

Trade Policy Dampens Investor Profitability in Exports

The National Trade Strategy put forward the well-conceived objectives of increasing exports to sustain growth and diversifying the export portfolio and

Figure O.9 High Nominal Rates, High Spreads, and High Real Interest Rates Constrain Investment

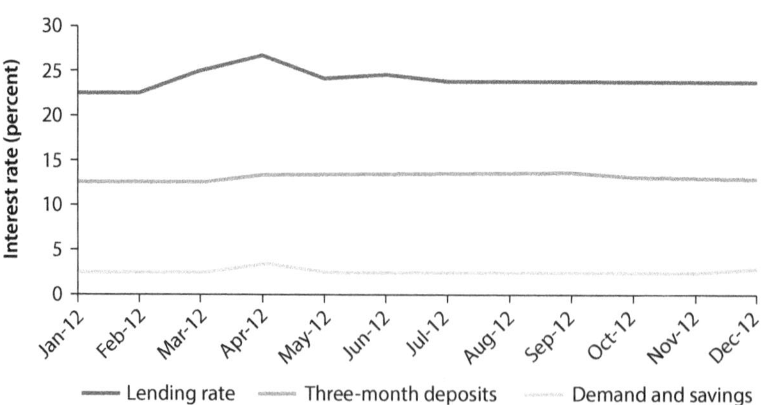

Source: Hove, Mawadza, and Vaez-Zadeh 2013.

increasing its technology content. However, the current structure of tariffs and other trade taxes shape prices in such a way that creates incentives to sell at home rather than selling abroad, and for those nonmineral exports that do find their way abroad, the tariff structure provides higher returns to sales in the region than on the global market. Tariffs and trade taxes form a wall of protection that makes it more profitable to sell at home and discourages exports. Estimates in chapter 2 highlight that selling at home behind a wall of most-favored nation tariffs and trade taxes is, on average, nearly twice as profitable as selling to the global market. Regional tariff walls are lower, but Zimbabwean producers find it more profitable to sell at home than in the region. By creating incentives to produce for sales at home rather than abroad, these border barriers weigh down overall expansion of the value-added goods industries.

Tariffs and trade taxes on intermediate inputs also undermine competitiveness. If Zimbabwean firms have to pay tariffs on their inputs, their costs rise and their products are less competitive on international markets. The evidence in chapter 2 shows that lower tariffs on inputs are associated with more exports. A decline in average most-favored nation input tariffs of 10 percent is associated with an average increase in total sector exports of 19 percent.

Another understudied area is nontariff measures, some of which have the same effect as tariffs. As of June 2013, Zimbabwe had 19 outstanding nontariff measure complaints based on the terminology registered in the Tripartite Monitoring Mechanism online portal. Most of these complaints relate to customs and transport and transit issues. In fact, during the first half of 2013 Zimbabwean traders registered six complaints on the Tripartite Trade Barriers website. One of the complaints related to transport issues and all the others concerned customs. Customs valuation emerged as a serious problem. In addition, several burdensome procedures, permits, and certifications impose costs on exporters, thereby impeding exports.

By giving the greatest protection to low-technology activities that are also slow growing in the world market—footwear, textiles, agricultural products—the incentive system encourages private investment to flow into these industries instead of into higher–value added sectors that are also fast growing in the international market. Moreover, the incentive system built into the tariff structure channels those firms that limit their exports toward preferential markets. Because regional markets have high levels of protection, inefficient, high-cost domestic industries are shielded from international competition, thereby lessening firms' incentives to invest in the latest, cost-lowering technologies—and passing the bill to consumers who have to pay higher prices. Moreover, this structure results in the growth of nonmining exports being highly dependent on the relatively small markets of the region. In sum, trade policies in Zimbabwe thus generally discourage exports, except when those exports are sheltered by preferential tariff agreements, most powerfully in the region.

In addition, if the objective of these trade policies had been to stimulate the growth of these low-technology industries, the results fell short, given that they have generally stagnated. These industries, while labor intensive, are not those envisioned in the National Trade Policy to propel Zimbabwe into the 21st century on a higher growth trajectory.

Industrial Policies Undermine Investor Confidence

Industrial policies comprise regulations, taxes, and subsidies intended to promote growth objectives for selected industries. In Zimbabwe, the government's most important initiative, as discussed in chapter 3, has been to use industry-specific policies to transfer ownership to indigenous populations as a way of empowering groups historically excluded from participating in rising incomes. The land reform launched in the 1990s was the first pillar of this policy, and it broke up many of the large commercial farms and transferred user rights to smallholders. This policy was later expanded in 2008–10 with the Indigenization and Economic Empowerment Act (IEEA) and its regulations to include manufacturing, and the government in 2011 announced it would seek to extend the indigenization effort to the mining and financial sectors. Businesses with capital of $500,000 or more are expected to transfer 51 percent ownership to indigenous Zimbabwean ownership.

The policy itself and the unevenness of its implementation have created considerable uncertainty about property rights in Zimbabwe, with the consequence of depressing domestic investment and deterring foreign investment. The country ranks nearly last on various measures of investor confidence (figure O.10).

For that reason, outside of mining, Zimbabwe has not been able to attract either foreign investors or to fully mobilize domestic investment. Zimbabwe's share of new foreign direct investment (FDI) going to low-income countries in the past decade is less than half its share during the 1990s, and would have been even lower were it not for the allure of natural resources (figure O.11). In addition to the missed opportunity to tap into foreign skills and technology for domestic production, the inability to attract FDI has cause Zimbabwe to miss out on possible connections to global and regional value chains. This scuttled opportunity has reduced the jobs open to low-income Zimbabweans, arguably the opposite of what empowerment objectives were intended to achieve.

Policies toward particular sectors dampen performance. In mining, the latest changes to the tax regime impose very high costs on new activities, in particular new exploration, and have led the business press to rank Zimbabwe last among mining destinations.[2]

In agriculture, credit policies and market extension are crucial to expanding exports, which argues for macroeconomic and financial reforms to bring down real interest rates, and for greater fiscal resources to be devoted to market extension work.

Inefficient Services Hamper Connectivity and Raise Trade Costs

Ease of connectivity to global and regional markets is a fundamental determinant of competitiveness, and connectivity hinges critically on efficient and modern services. Because of poor transport services, landlocked countries are at

Figure O.10 Investor Confidence in Zimbabwe and Other Countries
Global Competitiveness Index, 2013

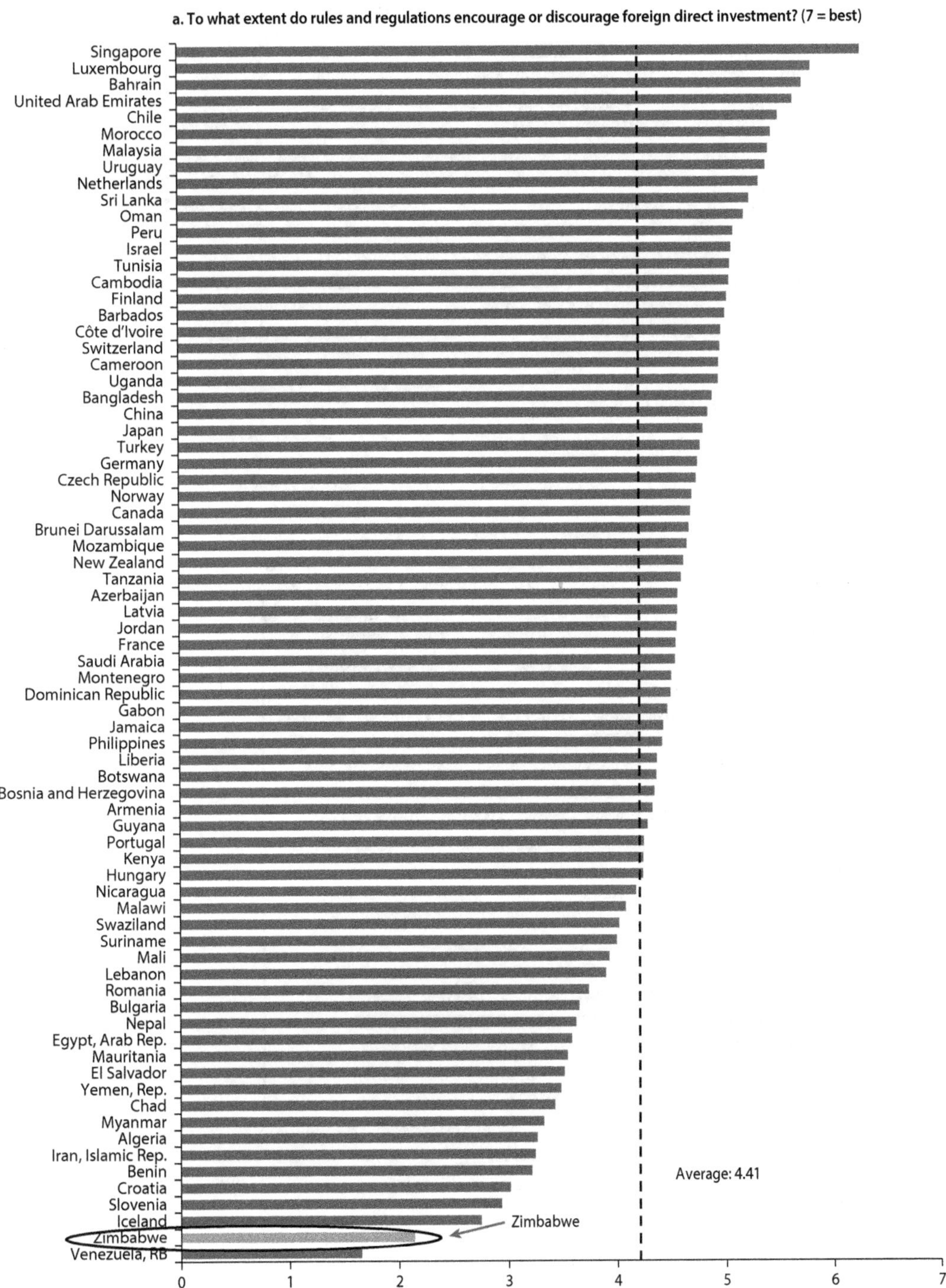

figure continues next page

Figure O.10 Investor Confidence in Zimbabwe and Other Countries *(continued)*

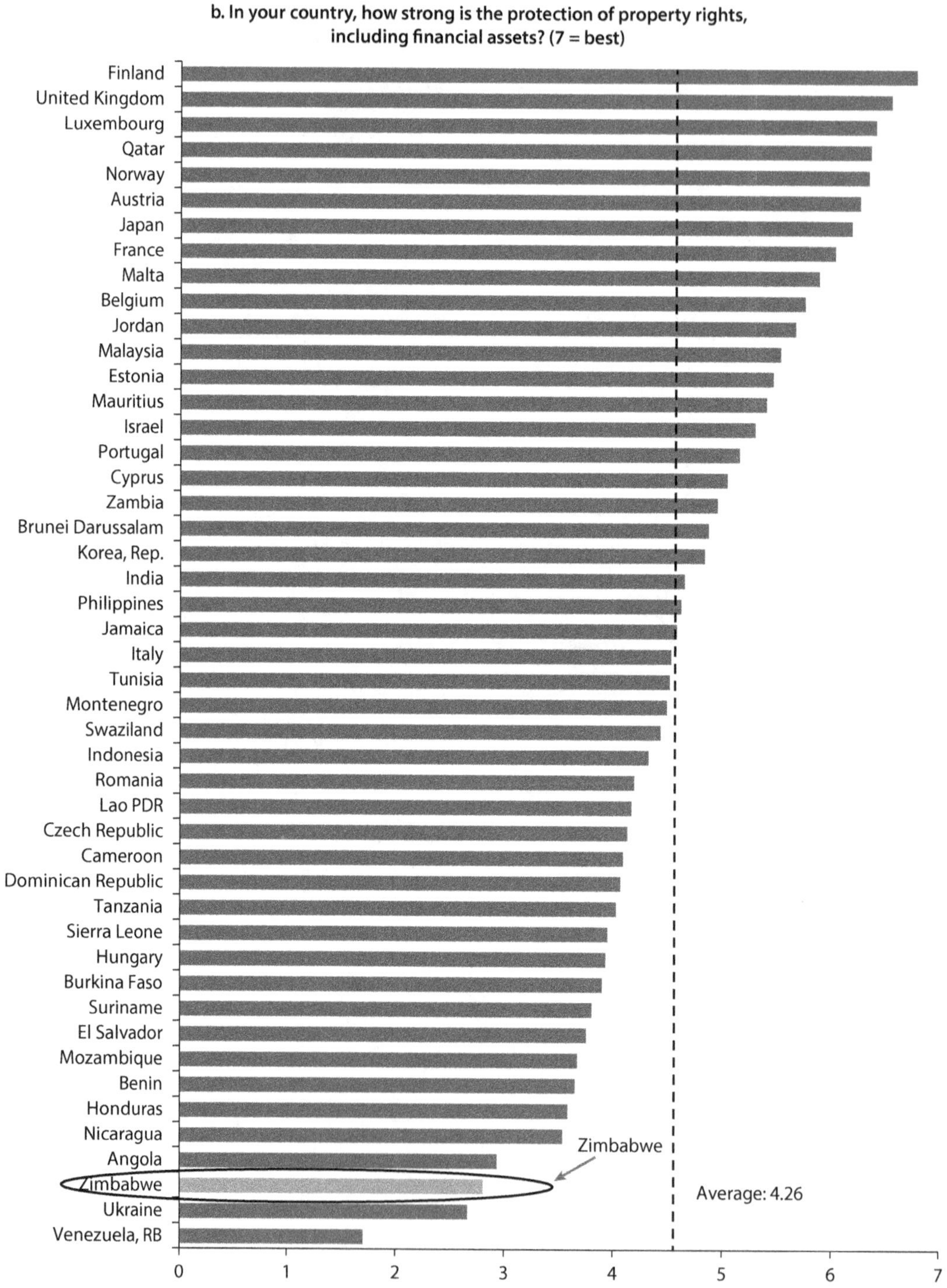

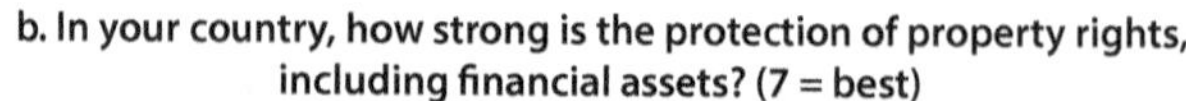

Source: World Economic Forum (WEF 2013).

Figure O.11 Zimbabwe's Share of Foreign Direct Investment Inflows

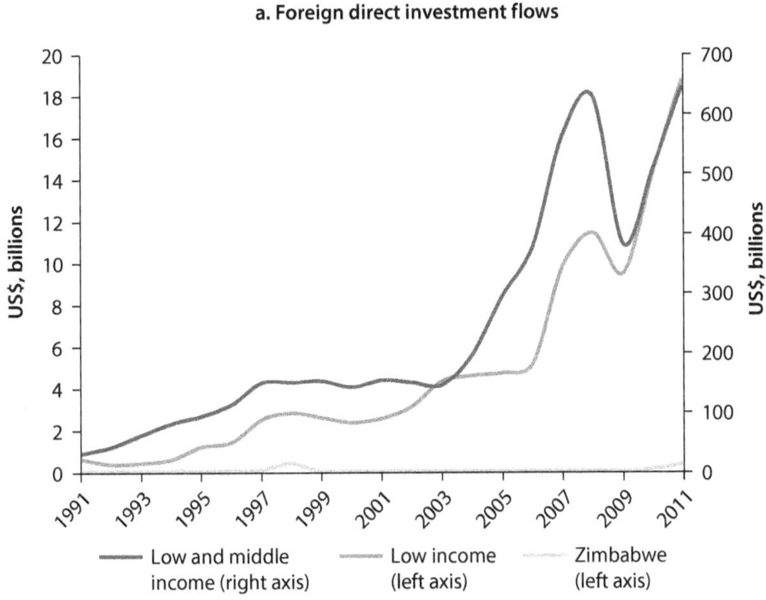

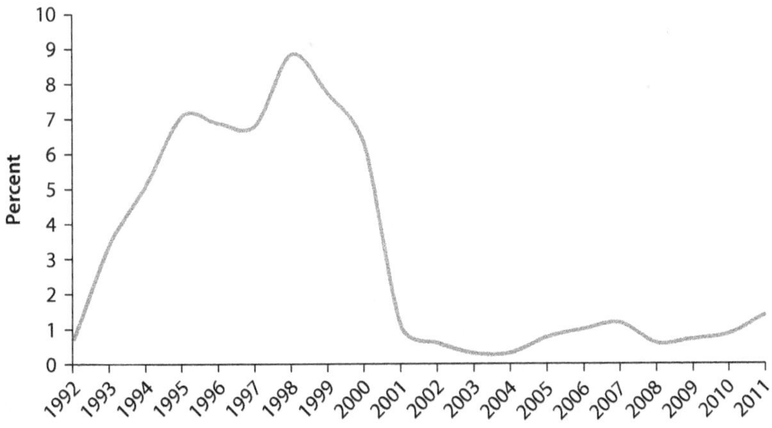

Source: World Bank, World Development Indicators, http://data.worldbank.org/data-catalog/world-development-indicators.

a particular disadvantage in accessing foreign markets. High transportation costs, delays at borders or in transit through third countries, and poor logistical arrangements can drive up the costs of exports in foreign markets, and price them out of the market. The emergence of global value chains of production as a central feature of world trade has compounded potential disadvantages of being landlocked because coastal countries have access to low-cost sea transport; at the same time, however, it has created new opportunities for centrally located landlocked countries like Zimbabwe to link into regional markets. Speed and low-cost transport services are key components of cost competitiveness in value chains.

Information connectivity is as important as transport connectivity. Telecommunications, finance, and other Internet-based services, as well as education, are crucial to the development of exports and productivity growth in general. On the one hand, these services are indispensable inputs into production. On the other hand, services such as tourism and BPO can be a direct source of export earnings. Several studies have shown that efficient services are associated with more rapid economic growth (Hoekman and Mattoo 2012; Mattoo and Fink 2002).

In Zimbabwe, these forms of connectivity are particularly important. Consider first transport of goods. As discussed in chapter 4, the costs of shipping a container laden with exports from Harare to Amsterdam are twice those of shipping from neighboring Malawi or South Africa. Since 2006, the costs of importing a container have more than doubled while the cost of exporting increased by 75 percent. Under standard assumptions, this would be equivalent to a 52 percent tariff (Masiiwa and Giersing 2012). For exports, the high shipping costs may be considered to be equivalent to an export tax. Although all countries have to pay transport costs to import and export their products, the incremental costs Zimbabwean firms have to pay relative to both their neighbors and other international competitors represent a significant disadvantage.

Although the problems associated with transportation costs are somewhat different for roads, rails, and air transport, the three sectors share common stories: policy barriers to competition (especially state monopolies and restrictions on foreign competition), high costs and underinvestment, and deteriorating infrastructure. Similarly, delays at the border are severe, and more severe coming into Zimbabwe than going from Zimbabwe into neighboring countries.

The availability of trade finance is limited, and, though large exporters in, say, mining can get suppliers' credits, the lack of trade finance is particularly prejudicial to small and medium businesses in manufacturing and agriculture. Its high cost and limited access stem mainly from the absence of a smoothly functioning, low interest rate financial system.

Other services are also expensive. From finance and accounting to telecommunications and international transport, access to services remains low and highly unequal—with availability at affordable prices limited primarily to the affluent in urban areas and to the larger firms. In telecommunications, for example, the lack of competition has hampered growth in the sector. A state enterprise monopolizes wire services (TelOne). As a result, consumers are penalized with high fees and poor-quality services. Fixed-line penetration is low (3 percent), and given TelOne's bad financial situation,[3] it is unlikely that expansion of lines or creation of a national backbone will take place. In mobile services, three cellular services operators, the privately owned Econet and Telecel and the state-owned NetOne, serve the market. Econet has about 70 percent of the market.[4] Each operator has its own network and is responsible for national and international traffic for its network, resulting in a fragmented wholesale market.[5] Operators continue to use very expensive satellite links for international communications, but that is beginning to change.

Although mobile penetration has dramatically increased to 68 percent from 13 percent between 2008 and 2011, prices are still high even by regional standards (Safdar 2013). The average price of a mobile call in Zimbabwe was US$0.24 per minute in 2011 (figure O.12, panel a), roughly 500 percent more than in comparator countries across the region. Although some reductions in prices for mobile broadband have occurred, prices are still high in Zimbabwe by

Figure O.12 Zimbabweans Pay More to Call or Surf the Web

a. Average price of mobile call per minute, 2011

U.S. dollars

0.30
0.25
0.20
0.15
0.10
0.05
0

Zimbabwe
Sub-Saharan Africa

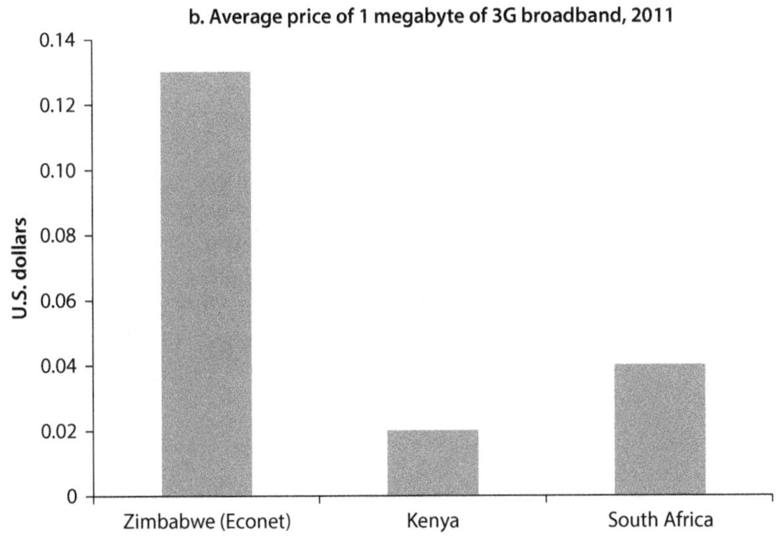

Source: Safdar 2013.

regional standards. For example, while mobile broadband (via 3G) is charged at US$0.08–US$0.17 per megabyte (MB) in Zimbabwe, in South Africa the price is US$0.03–US$0.04 per MB and US$0.015 per MB in Kenya (figure O.12, panel b).

Several factors explain the poor performance of Zimbabwean domestic and export services. One is that Zimbabwe restricts competition in services. Whether at a regional or global level, Zimbabwe has among the highest levels of restrictions in services (figure O.13).

Policy barriers to competition take four different forms in Zimbabwean services. First, policy tightly restricts the number of providers in sectors such as telecommunications and air transport. In part this is explained by the presence of state-owned companies that monopolize segments of the business and operate inefficiently. Second, some sectors have limitations on foreign investment that might otherwise provide competition, and in other sectors, the ownership limitation impedes foreign entry and ownership, and with it, the competition and technology that foreign investment would otherwise bring. Third, the requirement to demonstrate domestic unavailability in banking and insurance before allowing cross-border imports of services, as well as the application of labor

Figure O.13 Zimbabwe's Services Policy Is among the Most Restrictive
Services Trade Restrictiveness Index

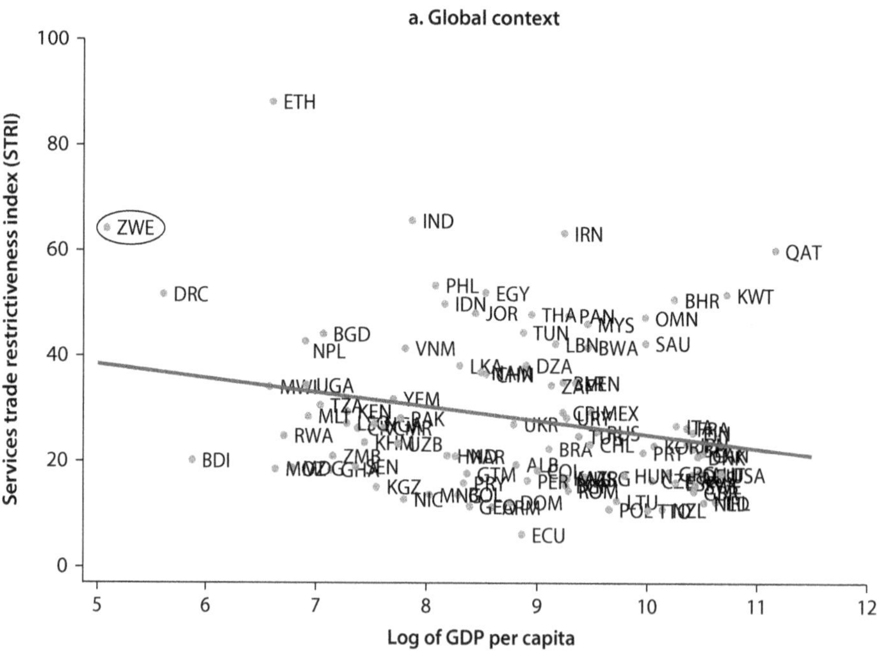

figure continues next page

Figure O.13 Zimbabwe's Services Policy Is among the Most Restrictive *(continued)*

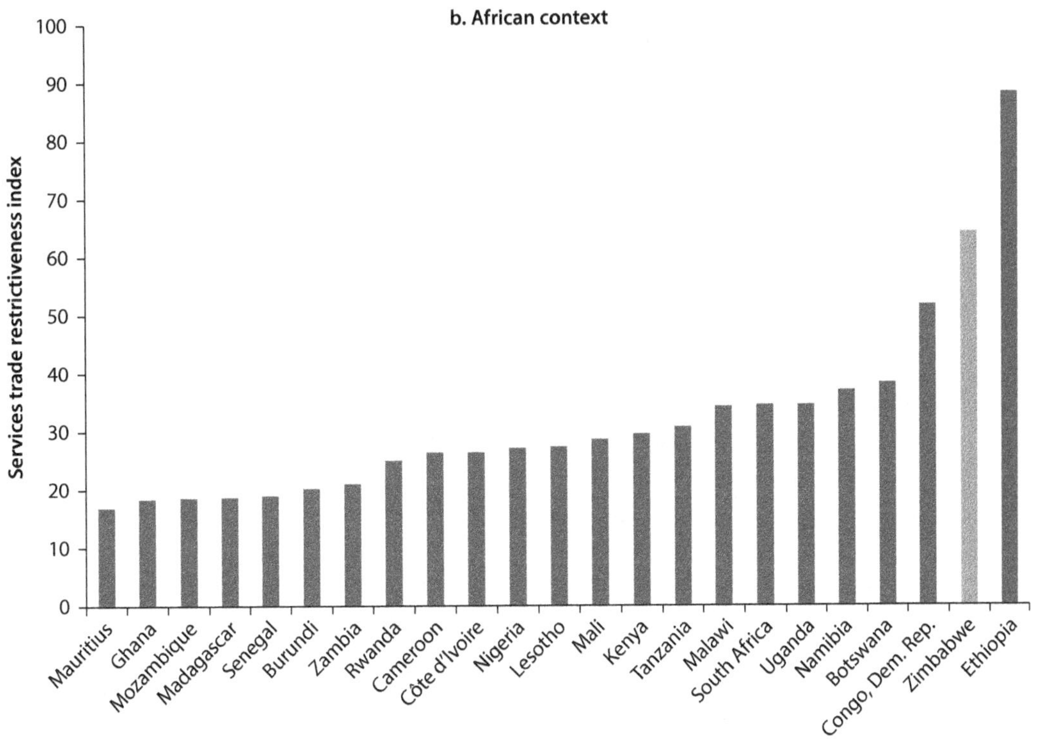

Source: Borchert, Gootiiz, and Mattoo 2012.
Note: In panel a, purchasing-power-parity 2007 GDP per capita in constant 2005 international U.S. dollars.

market tests in accounting and auditing, also limit competition. Finally, the high degree of regulatory and policy discretion in the implementation of policies discourages investment. For example, the allocation of new licenses remains opaque and discretionary across sectors. These policy impediments are common in varying degrees to five critical sectors: telecommunications, finance, tourism, air transport, and BPO.

A related problem has been the historically low investment rates in these sectors. Low investment in these sectors reflects the macroeconomic stresses on public finance noted above but also the inefficiency of poorly managed and regulated state enterprises in the sectors they dominate. Similarly, restrictions on foreign investment effectively preclude the mobilization of foreign savings and technological transfer to respond to the challenging investment needs. However, investing more in electric power, roads, rails, and telecommunications, as well as in the soft infrastructure and in improving border crossings and trade-related institutions such as customs, is imperative if Zimbabwe is to maintain recent export growth momentum and overcome downward trends in diversification.

The Forward-Looking Agenda

If the bad news of this report is that past economic policies have had a detrimental effect on exports and income growth, the good news is that today's problems can be addressed through policy reforms. This report presents a wide set of areas open to policy action. Already the country has taken the first, most basic step of reactivating the signaling effect of the price system through dollarization, which has allowed it to move out of hyperinflation and into renewed growth. This change allows the government to turn its attention to the prevailing incentives that could encourage private investment and deepen its connectivity to regional and global markets.[6]

Reconfiguring Economy-Wide Incentives Is Essential to Promoting Sustained Growth

As price stabilization and economic reactivation have started laying the foundation for a broad-based recovery and export expansion, the policy agenda to strengthen recovery, elaborated upon elsewhere in several World Bank reports and other documents (see World Bank 2012), entails efforts to reestablish creditworthiness with foreign lenders to tap into long-term foreign savings,[7] efforts to balance public sector accounts in such a way as to increase much-needed public investment, and efforts to reverse the widespread perceptions of incoherent and ineffective economic governance. Resolving these near-term issues would allow the country to begin looking for ways to channel rents from mining exports into investment in other sectors so as to diversify and to offset the potentially regressive distributional effects of growth based on mineral exports.

Reestablishing stable international relations with foreign governments and creditors outside the region is a priority for income growth *and* export growth. Such relations are necessary if Zimbabwe is to substantially expand exports outside the region. Although Zimbabwe does not currently qualify for access to the United States under the U.S. African Growth and Opportunity Act, access to the act's preferences is potentially an additional source of export growth and employment creation in Zimbabwean clothing firms. The Economic Partnership Agreement with the European Union signed in 2012 may also provide new market access. These efforts could go far toward allaying investor concerns and reversing existing macroeconomic incentives in a positive direction.

Aligning Trade Policies with National Objectives Could Propel Export Growth

Reversing recent trends so as to achieve objectives in the National Trade Strategy is possible, but would require removing the bias against exports and diversification embedded in the system of tariffs and taxes. Current policies make it much more profitable to sell only at home and more profitable to sell in the regional market than in the global market. Unless this pattern is reversed it will be hard to generate new sources of exports. Therefore, increasing exports to sustain growth and diversifying the export portfolio and increasing its technology content require several classes of actions:

- *Implement a duty drawback system.* A critical reason that the anti-export bias is so high in Zimbabwe is that domestic producers are compelled to pay tariffs on their inputs as well as shoulder other inefficiency-imposed transport costs that other competitors in the global market do not bear. In effect, this means Zimbabwe is "exporting its taxes," as they are embedded into the price of its exports. A key recommendation, therefore, is to implement an efficient and extensive duty drawback system as is suggested in the National Trade Policy document.[8]

- *Adopt efficient and lower tariffs.* Consideration should be given to adopting a major tariff reform that would bring Zimbabwe closer to regional practices. Analysis in chapter 2 shows that lower tariffs are positively correlated with exports. Lowering maximum tariffs to 15 percent, removing the import surcharge, and reducing the disparity in tariffs within sectors would contribute to eliminating the anti-export bias, and would allow greater import competition to drive productivity gains. Moreover, reducing the excessive number of tariff bands and replacing specific duties with ad valorem tariffs to conform to regional practices would reduce the opportunities for corruption that acts as a tax on trade.

- *Negotiate improved access to foreign markets.* Despite belonging to several preferential trade agreements, nontariff barriers remain a constraint to Zimbabwe's exports. In particular, the rules of origin that apply under the Southern African Development Community (SADC) free trade agreement constrain Zimbabwean firms' ability to gain access into the SADC (mainly South African) market. This affects the clothing sector in particular, where a double transformation rule (as opposed to the single transformation rule that applies to the Common Market for Eastern and Southern Africa [COMESA]). The government is already focused on negotiating a more relaxed SADC rule of origin for clothing, and these efforts should be intensified. Similarly, an important arena in which Zimbabwean policy makers may shape access to regional markets is the Tripartite Free Trade Agreement negotiations, which are expected to be completed in 2015.

Industrial Policies to Empower Zimbabweans

In a world increasingly populated with global value chains, expanding exports to take advantage of new opportunities, particularly in manufacturing and services exports, requires working closely with foreign companies. It is the growth of the economy and export sector that will create the jobs and income today and the opportunities of tomorrow that will empower millions of Zimbabweans.

New initiatives to ignite a broad-based recovery of exports—and the creation of new jobs and economic opportunities associated with them—include the following:

- *Review the implementation of the IEEA to reduce both domestic and foreign investor uncertainty.* The single most commonly cited obstacle deterring foreign investment is uncertainty about the short-term and long-term costs to investors of implementation of the IEEA. Exploring ways other countries as diverse as Malaysia, China, and even Mexico (in an earlier period) have used ownership rules to build a domestic entrepreneurial class without alienating prospective investors—domestic as well as foreign—could reveal models for sound policy implementation.

- *Review taxation of mining to reduce the tax burden.* Similarly, licensing should be reviewed so as to encourage competition and investment from whatever source.

- *Review the infrastructure needs of export sectors and adopt an investment program to remedy obstacles.* Each of the sectors has an acute need for greater public investment. Deficiencies in roads and rail transport and electric power are common impediments to the expansion of growth in mining and manufacturing. Correction of these deficiencies requires mobilization of greater public savings and improvement in relations with international creditors to access untapped, relatively inexpensive, international credit.

- *Adopt a framework for setting up a set of smart industrial incentives.* This framework should clearly state its objectives, quantify subsidies from tax expenditures and the treasury, provide transparency in annual budgets, and be subject to sunset clauses. These incentives would be subject to annual evaluation and parliamentary oversight as part of the normal budget process.

Improving Transport Connectivity and Reducing Trading Costs

Despite being landlocked, Zimbabwe has considerable scope for reducing transport costs. To some extent, high costs can be alleviated almost immediately with policies rather than money. For example, policies that increase competition will also increase the efficiency of the use of infrastructure. So, for example, rewriting regulations governing the use of roads could eliminate outdated cabotage rules that prevent truckers from hauling in both directions and driving up costs. Allowing more competition and private investment in railways can drive down costs and mobilize new sources of finance for investment. Some of these measures require regional collective action and may be subject to negotiation. Eliminating the drag of state-owned monopolies in air transport, telecommunications, and power generation can create new sources of efficiency and productivity gains.

Policy measures to improve transport can be grouped into three categories that require progressively greater persistence and effort: reducing policy barriers to competition, improving trade-related public institutions, and making necessary public investments to reduce costs. Measures include the following:

- *Opening sectors in which state enterprises have held monopoly positions to new competition and investment may enhance credibility and attract capital.* New competition in air transport, rail service, telecommunications, and power could lead to lower prices, better service, and greater access. In air transport, efforts to conclude maintenance partnerships between Air Zimbabwe and Air France–KLM provide examples of positive beginnings. In addition, pushing to open the skies could also increase competition in Zimbabwe and the region. Zimbabwe should support the full implementation of continent-wide liberalization up to and including Fifth Freedom rights.[9] Given the slow progress at the continental level, Zimbabwe could focus negotiation efforts regionally, on liberalization initiatives in COMESA and SADC, and in parallel, it could negotiate bilateral air service agreements. Revamping the board of directors and management of the rail system to make it an independent corporation with independent decision making designed to achieve specific profit and investment targets would mark an important beginning. Open entry and hard budget constraints for remaining state enterprises will be critical to success.

- *Implement regional protocols in road transport and work to make them more conducive to competition.* Implementing all regional transport protocol provisions, including those of the SADC Protocol on Transport, Communication, and Meteorology, would strengthen the regional integrated approach to transport management, thereby facilitating the provision of seamless regional traffic. Meanwhile, the bilateral agreement between Zimbabwe and South Africa restricts the transport of bilateral trade to carriers from the two countries. Zimbabwe has also signed bilateral road transport agreements (BRTAs) with Botswana, the Democratic Republic of Congo, Malawi, Mozambique, Namibia, South Africa, Tanzania, and Zambia. Undoing cabotage restrictions enshrined in the BRTAs is a priority. Other elements in regional accords include harmonization of road signs, harmonization of drivers' licenses, provision of one-stop border posts, and upgrading of trunk roads to comply with SADC technical design standards.

- *Push for regional cooperation in the rail system to lead to efficiencies and new competition.* Zimbabwe's railways are interconnected with other national networks along the North-South Corridor, but the lack of reciprocal access rights between operators prevents through train service, which means that locomotives need to be exchanged at national borders, often leading to extensive delays due to shortages in traction capacity. Negotiating a locomotive services agreement and wider access would reduce costs.

- *Reduce times at borders to improve competitiveness.* Institutional improvements in customs and other border agencies would be required to streamline procedures at the border posts. These improvements could include allowing for advance clearance and introducing the Authorized Economic Operator facility for precleared companies, eliminating licensing for all but the most sensitive products, developing an online trade information portal containing all required trade information, publishing data on cross-border delays, inviting dialogue with users and small businesses on trade facilitation, and establishing a process of subjecting all regulations to a regulatory impact assessment. These upgrades would allow the border agencies and Zimbabwe in particular to reduce forms and the number of agencies checking the same goods, collecting fees, and requiring identical information to be completed multiple times. Adopting more One Stop Border Posts based on the lessons from Chirundu (Chanda, n.d.) could reduce the long delays common at borders.

- *Increase investment in infrastructure.* Infrastructure is critical to exports. Rehabilitating existing infrastructure and building new roads, rail, and air links are imperative to reduce high transport costs in Zimbabwe. Several studies have proposed specific priorities that should be evaluated and, in a capital-scarce environment, ranked by estimated social rates of return; this process may require sophisticated techniques of capital budgeting and project planning in the public sector.

Enhancing Services Performance by Reducing Policy Barriers to Competition

The potential for trade in services in Zimbabwe is substantial and could counterbalance the regressive distributional effects of relying mainly on mineral-based growth. One impediment to investment and competition in telecommunications is the presence of debt-laden state-owned incumbents, struggling to expand services. Another general impediment is the unavailability of skilled labor. Zimbabwe is underinvesting in the higher education, especially the technical education, necessary to produce the skills needed for the domestic economy as well as to enhance earnings from tourism and to develop exports of information technology–enabled (IT-enabled) services. Finally, many of these services require public investment to unleash private productivity, but have gone wanting for lack of financing.

Overcoming these impediments to enhancing connectivity would arguably be the most effective way to empower formerly disenfranchised Zimbabweans. Whether it is the small business using the Internet to discover a new way to increase efficiency and profits; a smallholder farmer using a cell phone to receive weather forecasts that shape decisions as to when to plant, fertilize, and harvest and thereby increase yields; or a young girl exposed to new ideas that motivate her to gain an education, people can use global information to invest and raise their standards of living. In services sectors like telecommunications, transport, and finance, neither enhancing domestic ownership nor greater foreign ownership will by itself ensure the improved access and opportunities needed to empower Zimbabwean citizens, firms, and farms in the modern economy.

Rather, the key is setting up a maximally competitive environment that will foster investment and job creation in diverse activities.

Experience from a wide variety of countries has shown that meaningful development of domestic economies requires enhancing connectivity through three types of reform: encouraging competition between service providers by eliminating impediments to entry for all providers, domestic and foreign alike; improving domestic regulation so that it is both effective and appropriate; and strengthening incentives for service providers to create vital infrastructure, and to serve the poor and remote. (Borchert, Gootiiz, and Mattoo 2012)

Sector-specific policies could also be adopted to create new opportunities:

- In *telecommunications*, Zimbabwe stands to reap the development benefits of international integration by overcoming the handicap of being landlocked. It can unleash a connectivity revolution in services based on fiber optic broadband to boost the diffusion of knowledge and to facilitate exports of IT-enabled services. Pushing for deeper regional cooperation on infrastructure is crucial. Moreover, the regulatory framework could be improved through greater autonomy for the regulator and a more coherent distribution of responsibilities between regulatory agencies. In particular, a clearer interconnection policy could help foster more efficient interconnection between operators, and a policy toward infrastructure sharing can help avoid duplication of infrastructure, and help direct investment toward underserved areas. Finally, the Universal Services Fund (USF) to finance telecommmunication infrastructure in the country needs to be focused more closely on the priority needs of the sector, and the procurement and disbursement challenges that have plagued such funds in other countries need to be addressed.

- In *finance*, there are three priorities. First, consolidating macroeconomic stability is critical for maintaining the gains in the sector since dollarization. One key aspect of this, as noted previously, is implementing steps to regularize relationships with international creditors that would allow Zimbabwe to access international lending. Another key aspect is to take steps to redirect the composition of public spending toward public investment. Finally, removing the additional stress on the banking systems arising from indigenization requirements is paramount. Ownership requirements are increasing the cost of capital and dampening capital flows at a time when the sector requires recapitalization. Moreover, the involuntary expropriation could jeopardize interbank payments, interrupt credit lines (including trade finance), and lead to disruptive managerial inefficiencies that will result in further inhibiting both domestic and foreign investment. Stabilization and strengthening of the financial sector are necessary to pave the way to greater investment finance including trade finance for exporters.

- *Tourism*, a sector already on the rebound, could be further promoted by accelerating current government measures to improve marketing, image enhancement and rebranding, upgrading and diversification of the tourism product, and streamlined customs and immigration formalities, including through the introduction of the UNIVISA[10] for tourists. Specialized institutions are to be launched to train and upgrade personnel engaged in the tourism industry and direct financial support and marketing support chiefly to smaller resorts and small and medium tourism enterprises. The government plans to work with the private sector and international partners.

- In *BPO activities*, Zimbabwe has been handicapped by a massive brain drain of IT talent to advanced countries, such as the United Kingdom and the United States, and to neighboring South Africa. An improved domestic environment could lure some of this talent back, even as entrepreneurs, as has happened in other countries, and is needed to prevent further emigration of skills from Zimbabwe. Retaining IT talent has to be combined with investments and greater efficiency in telecommunications to be successful and internationally competitive.

Zimbabwe Has the Potential to Use Trade to Put Income Growth on a New Trajectory

Trade can be a vehicle for helping Zimbabwe move toward higher levels of growth. The country has a base of skills and vast natural resources that have the potential for driving sustained increases in incomes for decades to come. Revamping incentives to deepen connectivity and competitiveness is the key. If the government's current macroeconomic program is fully implemented in coming years, and is coupled with reestablishing relations with international agencies and donors, it would change the economy-wide incentives that today discourage investment and exports. Enacted in combination with the reforms suggested in this report, this macroeconomic program would markedly improve the positive incentives for domestic and foreign investors to produce in—and export from—Zimbabwe.

Annex OA: Trade Story Using UN Comtrade Mirror Data

Zimbabwean exports and imports of goods since the beginning of the new century have gone through three distinct phases (figure OA.1).[11] During the period 2000–07 the value of Zimbabwean exports grew by a comparatively slow 3.8 percent per year, much lower than growth in exports of its regional partners. Zimbabwean exports, for example, were equivalent to those of Kenya in 2001 and far exceeded those of Mozambique and Zambia (figure OA.2). By 2007 Zimbabwean exports had fallen behind those of Mozambique and Zambia and were only 77 percent those of Kenya. In other words, if Zimbabwean exports had grown as fast as those in Kenya, their value would have been 1.5 times higher in 2007 (or US$1.1 billion higher).[12]

The value of Zimbabwe's imports grew faster than the value of its exports during this period, and by 2007 the trade surplus of earlier years had been

Figure OA.1 Exports and Imports, 1990–2012

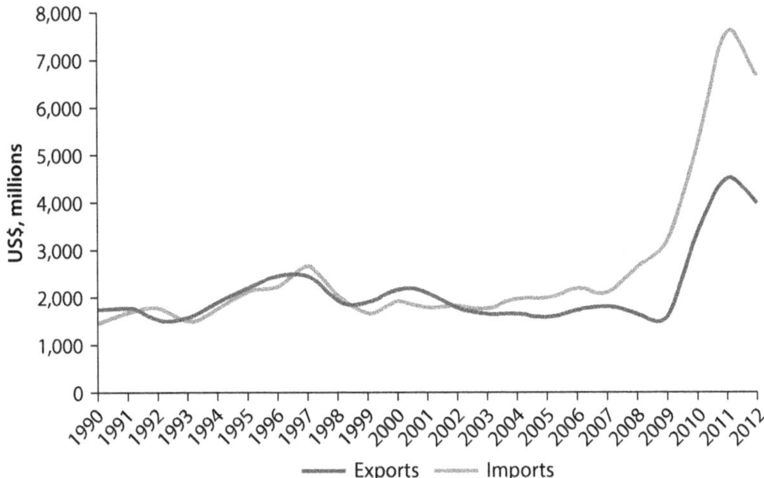

Source: Based on data from Reserve Bank of Zimbabwe at http://www.rbz.co.zw/.

Figure OA.2 Exports of Zimbabwe and Comparator Countries, 1990–2012

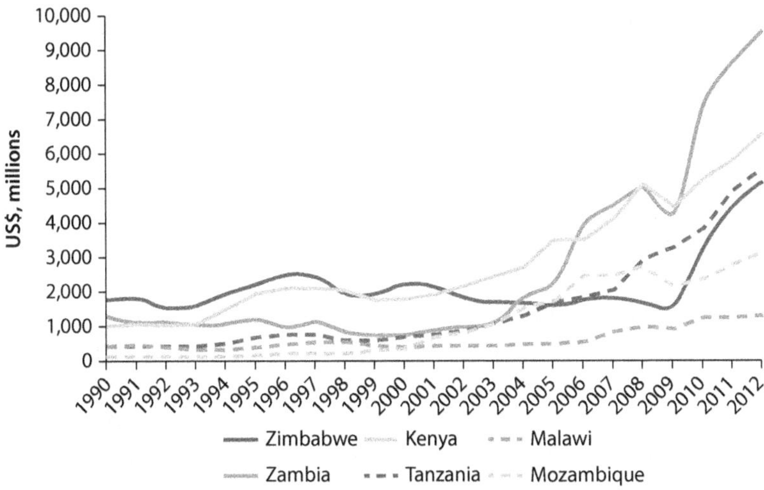

Source: Edwards and Kirk 2013.

eliminated. This growth in import value, however, still lagged behind that of the country's neighbors. Imports for the sample of African countries grew by an average of 15 percent per year, compared with 8.7 percent for Zimbabwe. The period 2000–07 was therefore a period of increasing isolation of the Zimbabwean economy from the international trading environment. As a share of GDP, however, trade rose in importance for the economy because the international markets provided a buffer or outlet for exports in response to the declining domestic market (Kaminski and Ng 2011). Still, Zimbabwe's share of global and regional trade declined during this period.

During the second phase, the deepening of the economic crisis in Zimbabwe in 2007 and 2008 coupled with a collapse in world trade and commodity prices in response to the global recession in 2008 and 2009 exacerbated Zimbabwe's trade position. Growth in the value of imports halted. Exports fell dramatically—by 54 percent between 2007 and 2009. The global recession in late 2008 drove exports in neighboring countries down as well, but the decline in export value for Zimbabwe was far greater.[13]

The decline in export value, however, exaggerates the volume response. The bulk of the decline in value can be attributed to three products: Metalliferous ores, mainly nickel ores (Standard International Trade Classification [SITC] 28), accounted for 50 percent of the decline. Iron and steel (SITC 67) made up 20 percent of the decline. And nonferrous metals, mainly nickel alloy (SITC 68), accounted for 14 percent of the decline. Prices of these commodities, particularly nickel ores and alloys, fell dramatically during the financial crisis. For example, the price of nickel (melting grade) fell from about US$100 per metric tonne in the beginning of 2008 to less than US$40 per metric tonne in the beginning of 2009 (IMF n.d.).

In the third postcrisis period, Zimbabwean trade flows rebounded strongly during the recovery in economic growth in 2009–11. Exports also rose rapidly—39 percent per year—but from a much lower base. By 2011, export values still fell short of their peak in 2007, but had converged back to 2008 levels. Imports rose particularly quickly, averaging 34 percent per year from 2009 to 2011, in response to a surge in domestic demand and inputs required for domestic production.

Mining accounted for the lion's share of export growth in recent years, and it accounted for 50 percent of total exports during the period 2010–12. This export growth reflects improvements in the domestic economy as well as the global recovery in demand, with its attendant price and volume effects. The agricultural sector has been expanding as well, but more slowly. The contribution of the agricultural sector to export growth remained positive in the period 2010–12. The manufacturing sector's share in total exports has been in persistent decline for more than a decade, and its contribution to export growth has been negative throughout the decade.

Notes

1. According to Christiaensen and others (2012), controlling for initial income distribution and other factors, a 1 percentage point increase in growth in resource-rich countries in Africa reduces poverty by 2.4 percent; in resource-poor countries the poverty reduction is substantially greater, 3.2 percent.

2. According to the trade press on diamonds, "The country has probably the most unfriendly mining laws in the world including a volatile policy-making framework. Zimbabwe recently inflated mining fees and prospectors will have to fork out US$1 million for a prospecting license and an additional $5 million to register a claim for three years. Once a company decides to proceed to actual mining activities it should be prepared to take up a maximum 49 percent shareholding while initially being expected to meet 100 percent of the costs. Furthermore, alluvial mining of diamonds is only possible at the invitation of the Zimbabwean Government" (Manyengavana and Takafuma 2013).
3. TelOne inherited a large foreign currency debt when the government separated post and telecommunications as part of a restructuring process that took place in 2001.
4. As within the fixed-line segment, it has been difficult for NetOne to raise capital to invest. The indigenization requirement has affected investment in Telecel. Although there is ostensibly more than one competitor, the degree of effective competition may be limited. Safdar (2013) argues that the relatively high prices of mobile services, and the dominant position of Econet, suggest that competition is not yet fully effective in the cellular telephone segment.
5. NetOne is licensed to operate international gateway services but is not carrying out these operations. Econet Wireless has its own international gateway.
6. Investment climate policies—protecting property rights, honoring debt obligations to retain access to credit, and providing a stable policy and political environment—create the economy-wide contours of the incentives framework. These incentives influence the decisions of private investors by affecting the risks and returns associated with an investment. Trade, industrial, and services policies can play a fundamental role in shaping firms' decisions to invest and trade.
7. In the near term, the government has indicated that it will undertake sufficient reforms to begin to redress the underlying macroeconomic problems, and work with the International Monetary Fund, the World Bank Group, and other international creditors to reestablish its long-term creditworthiness.
8. Various rebates are provided for by the Zimbabwe Revenue Authority (ZIMRA), but access is confined largely to mining-related projects or specific approved projects. These include (1) rebate of duty on chemicals for the mining industry, (2) rebate of duty on goods imported under a special mining lease, (3) suspension of duty on goods imported for specific mine development operations, (4) rebate of duty on goods temporarily imported or to be incorporated in approved projects, and various others (see http://www.zimra.co.zw/ for further information).
9. The Fifth Freedom allows an airline to carry revenue traffic between foreign countries as a part of services connecting to the airline's own country (Rowell 2002).
10. A single shared visa between Zimbabwe and Zambia, aimed at increasing tourism in both countries, with other countries (Namibia, Angola, Botswana) set to join the program in the future.
11. Data come from mirror statistics taken from a sample of 128 importing countries with reported trade data in the UN Comtrade database in each year from 2000 to 2011. Countries for which there are no data account for between 1 percent and 3 percent of total imports from Zimbabwe. Some 43 countries that report imports from Zimbabwe are eliminated.

12. This analysis is based on mirror data. The relatively poor growth in the value of Zimbabwean exports during the period 2000–07 can be attributed to strong declines in the volume of exports (all major commodities apart from Platinum Group Metals [PGM] and cotton lint) that were offset by increases in commodity prices (platinum, sugar, gold, nickel, chrome) (Kaminski and Ng 2011).
13. Zimbabwe reported that exports fell more sharply in 2008 and then grew in 2009.

References

Borchert, I., B. Gootiiz, and A. Mattoo. 2012. "Guide to the Services Trade Restrictions Database." Policy Research Working Paper 6108, World Bank, Washington, DC.

Buiter, W. H. 2013. "Global Economic Outlook and Strategy." Citigroup Global Markets.

Chanda, K. n.d. "Modern and Efficient Border Controls: The Theory of One Stop Border Posts (OSBP) and Lessons Learnt on the Chirundu OSBP Project." http://www.rtfp.org/media/chirundu_one_stop_border_aug_07.pdf.

Christiaensen, Luc, Peter Lanjouw, Jill Luoto, and David Stifel. 2012. "Small Area Estimation-Based Prediction Methods to Track Poverty: Validation and Applications." *Journal of Economic Inequality* 10 (2): 267–97.

Edwards, Lawrence, and Robert Kirk. 2013. "The Opportunities and Constraints for Stronger Regional and Global Integration of Zimbabwe." Unpublished, World Bank, Washington, DC.

Hoekman, B., and A. Mattoo. 2012. "Services Trade and Growth." *International Journal of Services Technology and Management* 17 (2/3/4): 232–50.

Hove, S., C. Mawadza, and R. Vaez-Zadeh. 2013. "Zimbabwe—Trade Finance as an Instrument of Trade Openness: Issues and Challenges in a Dollarized Economy." Unpublished, World Bank, Washington, DC.

IMF (International Monetary Fund). 2012. *Zimbabwe: Staff Report for the 2012 Article IV Consultation*. Country Report 12-279. Washington, DC: International Monetary Fund.

IMF (International Monetary Fund). n.d. "IMF Primary Commodity Prices." http://www.imf.org/external/np/res/commod/index.aspx.

Kaminski, Bartlomiej, and Francis Ng. 2011. *Zimbabwe's Foreign Trade Performance during the Decade of Economic Turmoil*. Washington, DC: World Bank.

Manyengavana, Gerald, and Tinashe Takafuma. 2013. "Zimbabwe Diamond Mining." Equity Communications, Singapore.

Masiiwa, M., and B. Giersing. 2012. "Trade and Transport Facilitation Assessment in Zimbabwe." World Bank, Washington, DC.

Mattoo, Aaditya, and Carsten Fink. 2002. "Regional Agreements and Trade Services—Policy Issues." Policy Research Working Paper Series 2852, World Bank, Washington, DC.

Mattoo, Aaditya, and Eshrat Waris. 2013. "Zimbabwe: Empowerment through Services Trade Reform." Unpublished, World Bank, Washington, DC.

Rowell, David. 2002, updated 2013. "Freedoms of the Air." *The Travel Insider*. http://www.thetravelinsider.info.

Safdar, Z. 2013. "Telecommunication Sector Draft." Unpublished, World Bank, Washington, DC.

World Bank. 2012. "Zimbabwe: From Economic Rebound to Sustained Growth: Growth Recovery Notes." World Bank, Washington, DC.

———. 2013a. Worldwide Governance Indicators (database), World Bank, Washington, DC.

———. 2013b. "Zimbabwe Economic Briefing." Unpublished, World Bank, Washington, DC.

WEF (World Economic Forum). 2013. *The Global Competitiveness Report 2013–2014.* Geneva: World Economic Forum.

CHAPTER 1

Trade as an Engine of Growth: Patterns, Potential, and Problems

Introduction

Trade has been integral to Zimbabwe's growth since the days of antiquity. The Great Zimbabwe Kingdom and the Mutapa Empire from the 13th century and later based their astounding civilizations on trading gold, copper, and ivory in exchange for cloth and other artifacts from as far away as China. Today, trade is more important than ever. Modern day Zimbabwe enjoys one of the highest trade shares in GDP of continental Africa (figure 1.1, panel a). And since 1990, increases in exports have been positively associated with growth in standards of living as measured by GDP growth (figure 1.1, panel b). Trade is vital to growth in Zimbabwe. Without export growth, the economy as a whole cannot long prosper.

Several econometric studies have shown that trade has been an engine of growth in other countries as well as in Zimbabwe. Of 14 major econometric studies since 2000 exploring the relationship of trade to growth, 13 find a strong positive relationship.[1] Brückner and Lederman (2012) find that a 1 percentage point increase in the ratio of trade to GDP is associated with a short-term increase in growth of approximately 0.5 percent per year, and an even larger effect in the long term, reaching about 0.8 percent after 10 years.

In Zimbabwe, trade has once again begun to power economic growth. Since dollarization and liberalization in 2009, exports have grown at an average annual rate of 39 percent through 2012. This growth coincided with the incipient global recovery from the Great Recession, resurgent commodity prices, and increasing demand from China for raw materials, but the domestic revival of the price and payment systems were arguably more important.

The government has recognized the importance of trade to economic prosperity. In its *National Trade Policy (2012–2016)* (Ministry of Industry and

Figure 1.1 The Importance of Trade in Zimbabwe

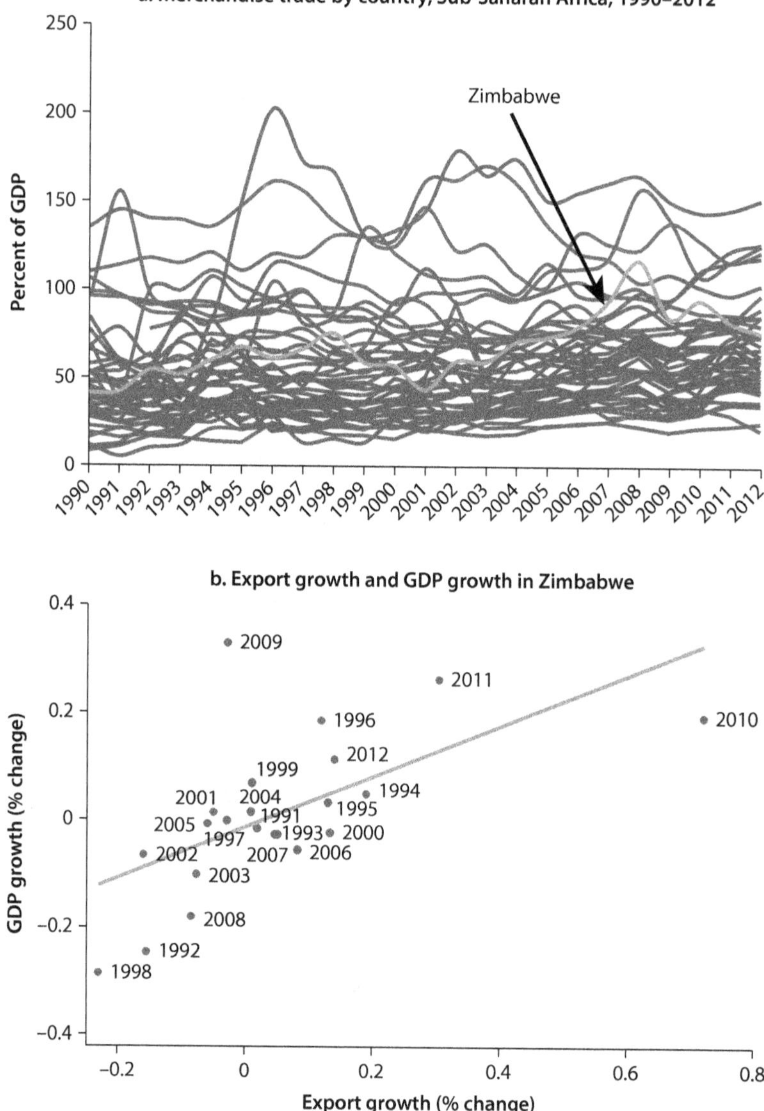

Source: World Bank, World Development Indicators, http://data.worldbank.org/data-catalog/world-development-indicators.

Commerce, n.d., vii), it set out important trade-related objectives as in the following statements:

- "strategies that will enable trade to be the engine for sustainable economic growth and development"
- "transform Zimbabwe from being an exporter of primary commodities to an exporter of value added high quality processed goods and services"

- "seeks to diversify the country's exports, expand and explore new markets, as well as promote the consumption of locally produced goods and services"

This chapter explores Zimbabwe's major trading patterns. It focuses on three questions:

- What trends dominate Zimbabwe's trade performance?
- Have exports become more diversified and with increasing value added and greater technological content?
- Is the recent export surge the harbinger of a sustained export-driven expansion?

The first section explores patterns of Zimbabwe's trade performance, focusing on trend expansion of exports and changes in its major trading partners. The second section zeros in on the composition of Zimbabwean exports to look at diversification, technological content, and employment intensity. The third section looks forward to briefly review the macroeconomic and investment climate prerequisites for mounting an export-led surge to a sustained higher-growth plateau.

Zimbabwe's Trade Performance: Growth and Direction

Mining Has Led the Rebound

The trade rebound since 2009—for both exports and imports—has been astonishing (figure 1.2).[2] Exports surged from US$1.6 billion to US$5.2 billion in 2011. Imports grew somewhat more slowly but more in total value, from about

Figure 1.2 Zimbabwe's Exports and Imports, 1990–2012

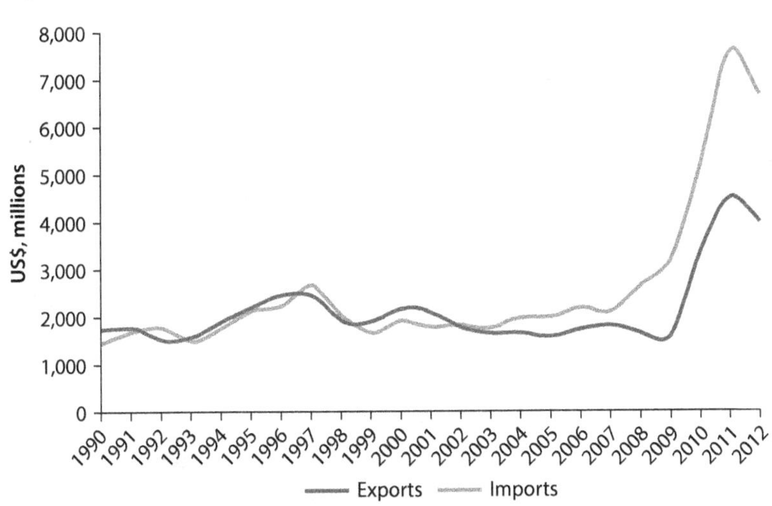

Source: Based on data from Reserve Bank of Zimbabwe at http://www.rbz.co.zw/.

US$3.2 billion to more than US$7.2 billion in 2011. Mineral exports drove two-thirds of the increase, led by substantial increases in diamonds, platinum, and gold. Agriculture, mainly tobacco and cotton lint, accounted for virtually all of the remaining increase. The contribution of manufacturing actually declined during this period, continuing its decade-long slide.

The impressive increase in nominal exports resulted from a mixture of both volume and price effects in minerals and agriculture (figure 1.3).[3] Mining volumes rose eightfold and prices of precious metals on world markets nearly doubled, supported by the coming on stream of diamond mines from the

Figure 1.3 Volumes and Prices of Exports

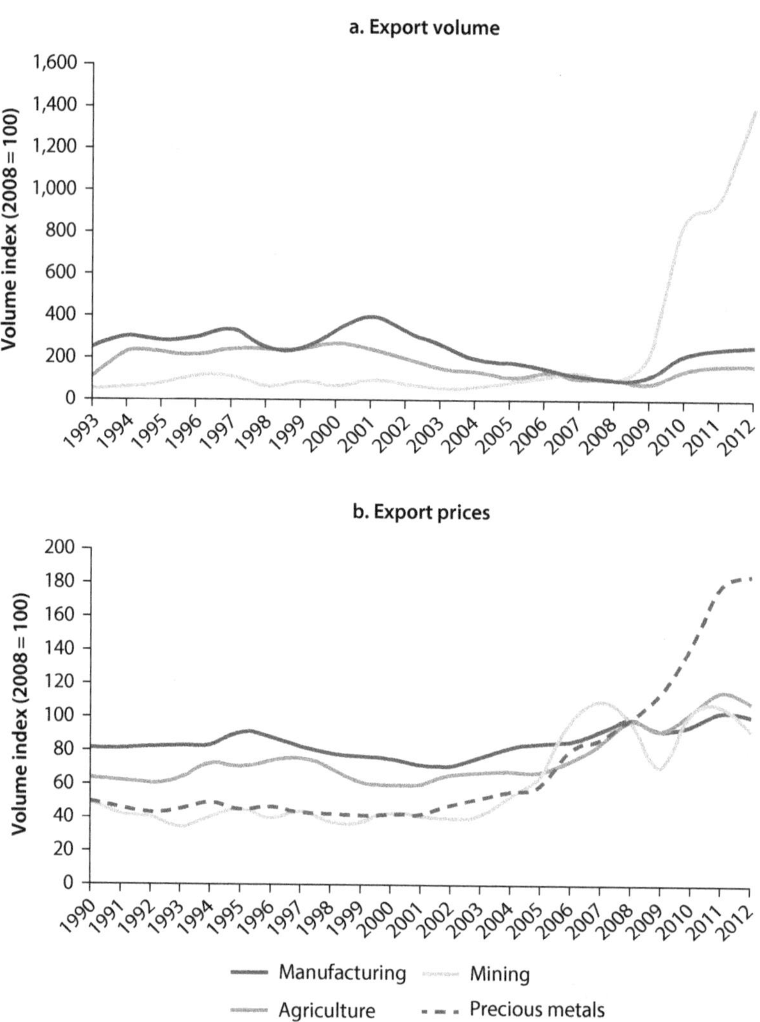

Sources: Based on Reserve Bank of Zimbabwe data at http://www.rbz.co.zw/; World Bank, World Development Indicators, at http://data.worldbank.org/data-catalog/world-development-indicators.

Marange deposits. Similarly, agriculture experienced sharp increases in volumes—nearly double 2009 levels—and price rises contributed another 10 percent to nominal values during the period. The small increase in manufacturing nominal export values was explained almost entirely by the recovery in volume.

The Long-Term Picture Reveals Disquieting Trends

Despite the recent increase, export performance since 1990 has been lackluster. Exports declined from 1996 to 2009 (figure 1.2). Mining volumes were flat through 2009, and agricultural volumes contracted by nearly two-thirds relative to 2001;[4] even with the export surge after 2009 agricultural volumes achieved levels still one-third lower than their levels in 2001. Manufacturing performance was even worse. The sector fell by two-thirds relative to its peak in 1995, and even after the rebound through 2011, export production stood some 60 percent lower than peak levels.

On the surface, when distinguishing between the effects of changes in world prices and changes in volumes, the underlying picture is much bleaker: volumes in agriculture and manufacturing remain well below their peaks in the mid to late 1990s (figure 1.3). Agricultural exports, other than tobacco and cotton, have lost their once dominant role in the region, and have made only a marginal contribution to the post-2009 recovery. They are no longer a source of diversification. Manufacturing has continued to wither in secular decline, and even though many firms are operating at less than 60 percent capacity, manufacturing firms seem unwilling or unable to sell their wares abroad. Services exports also have grown slowly.

This sluggish long-term performance stands in sharp contrast to the progressive increases in the total value of exports from neighboring and comparator countries. Since 2000, Zimbabwe has lagged behind Kenya, Zambia, Malawi, and Tanzania in export growth (figure 1.4). If Zimbabwe's exports had grown at a pace as rapid as Kenya's and Zambia's, their value could have surpassed US$20 billion instead of topping out at US$5.2 billion.

A careful decomposition of export growth underscores this point (figure 1.5). During the 1990s, the contribution to export growth of the four potential sectoral drivers—agriculture, mining, manufacturing, and services—was relatively balanced. However, by the start of the new century, a new pattern emerged. Only minerals contributed significantly and positively to export growth before the poststabilization period. The manufacturing sector's contribution to export growth has been persistently negative throughout the past decade.

Changing Export Destinations: South Africa and China Up, European Union Down

The direction of Zimbabwean trade shifted sharply from the European Union (EU) to South Africa between 2000 and 2008.[5] The share of South Africa in

Figure 1.4 Exports of Zimbabwe and Comparator Countries, 1990–2012

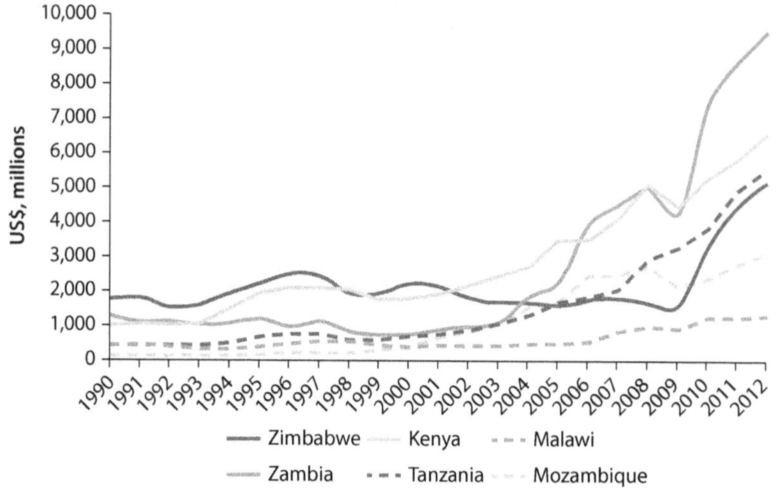

Source: Edwards and Kirk 2013.

Figure 1.5 Mining Drives Postrecovery Export Rebound

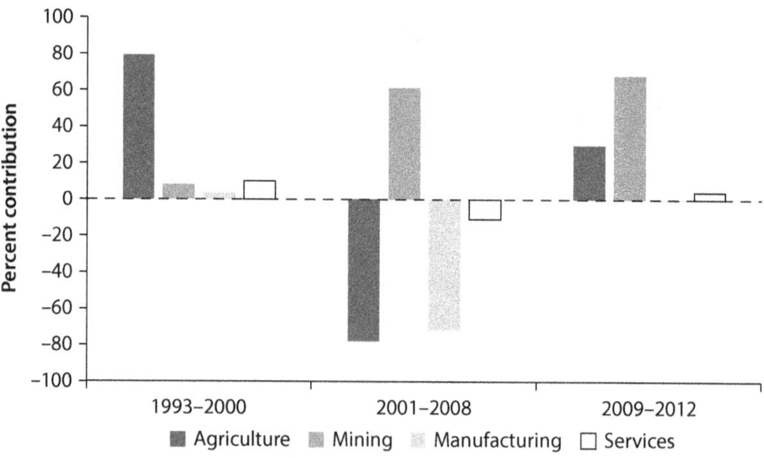

Source: Based on Reserve Bank of Zimbabwe data at http://www.rbz.co.zw/.

Zimbabwean exports rose from 10.2 percent in 2000 to 35.6 percent in 2008, before falling to 20 percent in 2011. Meanwhile, the share of exports destined for the EU fell from 41.1 percent to 23.6 percent in 2008 before reviving to 30.0 percent in 2011. The main contributing factor to the decline in South Africa's share appears to be Standard International Trade Classification category 28-metalliferous ores and metal scrap, which is made up largely of nickel ore, the price of which plummeted in 2009 (Edwards and Kirk 2013).

The other big shift occurred with China. Zimbabwe's exports to China rose from 5.7 percent to 7.0 percent in 2008 then surged to 22.0 percent in 2011

Figure 1.6 Trade Partners: Consolidating Regional Partners and Gaining Others

a. Exports to China

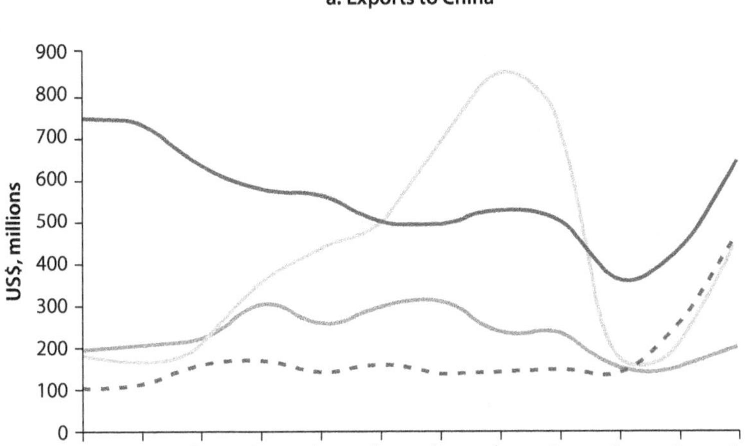

b. Imports from South Africa

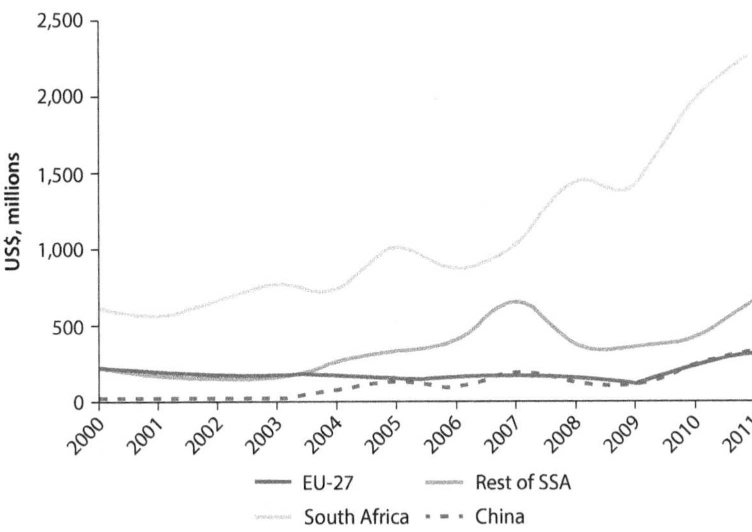

Source: Edwards and Kirk 2013.
Note: EU-27 = European Union 27; SSA = Sub-Saharan Africa.

(figure 1.6, panel a). Exports to China rose dramatically from 2010 on the strength of huge mineral exports. As of 2011, China is the second biggest destination for Zimbabwean exports.

South Africa continues to dominate as the primary source of Zimbabwean imports, making up 57 percent of the value of imports in 2011. This number is slightly lower than South Africa's 2008 share, given that imports from China and the rest of the world have increased.

Regional Trade: Rebound to Neighboring Economies

Zimbabwe's neighbors account for a high share of exports and an unusually high share of its imports. Sub-Saharan Africa accounted for nearly 30 percent of Zimbabwe's exports. South Africa alone accounted for 20 percent of Zimbabwean exports and 57 percent of its imports in 2011 (Edwards and Kirk 2013). However, the relative importance of Sub-Saharan Africa as a destination for Zimbabwean exports has declined with the growth recovery. Much of this decline can be attributed to the dramatic decline in the value of exports to China from South Africa in 2008. Although exports to South Africa recovered in 2011, the increase was not sufficient to offset the earlier fall (figure 1.6, panel a). The value and share of exports to the rest of Sub-Saharan Africa have also fallen. In the middle of the first decade of the 2000s, the rest of Sub-Saharan Africa made up 15 percent of Zimbabwean exports. By 2011, this share had fallen to slightly less than 10 percent. The main contributors to this decline were Zambia and Malawi, where export values fell sharply. Exports to the rest of Sub-Saharan Africa recovered slightly from the trough of 2009, but this growth in exports lagged behind growth of exports to other regions (China and the EU-27).

Zimbabwean imports are even more dependent on the region than are exports (figure 1.6, panel b). As the Zimbabwean economy has recovered, imports have risen from all major sources, including Sub-Saharan Africa. Five of the top 10 import sources are in Sub-Saharan Africa and include (in order of importance) South Africa, Zambia, Botswana, Malawi, and Mozambique. Altogether, 74 percent of Zimbabwean imports are sourced from Sub-Saharan Africa, although the bulk of this share (57 percentage points) is sourced from South Africa. Nevertheless, the share of total imports sourced from the rest of Sub-Saharan Africa is substantially higher than the share of the rest of Sub-Saharan Africa in total Zimbabwean exports.

Composition of Trade: Lingering Vulnerabilities

Increasing the volume of exports is an important objective, but the composition of those exports is no less important. The government has consistently held the objective of diversifying away from commodity dependence and upgrading the technological content of exports and the labor intensity of trade as a way to improve the sustainability of trade-led growth.

Export Diversification: Unintended Reversal

The Zimbabwean government's *National Trade Policy (2012–16)* (Ministry of Industry and Commerce, n.d.) put significant emphasis on diversification. The literature suggests that this focus is well founded. Export diversification may improve growth through several channels. For example, diversification makes countries less vulnerable to adverse terms-of-trade shocks by stabilizing export revenues (Ghosh and Ostry 1994; Lederman and Maloney 2012). Other studies have found that terms-of-trade-induced income volatility depresses long-term growth, in part by impairing human capital through ratchet effects, as unemployed workers lose contacts and skills and younger workers forgo education to support themselves during downturns (Lutz and Singer 1994; Easterly and Kraay 2000). Furthermore, cumulative investment in traditional products will in most cases eventually exhaust the activity-specific economies of scale and lead to stagnating or decreasing returns. In addition, knowledge spillovers from exporters (such as information on foreign quality specifications, production processes, and management techniques), combined with increasing returns to scale, create learning opportunities that lead to new forms of comparative advantage, and these spillovers tend to be more common in manufactures than in primary commodities. Finally, Pritchett and others (2005) argue that when exports are limited to a few minerals, rents from primary commodities are associated with poor governance.

Some studies have found an empirical relationship between export diversification and growth. Al-Marhubi (2000) finds using cross-section data that export diversification boosts growth; Piñeres and Ferrantino (1999) establish that export diversification is associated with income growth in Latin America; and Feenstra and Kee (2004) estimate that export product variety explains 13 percent of productivity gains in 34 industrial and developing countries. Hammouda and others (2009) find that deepening diversification has been associated with increases in total factor productivity in Sub-Saharan Africa.[6] Hesse (2008) provides robust empirical evidence of a positive effect of export diversification on growth of per capita income in developing countries.

Diversification through a Prism

Export diversification can be analyzed through the prism of three lenses. The first is the calculation of a simple Herfindahl concentration ratio that captures the dominance of the leading products—platinum, gold, diamonds, tobacco, cotton lint, and other processed commodities—in the total export basket. By this measure and using Reserve Bank of Zimbabwe (RBZ) data on the portfolio of product exports, the export basket of Zimbabwe has become markedly more concentrated during the past decade (figure 1.7).

Variety Counts: Fewer Products Sold in Fewer Markets

Peering beneath the aggregate trends using a second lens illuminates the diversification process. Zimbabwe exports a comparatively broad range of products to a relatively wide range of countries. For example, Zimbabwe exported 564 out of 780 possible products in 2011. Many of the trade values are low and some of these products may be reexported, but the trade data suggest a relatively broad base from which exports can grow.

However, during the past decade Zimbabwe has experienced a steady retreat from diversification. Diversification can take the form of adding a new product to the export basket, or selling an established export product to a new market (that is, a new country trading partner). One way to measure product and market diversification is to simply count the number of product-markets that Zimbabwe reaches, referring to each product-market combination as a different "variety."[7]

Figure 1.7 Rising Product Concentration

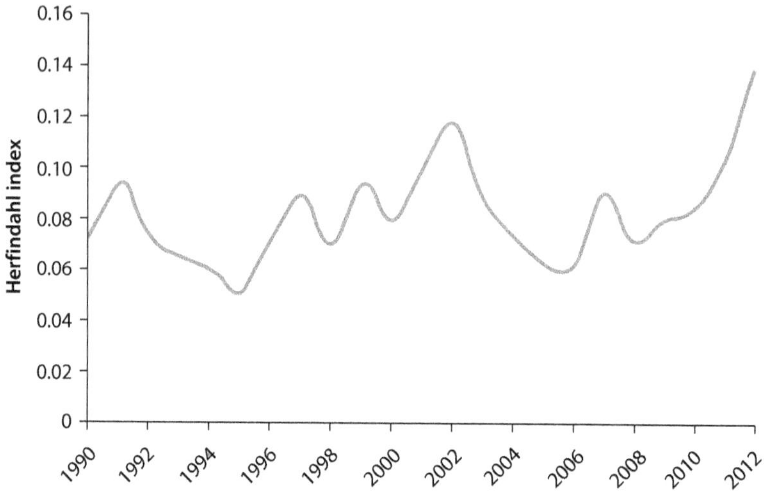

Source: Based on UN Comtrade mirror data at http://comtrade.un.org/.

Figure 1.8 The Export Portfolio Is Becoming Less Diversified

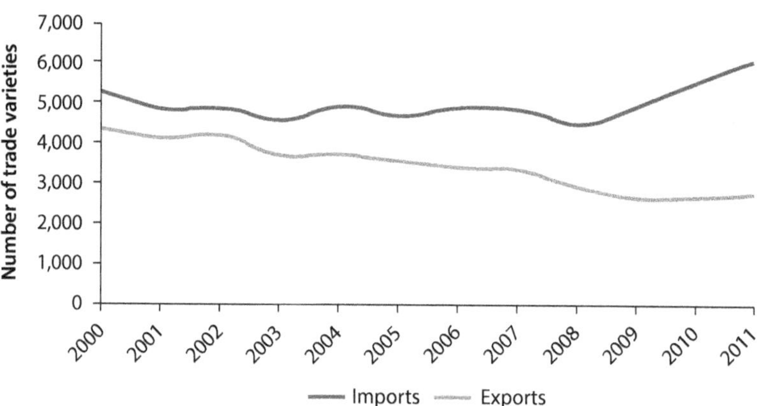

Source: Edwards and Kirk 2013.

Although the number of import varieties has ranged between 5,000 and 6,000 since 2000, exports show a steady retreat from diversification (figure 1.8). The number of export varieties fell consistently nearly every year. In 2000, Zimbabwe exported 4,377 varieties. By 2008, this number had fallen to 2,715 and has risen only slightly with the economic rebound. The decade-long trend in Zimbabwe, contrary to the objective boldly set forth in the national export strategy of increasing diversification, is headed downward.

The key driver of this decline is the ever-narrower range of products exported. Although the number of country partners held steady, the number of products exported fell from 681 to 552. The decline in the number of export varieties

Figure 1.9 Zimbabwe's Export Diversification in Contrast with That of Other African Countries

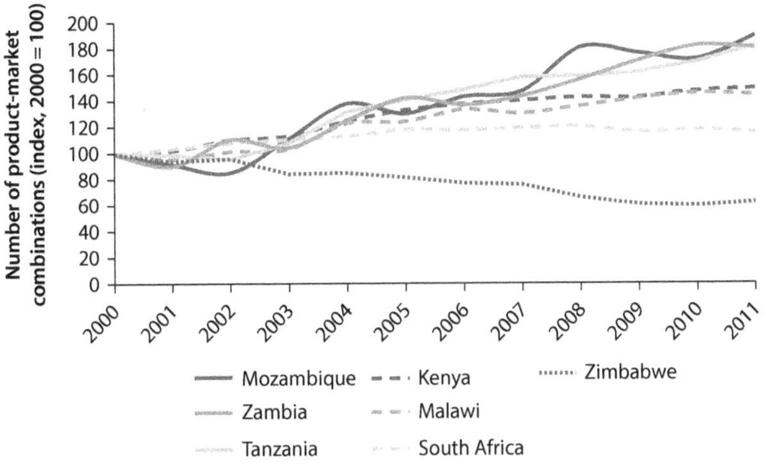

Source: Edwards and Kirk 2013.

tapered off in 2008 and since 2010 has risen very slightly, driven by a slight recovery in the number of export destinations and the range of products exported. The implication is that the strong growth in the value of exports during the economic recovery appears to have been driven by exports of existing products rather than by diversification.

This trend for Zimbabwean exports contrasts starkly with comparator countries, all of which experienced a rise in export varieties (figure 1.9). For example, Kenya, a larger and more diversified economy, increased the number of export varieties by more than 40 percent during 2000–08. But even smaller African countries that began the period with far less diversified export portfolios than Zimbabwe trended sharply toward greater diversification. This situation also holds in the post-2009 period, in which only South Africa and Malawi experienced slower growth in export varieties.

Traditional Goods to Known Markets Drive Exports

A third lens for analyzing diversification is a decomposition of the value that existing products and existing markets (the "intensive margin") contribute to growth compared with the contribution of new products and new markets (the "extensive margin"). Whereas the previous analysis simply counts the number of product-market combinations, this decomposition highlights the contribution of diversification to export growth. Table 1.1 decomposes Zimbabwean exports into growth between new destinations and new products, and growth in value of old varieties. The intensive margin denotes the growth in trade value that can be attributed to product varieties that Zimbabwe exported (or imported) at the beginning of the period in 2000. The extensive margin is made up of trade in new products or new destinations.

Table 1.1 Growth of Extensive and Intensive Margins in Zimbabwean Exports and Imports

Percentage change from base year

		Intensive margin			*Extensive margin*	
			Of which:			
	Growth	*Net growth of initial year varieties*	*Growth of surviving varieties*	*Death of initial year varieties*	*New destinations (new origins for imports)*	*New products*
Exports						
2000–08	21.8	6.9	31.2	−24.2	14.7	0.1
2008–09	−50.3	−53.6	−19.9	−33.7	3.1	0.2
2009–11	89.9	52.1	65.0	−12.9	37.3	0.5
Imports						
2000–08	76.8	52.0	69.4	−17.5	24.6	0.2
2008–09	−4.1	−7.2	−2.8	−4.3	3.0	0
2009–11	79.5	70.9	74.7	−3.8	8.5	0

Source: Edwards and Kirk 2013.

Note: Sample consists of 129 importing countries with reported trade data in the UN Comtrade database in each year from 2000 to 2011. Data are at four-digit level of Standard International Trade Classification Rev.2. The intensive margin is made up of (1) growth of surviving varieties and (2) death of initial year varieties. New destinations extensive margin refers to exports of existing products to new destinations. New products extensive margins refers to entry into new product categories.

The decomposition reveals a high degree of churning or export dynamics that underpin aggregate export performance. Between 2000 and 2008, merchandise exports grew by only 21.8 percent (or an average of 2.1 percent per year). This slow growth can be attributed to two factors. At the intensive margin, the discontinuation of export varieties present at the outset of the period lowered the value of exports by 24.2 percent. This impact was offset by increases in the value of surviving variety exports, but with a contribution of only 31.2 percent, the net effect on overall export growth was low (6.9 percent).

Looking at the extensive margin, new variety exports raised the value of exports by 14.8 percent (14.7 percent + 0.1 percent) from 2000 to 2008. Most of this margin is made up of the export of existing products to destinations with which trade in other products already occurred. Existing channels of information, market linkages, or preference agreements (see chapter 2) developed through the export of one product may therefore reduce the cost of exporting other existing products into that market. The contribution to export growth of *new products* to *new destinations* is less than half a percentage point. Diversification into new products has therefore contributed little to export growth.[8] Overall, therefore, the failure to diversify sufficiently into new products, combined with the death of initial year varieties and slow growth of surviving varieties, contributed to weak export growth from 2000 to 2008.

The period 2008–09 differs from the earlier period in that the value of exports fell by more than 50 percent. This decline was driven by negative growth in surviving varieties (19.9 percent), but even more so by the exit from existing varieties (33.7 percent). New products and new destinations (extensive margin) raised exports marginally. These outcomes are not unexpected. The decline in world growth led to a sharp reduction in global imports, which negatively affected Zimbabwean exports through reductions in commodity prices and reductions in demand. The decline, however, also arose from particular supply constraints faced by domestic exporters (see chapter 2).

The post-2009 recovery period has been driven by improved export performance along both the intensive and extensive margins. Exports have risen by close to 90 percent in this period with more than two-thirds of this growth arising from growth in exports of surviving varieties. Exports of existing products to new destinations also contributed strongly to growth, raising exports by 37.3 percent. The contribution of new product categories, however, remained very low.

In summary, by all three measures, Zimbabwean exports appear to be becoming less diversified. Not only is Zimbabwe becoming more dependent on a few, mainly mineral, exports but it is failing to introduce new varieties and develop new products. No less disheartening, it seems comparator countries are diversifying at a faster pace.

Factor Intensity: Retreat from Technology Intensity and Labor Intensity

Another objective of policy is to increase the technological content of exports. Adapting the optic developed by Landesmann and Stehrer (2002) provides insight into the technology and labor content of exports. Their work distinguishes among three broad categories of production activities: (1) low-technology and labor-intensive activities, (2) resource-intensive activities, and (3) medium- to high-technology production activities. Low-technology and labor-intensive activities include, among others, agricultural foods and feeds, some animal and vegetable oils, simple manufactured goods, and textiles and clothing. Resource-intensive activities, accounting now for about two-thirds of Zimbabwe's total exports, cover such sectors as mining, steel and iron, and simple industrial products based on intensive use of natural resources (for example, wood materials, cement, alloys, and so forth). Medium- to high-technology-intensive products include machinery and transport equipment as well as some miscellaneous manufactures such as furniture parts and medical instruments.

In the long term, the technology content of Zimbabwe's exports has barely registered on export charts (figure 1.10 and table 1.2). Through 2011, exports of low-technology and labor-intensive products exhibited little growth from its peak in 1997. Although the post-stabilization bounce was high, figures since seem to have regressed to the mean.[9]

An implication of this pattern of export growth is that the impulse to create jobs, particularly for unskilled labor, has attenuated over time. As manufactures, and to a lesser extent, diversified agriculture, have given way to mining in export composition, the capital intensity of production has risen. One offsetting factor has been the revived output of smallholder tobacco production, which has created some jobs in the rural sector although it has done little to help raise the technological content of exports. Still, this trade pattern has created demand for

Figure 1.10 Increasing Dominance of Resource-Intensive Exports

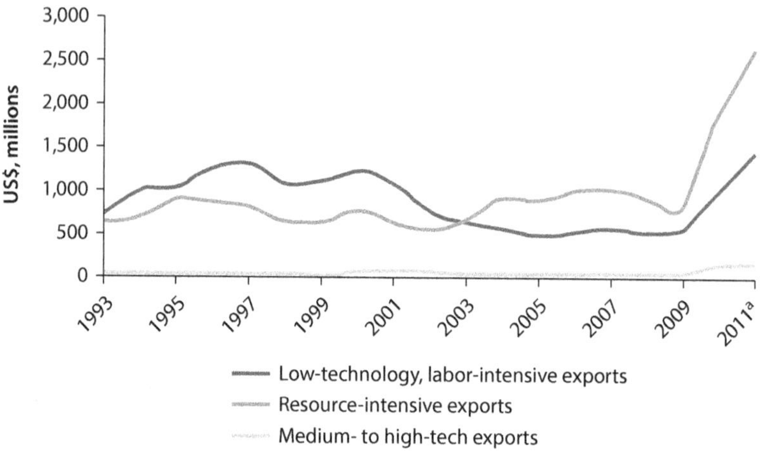

Source: Reserve Bank of Zimbabwe data at http://www.rbz.co.zw/.
a. Projected data.

more-skilled labor and imparted a skill-bias to the growth path, and with it, tendencies toward greater income inequality.

Looking Forward: Consolidating Current Stability to Accelerate Export Growth

The outlook for sustained export growth that might in turn power more rapid economic growth is heavily dependent on global developments and the domestic macroeconomic environment. Both give cause for concern. Even though the global recovery is slowly building momentum, the international environment is exposed to new uncertainties arising from slowing growth in China, persistent slow growth in Europe associated with deep recession in its south, and the course of monetary and fiscal policy in the United States. These conditions weigh heavily on prices of Zimbabwe's commodity exports: prices are projected to fall relative to 2012 levels for platinum, gold, maize, and tobacco while cotton prices are predicted to remain flat (World Bank 2013b). Moreover, higher interest rates in the United States and internationally associated with the U.S. Federal Reserve's tapering of its purchases of bonds seems likely to slow the flow of capital to developing countries.

The exchange rate casts a further shadow over export prospects. The U.S. dollar has appreciated by almost 30 percent relative to the South African rand since early 2012 and is forecast to fall further in 2014 (Buiter 2013). Because such a large share of Zimbabwe's trade is with South Africa, this appreciation undermines the competitiveness of Zimbabwe's exports because dollarized exports are now priced higher in the regional market.

There are also domestic headwinds. Three interrelated pressures threaten export performance and growth. First, the financing of the large and persistent

Table 1.2 Export Composition by Type of Product Exported

	1993–99	*2000–04*	*2005–09*	*2010*	*2011[a]*	*2012[b]*
			US$, millions			
Low-tech, labor-intensive exports	1,085.5	858.3	543.6	1,001.5	1,431.4	1,344.9
Tobacco	540.7	437.3	243.2	475.5	830.5	821.6
Cotton lint	90.9	96.1	98.7	119.2	142.5	198.0
Resource-intensive exports	753.1	697.3	932.5	1,890.3	2,604.7	2,542.3
Platinum	1.5	57.4	343.5	700.6	898.9	854.9
Gold	260.1	203.2	159.0	334.2	598.7	714.9
Diamonds	4.2	1.3	30.8	344.4	419.0	657.9
Ferro-alloys	168.6	129.7	138.6	118.3	260.0	126.0
Medium- to high-tech exports	28.6	47.5	28.6	143.1	155.9	16.6
Transport equipment	7.8	5.9	4.6	69.0	75.2	0.9
Electrical machinery and appliances	8.1	8.6	8.4	25.8	28.1	9.0
Other	77.0	188.6	80.5	153.9	167.8	29.4
	1993–99	*2000–04*	*2005–09*	*2010*	*2011[a]*	*2012[b]*
			Percent			
Low-tech, labor-intensive exports	56	48	34	31	33	34
Tobacco	28	24	15	15	19	21
Cotton lint	5	5	6	4	3	5
Resource-intensive exports	39	39	59	59	60	65
Platinum	0	3	22	22	21	22
Gold	13	11	10	10	14	18
Diamonds	0	0	2	11	10	17
Ferro-alloys	9	7	9	4	6	3
Medium-to high-tech exports	1	3	2	4	4	0
Transport equipment	0	0	0	2	2	0
Electrical machinery and appliances	0	0	1	1	1	0
Other	4	11	5	5	4	1

Source: Reserve Bank of Zimbabwe data at http://www.rbz.co.zw/.
a. estimated.
b. projected.

current account deficit is unlikely to continue to sustain imports at current levels; the bulk of current account financing comes from short-term capital inflows (including errors and omissions) and arrears accumulation. The external debt is estimated to be 82 percent of GDP at the end of 2013 (IMF 2012). About half of this debt is arrears to creditors. If global interest rates were to rise and raise the return to capital elsewhere relative to Zimbabwe, the country would be vulnerable to a sudden reversal of capital inflows. Absent the ability to adjust relative prices through devaluation, the burden of adjustment will fall on import volumes, including machinery imports and intermediate inputs to export activities. This will put a tourniquet on domestic investment and growth.

Figure 1.11 High Nominal Rates, High Spreads, and High Real Interest Rates Constrain Investment

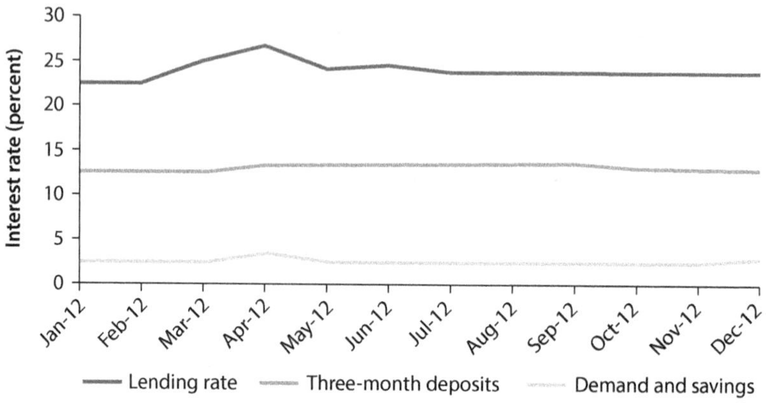

Source: Hove, Mawadza, and Vaez-Zadeh 2013.

Second, pressures are likely to develop in the national budget because the primary fiscal deficit is rising while the very high level of the wage bill as a percentage of GDP is constraining fiscal space for public infrastructure.

Third, investor concerns about ownership policies and weak levels of domestic confidence are dampening the financial system's ability to mobilize savings for investment. Credit conditions are tightening further—nonperforming loans in the banking sector rose to 15.9 percent at the end of 2013. Real interest rates remain high. Nominal lending rates are running between 20 percent and 25 percent, while inflation hovers between 2.0 percent and 2.5 percent (World Bank 2013b). Bank spreads are extremely large (figure 1.11), reflecting a combination of factors, including a low level of savings and very high perceived risk. The widespread perception of high risk has led to a low-level equilibrium in which the public's desire to place funds at the banks is constrained. As a result, real interest rates remain stiflingly high.

Behind these numbers linger concerns about property rights, asset protection, weak governance, and corruption. Investor behavior shows strong inertia following the decade-long decline. Among the 139 countries that the World Economic Forum's Competitiveness Index tracks, Zimbabwe ranked 118 in overall score in 2013, and near the bottom in matters affecting investor confidence: 135 in property rights, 138 in policies and regulations, and 139 in policies affecting foreign investors (WEF 2013). These rankings mark a considerable deterioration since the mid-1990s. Similarly, according to the World Bank Worldwide Governance Indicators, Zimbabwe had fallen to the 7th percentile of all countries in 2011, down from the 37th percentile in 1996, the first year of the index; and ranks at the lowest levels in various governance indicators that affect investor perception and confidence in the economy (figure 1.12). As investor confidence remains weak, investment rates continue to hover at levels insufficient to propel growth in every sector, possibly save mining.

Figure 1.12 Zimbabwe's Rankings in Matters Affecting Investor Confidence, 1996–2011

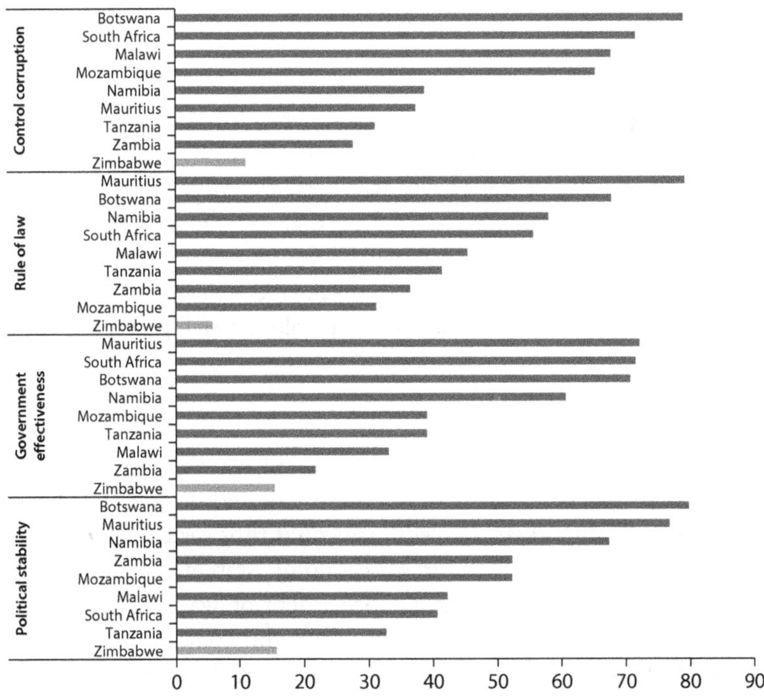

Source: World Bank 2013a.

Note: Average percentile rank values, 1996–2011; higher number reflects better governance. Data available at two-year intervals prior to 2002; annually thereafter.

Patterns Point to Promise and Policy Possibilities

Zimbabwean standards of living are closely tied to the country's trade performance. Its location and resource base, together with a low-cost but relatively well-educated labor force, have endowed it with a naturally high trade ratio built on a diversified base that facilitates using trade as an engine of growth. Two bright spots in recent performance are underscoring the promise of Zimbabwean exports for future growth: the surge of mining exports and the emergence of China as a major export destination.

However, patterns of the past decade point to a slow erosion of the country's natural comparative advantages. Trade volumes have rebounded smartly from the deep recession of 2007–08, but not sufficiently to offset other worrisome longer-term trends: Agricultural exports, other than tobacco, have lost their once prominent role in the region, and have made only a marginal contribution to the post-2009 recovery. They are no longer a source of diversification. Manufacturing, especially when resource-based manufactures are discounted, has continued to wither in secular decline. In contrast to other countries in the region, Zimbabwe has failed to introduce new products and expand to new markets with sufficient vigor to power diversification. As a result of these trends, exports have become less diversified, less technologically sophisticated, and less labor intensive—and ever more dependent on a few large mining activities to provide foreign exchange and employment.

The underlying causes of these patterns, while diverse and complex, are deeply rooted in Zimbabwe's policy framework. Indeed, that is both the bad news and the good news of this report. It is bad news because policy was at the center of the perfect storm in 2007–08: ill-conceived trade and industrial policies came together with ultimately destructive macroeconomic and fiscal policies and the global recession to propel Zimbabwe into the recessionary jaws of hyperinflation. It is good news because remedies are available through policy shifts, and the country has already taken the first, most basic step of reactivating the price system through dollarization, which has allowed it to move out of high inflation and into renewed growth.

The growth revival provides room for turning attention to the prevailing incentives that could encourage private investment and deepen its connectivity to regional and global markets. The country could thus seize opportunities now open to it because of its newfound macroeconomic stability. Investment climate policies—protecting property rights, honoring debt obligations, and providing a stable policy and political environment—create the contours of the incentive framework. Without improvements in these policies, the economy will not be able to generate the much-needed new investment and productivity increases that drive exports.

The government has indicated that it will undertake sufficient reforms to begin to redress the underlying macroeconomic problems, and will work with the International Monetary Fund (IMF), the World Bank Group, and other international creditors to reestablish its long-term creditworthiness.[10]

Successful stabilization would lay the groundwork for reopening access to international financial markets. Enacted in combination with the reforms suggested in this report and other World Bank reports (see World Bank 2012), stabilization would markedly improve the positive incentives for domestic and foreign investors to produce in, and export from, Zimbabwe.

This report focuses on trade-related policy levers that the government could use to make trade a driver of rapid growth, diversification, and poverty reduction. These policies include revamping incentives and deepening connectivity through trade policies (chapter 2), industrial policies (chapter 3), reducing trade costs (chapter 4), and fostering services growth and exports (chapter 5). Taken together, policy changes in these areas as well as in the investment climate can allow Zimbabwe to take advantage of new export opportunities to drive growth and poverty reduction.

Notes

1. See Newfarmer and Sztajerowska (2012) for a review of these studies.
2. Trade performance analysis is hampered by an immediate problem: an inadequacy of statistics. As explained in box O.1, a wide discrepancy exists between Zimbabwean reported trade flows and those reported by its trading partners. This report relies on a combination of government-reported statistics from the Reserve Bank of Zimbabwe (RBZ) to analyze aggregate trends and on UN Comtrade mirror data for the more detailed product, destination, and econometric analyses in chapters 1 and 2.
3. Volume numbers in this section are from RBZ; price information is from the World Bank commodities section in the Development Economics Prospects Group.
4. This is relative to 2001, the first year for which data are available.
5. The analysis in this section is based on UN Comtrade mirror data at http://comtrade.un.org/.
6. Other studies could be added to the list: In Bangladesh and Nepal, export diversification is estimated to raise export growth, which increases GDP growth (Hasan and Toda 2004). Herzer and Nowak-Lehnmann (2006) find that export diversification played an important role in growth in Chile. Lederman and Maloney (2008) present econometric evidence that slow growth associated with dependence on natural resources is likely a result of export concentration rather than dependence on natural resources per se.
7. See Schott (2004) on within-product variety in U.S. imports.
8. The small contribution of entry into new product categories is consistent with the findings of Zahler, Sheu, and Morales (2011), although the contribution for Zimbabwe is substantially lower than the average of 7 percent of export growth.
9. This regression to the mean could also be related to the fact that the original rebound may have only been the result of one-time transactions of donations or second-hand exports, which was observed in a more detailed inspection of the data at the product level for the years of increased exports in this category.
10. The Finance Minister, according to press reports, indicated that the new Mugabe administration will adhere to the IMF monitoring program established in June 2013 and set to expire at the end of the year. Reuters, "Zimbabwe Finance Minister Says to Stick with IMF Program," October 3, 2013.

References

Al-Marhubi, F. A. 2000. "Corruption and Inflation." *Economics Letters* 66 (2): 199–202.

Brückner, M., and D. Lederman. 2012. "Trade Causes Growth in Sub-Saharan Africa." Policy Research Working Paper 6007, World Bank, Washington, DC.

Buiter, W. H. 2013. "Global Economic Outlook and Strategy." Citigroup Global Markets.

Easterly, W., and A. Kraay. 2000. "Small States, Small Problems? Income, Growth, and Volatility in Small States." *World Development* 28 (11): 2013–27.

Edwards, Lawrence, and Robert Kirk. 2013. "The Opportunities and Constraints for Stronger Regional and Global Integration of Zimbabwe." Unpublished, World Bank, Washington, DC.

Feenstra, R., and H. L. Kee. 2004. "Export Variety and Country Productivity." Policy Research Working Paper 3412, World Bank, Washington, DC.

Ghosh, A., and J. D. Ostry. 1994. "Export Instability and the External Balance in Developing Countries." *IMF Staff Papers* 41 (2): 214–35.

Hammouda, H. B., S. N. Karingi, A. E. Njuguna, and M. S. Jallab. 2009. "Why Doesn't Regional Integration Improve Income Convergence in Africa?" *African Development Review* 21 (2): 291–330.

Hasan, M. Aynul, and Hirohito Toda. 2004. *Export Diversification and Economic Growth: The Experience of Selected Least Developed Countries*. New York: United Nations Economic and Social Commission for Asia and the Pacific.

Herzer, D., and D. F. Nowak-Lehnmann. 2006. "What Does Export Diversification Do for Growth? An Econometric Analysis." *Applied Economics* 38 (15): 1825–38.

Hesse, H. 2008. "Export Diversification and Economic Growth." Commission on Growth and Development Working Paper 21, World Bank, Washington, DC.

Hove, Seedwell, Crispen Mawadza, and Reza Vaez-Zadeh. 2013. "Zimbabwe—Trade Finance as an Instrument of Trade Openness: Issues and Challenges in a Dollarized Economy." Unpublished, World Bank, Washington, DC.

IMF (International Monetary Fund). 2012. *Zimbabwe: Staff Report for the 2012 Article IV Consultation*. Country Report 12-279. Washington, DC: International Monetary Fund.

Landesmann, M., and R. Stehrer. 2002. *The CEECs in the Enlarged Europe: Convergence Patterns, Specialization and Labour Market Implications*. Research Report 286, Vienna Institute for International Economic Studies, Vienna.

Lederman, D., and W. Maloney. 2008. "In Search of the Missing Resource Curse." Policy Research Working Paper 4766, World Bank, Washington, DC.

———. 2012. *Does What You Export Matter? In Search of Empirical Guidance for Industrial Policy*. Washington, DC: World Bank.

Lutz, M., and H. W. Singer. 1994. "The Link between Increased Trade Openness and the Terms of Trade: An Empirical Investigation." *World Development* 22 (11): 1697–709.

Ministry of Industry and Commerce. n.d. *National Trade Strategy (2012–2016)*. Harare, Zimbabwe.

Newfarmer, R., and M. Sztajerowska. 2012. "Trade and Employment in a Fast-Changing World." In *Policy Priorities for International Trade and Jobs*, edited by Douglas Lippoldt. Paris: Organisation for Economic Co-operation and Development.

Piñeres, S. A. G. D., and M. Ferrantino. 1999. "Export Sector Dynamics and Domestic Growth: The Case of Colombia." *Review of Development Economics* 3 (3): 268–80.

Pritchett, L., J. Isham, M. Woolcock, and G. Busby. 2005. "The Varieties of Resource Experience: Natural Resource Export Structures and the Political Economy of Economic Growth." *World Bank Economic Review* 19 (2): 141–74.

Schott, P. K. 2004. "Across-Product versus Within-Product Specialization in International Trade." *Quarterly Journal of Economics* 119 (2): 647–78.

WEF (World Economic Forum). 2013. *The Global Competitiveness Report 2013–2014*. Geneva, Switzerland: World Economic Forum.

World Bank. 2012. *Zimbabwe: From Economic Rebound to Sustained Growth: Growth Recovery Notes*. Washington, DC: World Bank.

———. 2013a. Worldwide Governance Indicators (database). World Bank, Washington, DC.

———. 2013b. "Zimbabwe Economic Briefing." Unpublished, World Bank, Washington, DC.

Zahler, A., G. Sheu, and E. Morales. 2011. "Gravity and Extended Gravity: Estimating a Structural Model of Export Entry." MPRA Paper 30311, University Library of Munich, Germany.

CHAPTER 2

Revamping Incentives: Trade Policies

Introduction

Government policies affect relative prices in the economy and thereby transmit profit incentives to private investors. Economy-wide policies convey incentives to investors that affect whether to invest based on perceptions of risk, and in Zimbabwe, economy-wide incentives have tended to discourage overall investment to the detriment of export growth and diversification (see chapter 1). Trade and industrial policies transmit price incentives to invest in favored economic activities, even though they come at the expense of other activities, because consumers, other producers, or taxpayers have to pay for the cost of protection or subsidies. In Zimbabwe, trade policy such as tariffs and other border barriers appear to be motivated by a concern to protect local industry, encourage infant industries, stimulate exporting and regional integration, and favor economic activities that have broad social impacts or have the potential to become competitive.[1]

The National Export Strategy aspired to increase the pace of export growth, increase local value added, and diversify the export basket. The country has had limited success in achieving these objectives. Chapter 1 concludes that this lack of success was due not only to the macroeconomic turmoil at the end of the decade, but to economy-wide incentives associated with policy shortcomings that had depressed trend performance over several years. The government's trade policy is now at a crossroads on its strategy for incentives in the future: to revitalize dismal nonmineral export performance, it can respond to political demands to further increase existing border barriers in an effort to shield producers from foreign competition, or it can adopt new policies that would more assertively open the economy to tap into lower-cost inputs, which in turn would boost domestic productivity and new exports.

To inform this strategic choice, this chapter explores whether existing trade policies are consistent with the trade objectives of rapid export growth, diversification, and heightened technological content. The first section maps trade policies—tariff policies as well as selected nontariff barriers (NTBs)—according to various sectors and economic activities, analyzes the complexity of the tariff code, and describes preferences applicable to Zimbabwean producers. The second section reviews the incentives the tariff system conveys to private firms by using border barriers to raise the profitability of selected activities, and finds that the system discourages producing for export relative to the domestic market. The third and fourth sections trace the effects of these incentives on export performance, and conclude that indeed those sectors facing the highest tariffs on their inputs sell less abroad. A final section presents some conclusions and a suggested way forward.

Structure of Tariffs and Preferences

Cascading Structure of Most Favored Nation Tariffs

The National Trade Policy (NTP) outlines the strategies for promoting international competitiveness and diversification of both products and markets. Within the NTP, tariffs are regarded as a policy tool for encouraging domestic production and diversification. Finance Minister Patrick Chinamasa was quoted in late 2013 as saying that policy makers were looking at ways to regulate imports to both curb the influx of cheap imports and to help local industries operate viably.[2]

Zimbabwe's tariff regime is shaped by the country's commitments under multilateral, regional, and bilateral trading arrangements. Zimbabwe is a member of the World Trade Organization, the Common Market for Eastern and Southern Africa (COMESA), the Southern African Development Community (SADC), and an interim Economic Partnership Agreement with the European Union (EU), as well as bilateral trade agreements with Botswana, Mozambique, Namibia, and South Africa. Zimbabwe therefore operates multiple tariff schedules: a standard most favored nation (MFN) rate extended to all nonpreferential partners; and tariff rates under preferential trade agreements such as the COMESA free trade area, the SADC trade protocol; and bilateral trade agreements with Botswana, Mozambique, Namibia, and South Africa.

Zimbabwe's simple average MFN tariff rate is 15.3 percent as of 2012 (table 2.1). Its maximum MFN tariff rate is 125 percent, and the standard deviation of rates is 16.2 percent. It should be noted that these MFN tariff indicators cover both products whose tariffs are applied as ad valorem duties (5,702 tariff lines) and products on which compound duties are applied but that include an ad valorem component (331 tariff lines). Moreover, the 25 percent surtax imposed by the Zimbabwe government from January 2012 onward for a list of 103 selected products has also been added to the MFN tariff.

Zimbabwe's agricultural products are more protected than other products: the average applied MFN rate on agricultural imports (23.5 percent) is much higher than that on nonagricultural imports (14.1 percent). Tariff peaks, that is, rates greater than 15 percent, are more commonly found in agriculture than in nonagriculture (45.1 percent versus 34.6 percent). In addition, agriculture holds the largest share of products with duties in forms other than ad valorem that, if converted to tariff equivalents, would likely push the average nominal protection rate in the sector to an even higher level.

Table 2.1 Zimbabwe's Import Tariffs, MFN Tariff Data at Harmonized System 8-Digit Level, 2012

		Simple average MFN rates (%)	*Share of HS 8-digit tariff lines with compound duties and excise taxes (%)*	*Share of HS 8-digit tariff lines with duties > 15% (%)*	*Share in total imports (%)*	*Total imports (million US$)*
Overall		15.3	1.1	36.1		3,567
Agriculture		23.5	5.4	45.1	18.2	651
Nonagriculture		14.1	0.4	34.6	81.8	2,917
By sector groups						
01–05	Animal products	17.0	0	39.5	1.6	57.5
06–15	Vegetable products	19.1	0	42.0	9.8	348.3
16–24	Foodstuffs	37.2	17.7	56.2	7.2	256.1
25–26	Minerals	6.3	0	6.5	0.3	10.6
27	Mineral fuels	10.0	3.1	29.7	2.9	103.9
28–38	Chemicals	7.2	0	8.5	14.7	524.1
39–40	Plastic and rubber	12.1	0	46.4	6.5	233.1
41–43	Hides and skins	22.9	0	77.1	0.2	5.8
44–49	Wood	15.3	0	29.8	3.7	130.7
50–63	Textiles and clothing	19.8	0	44.6	3.4	120.6
64–67	Footwear	35.7	0	83.7	0.7	24.1
68–71	Stone and glass	19.5	0	56.1	1.6	58.0
72–83	Metals	13.6	0	42.3	8.7	310.6
84–85	Machinery and electrical	9.3	0.5	21.9	25.1	896.7
86–89	Transport equipment	14.4	0	40.2	10.1	358.7
90–98	Miscellaneous	16.6	0	47.9	3.1	112.4

Source: Fernandes and Kirk 2013.
Note: HS = Harmonized System; MFN = most favored nation.

Zimbabwe's tariff regime fosters the domestic development of some finished goods industries (for example, foodstuffs and footwear) by imposing higher barriers on imports of competing goods. It also supports production of animals, seeds, and unprocessed foods as well as chemicals, machinery, and electrical equipment.[3] Even though the tariff regime changed substantially during the first decade of the 2000s, since 2010 changes have been limited to fewer than 6 percent of tariff lines. Between 2010 and 2011, 3 percent of lines experienced increases of 0–10 percentage points and 1.5 percent experienced declines of that magnitude, whereas between 2011 and 2012, 2.1 percent of lines experienced increases of more than 20 percentage points, essentially due to the application of the 25 percent surtax (Fernandes and Kirk 2013).

The rationale for tariffs can be inferred from the Annual Reports of the Competition and Tariff Commission and interviews with the Tariff Operations staff. Changes and levels appear to be motivated by a concern to "protect local industry through using tariffs" (Fernandes and Kirk 2013, 10). In particular, the Tariff Commission makes recommendations to the Ministry of Industry and Commerce and the Ministry of Finance on import duty reductions and waivers (for imported inputs), tariff splits (targeted to specific users), and tariff protection for domestic firms. The Annual Report eschews across-the-board tariff protection and recommends that it should be targeted to selected industries that (1) manufacture quality and cost-competitive products, (2) are infant industries, (3) are exporting firms and those with export potential, (4) have development projects and programs with broad social impact, and (5) have exhibited potential for future cost competitiveness. Although these categories have fostered a permissive approach to tariff protection, the Tariff Commission has noted that they have considered applications for tariff reductions or zero rating on inputs more favorably than requests for tariff protection on finished products.

Based on the situation prevailing in 2008, Zimbabwe appears to have one of the most complex tariff codes in SADC, with the highest average rates and the greatest dispersion (Behar and Edward 2011) (table 2.2). It is complex because the number of tariff bands and non–ad valorem lines are more than triple the average for the region. Tariff rates are more than double the average of the regional group, and dispersion is greater, though this may have changed since 2008 given that Fernandes and Kirk (2013) report lower maximum and average rates by 2012. Aside from the problems associated with high levels of protection, complexity usually slows down the process of entry. More important, in some situations, protection creates an incentive for corruption when customs officials have scope to use their discretion in classifying a product in a high or low tariff band category.

Different Preference Regimes, Different Degrees of Protection

Because Zimbabwe is a member of SADC and COMESA and has a series of bilateral agreements with main regional partners such as Botswana, Mozambique, Namibia, and South Africa, actual nominal protection is far lower than MFN statutory rates. Within preference regimes, nominal protection is much lower under SADC's preferences than under the bilateral agreement with South Africa (table 2.3).

Table 2.2 Structure of MFN Tariffs Applied by SADC Economies, 2008

		Angola	Botswana	Congo, Dem. Rep.	Lesotho	Madagascar	Malawi	Mauritius	Mozambique	Namibia	Seychelles	South Africa	Swaziland	Tanzania	Zambia	Zimbabwe	SADC average
Complexity	Number of tariff lines	5,201	6,671	5,794	13,348	6,362	5,397	12,516	5,203	6,671	5,122	6,671	6,671	5,260	5,984	5,899	6,851
	Number of bands	7	157	4	157	5	6	283	6	157	51	169	157	14	31	372	105
	Duty-free lines (% of total)	0	59.5	0	59.5	1.9	9.8	87.7	2.9	59.5	87.2	59.5	59.5	37.2	19.3	6.2	36.6
	Non–ad valorem (% of lines)	0	2.3	0	2.6	0	0	2.8	0	2.3	0.6	2.3	2.3	0.2	2.1	6.8	1.6
	Binding coverage (%)	100	96.6	100	100	29.7	31.2	17.9	13.6	96.6	n.a.	96.6	96.6	13.4	16.8	21.2	59.3
Average rates	All products	7.3	7.8	12	7.8	12.5	13	2.9	10.1	7.8	8.2	7.8	7.8	12.6	13.8	25.5	10.5
	Nonagriculture	6.9	7.6	11.9	7.5	12.1	12.6	2.7	9.5	7.6	6.4	7.6	7.6	11.5	13	25.5	10
	Agriculture	10	9.4	12.8	9.4	14.7	15.5	4.2	13.8	9.4	19.7	9.3	9.4	19.9	19.3	25.4	13.48
	Maximum rate	30	346	30	141	20	25	286	20	346	786	>1,000	346	113	66	>1,000	197
Dispersion	Domestic spikes	2.5	9	0	9	0	0	11.7	0	9	10.8	9	9	0.7	0.1	5.6	5.1
	International (>15%) (% lines)	10	21	35.2	21	38.3	36.9	5.5	33.5	21	10.8	21	21	40.7	33.2	35	25.6
	Coefficients of variation	92	154	51	138	50	73	333	72	154	422	206	154	95	73	215	152

Source: World Trade Organization World Tariff Profiles 2009 as reported in Behar and Edwards (2011).
Note: MFN = most favored nation; n.a. = not applicable; SADC = Southern African Development Community.

Table 2.3 Zimbabwe's Import Tariffs, Preferential Tariff Data, Harmonized System 8-Digit Level, 2012
Percent

		Simple average rates, South Africa under bilateral agreement	*Simple average rates, South Africa under SADC*	*Simple average rates, SADC excluding South Africa*	*Simple average rates, COMESA*	*Share of HS 8-digit tariff lines duty-free, South Africa under bilateral agreement*	*Share of HS 8-digit tariff lines duty-free, South Africa under SADC*	*Share of HS 8-digit tariff lines duty-free, SADC excluding South Africa*
Overall		12.6	2.7	1.0	3.7	9.0	84.6	94.8
Agriculture		9.4	8.5	4.7	5.5	29.1	61.7	79.3
Nonagriculture		13.6	1.8	0.5	3.4	5.9	88.1	97.2
By sector groups								
01–05	Animal products	4.5	4.2	1.9	1.9	25.2	77.2	91.4
06–15	Vegetable products	7.0	4.6	3.0	3.6	34.9	72.7	83.7
16–24	Foodstuffs	20.4	16.6	8.0	13.2	10.7	42.4	68.0
25–26	Minerals	0	0.5	0.1	2.2	0.9	96.3	97.2
27	Mineral fuels	17.5	2.0	2.3	2.8	0	87.5	84.4
28–38	Chemicals	7.9	0.8	0.4	2.4	2.4	96.7	98.1
39–40	Plastic and rubber	15.1	1.4	0	1.6	2.5	87.1	100.0
41–43	Hides and skins	36.5	1.2	0	4.2	4.1	76.7	100.0
44–49	Wood	11.0	2.1	0.1	2.9	13.2	75.6	99.3
50–63	Textiles and clothing	12.1	0.3	0.1	5.5	4.2	97.5	99.6
64–67	Footwear	31.3	2.5	1.7	8.1	0	84.0	92.0
68–71	Stone and glass	17.7	1.8	0	4.0	5.8	87.5	100.0
72–83	Metals	14.0	1.4	0	2.3	5.4	89.8	99.8
84–85	Machinery and electrical	9.4	2.2	0.2	2.0	13.5	90.5	99.1
86–89	Transport equipment	15.0	6.3	5.5	4.7	5.9	58.9	71.3
90–98	Miscellaneous	16.6	2.4	0	4.6	2.3	73.8	97.4

Source: Fernandes and Kirk 2013.
Note: COMESA = Common Market for Eastern and Southern Africa; HS = Harmonized System; SADC = Southern African Development Community.

Share of HS 8-digit tariff lines duty-free, COMESA	*Maximum rate, South Africa under bilateral agreement*	*Maximum rate, South Africa under SADC*	*Maximum rate, SADC excluding South Africa*	*Maximum rate, COMESA*	*Share of HS 8-digit tariff lines with duties > 15%, South Africa under bilateral agreement*	*Share of HS 8-digit tariff lines with duties >15%, South Africa under SADC*	*Share of HS 8-digit tariff lines with duties >15%, SADC excluding South Africa*	*Share of HS 8-digit tariff lines with duties >15%, COMESA*
31.8	80.0	100.0	40.0	80.0	8.7	3.7	2.9	2.4
27.6	55.0	50.0	40.0	65.0	13.2	16.9	14.8	9.1
32.4	80.0	100.0	40.0	80.0	8.0	1.7	1.1	1.4
58.2	37.5	40.0	40.0	31.5	5.0	5.0	5.0	4.5
40.6	55.0	50.0	35.0	33.0	10.7	6.8	5.4	5.4
8.7	55.0	100.0	30.0	80.0	20.1	36.9	31.7	20.7
44.9	0	15.0	5.0	5.0	0	0	0	0
45.3	22.5	40.0	40.0	45.0	1.6	1.6	1.6	4.7
33.8	47.5	40.0	25.0	34.5	0.9	1.8	1.8	1.8
56.1	37.5	20.0	0	11.0	8.9	0.7	0	0
13.7	47.5	5.0	0	9.5	13.7	0	0	0
36.9	37.5	15.0	15.0	9.5	6.8	0	0	0
15.9	37.5	40.0	25.0	25.0	5.1	0.2	0.2	0.1
4.0	37.5	25.0	25.0	34.0	28.0	6.0	6.0	6.0
19.7	35.0	40.0	0	9.5	12.0	0.5	0	0
29.9	62.5	20.0	15.0	9.5	18.1	0.8	0	0
46.6	80.0	55.0	25.0	31.5	5.1	3.7	0.9	0.8
18.8	75.0	40.0	40.0	29.0	7.4	4.0	5.0	9.4
16.8	37.5	15.0	0	15.0	18.9	0	0	0

Note that the 25 percentage point import surtax imposed by the Zimbabwean government is also included in the preferential tariffs reported in table 2.3 given that, according to the Zimbabwe Revenue Authority's (ZIMRA's) Public Notice No. 2 of 2012, this surtax is levied on all imports regardless of source. Although no official legal basis suggests that some preferential partners could be exempt from that surtax, South African sources informally suggest that, in practice, among imports from preferential partners, the surtax has been levied just on imports from South Africa (not from COMESA partners nor from other SADC partners). If this practice is confirmed, it would raise serious issues of transparency and absence of information on trade regulations applying to firms in Zimbabwe.

Average tariffs for imports from South Africa are 12.6 percent compared with 2.7 percent under SADC. Moreover, although only 9.8 percent of 8-digit Harmonized System (HS) tariff lines are duty-free under the bilateral agreement with South Africa, 85.6 percent of lines are duty-free for imports from South Africa under SADC.

Under the bilateral agreement with South Africa, imports of agricultural products face lower tariffs than nonagricultural products. The opposite is true under SADC, although again, in absolute terms, preferences under SADC grant far less protection than under the bilateral agreement with South Africa. For imports from South Africa, the highest average tariffs apply to hides and skins under the bilateral agreement (36.5 percent) and foodstuffs (16.6 percent) and transport equipment under SADC (6.3 percent). It is important to note that no goods exported by Zimbabwe are entering South Africa under the bilateral agreement because South Africa has formally stated that the agreement has been superseded by SADC, under which a wider range of products are eligible to enter duty-free, subject to meeting the rules-of-origin requirements. However, some goods from South Africa are being imported by Zimbabwe under the bilateral agreement because Zimbabwe has yet to reduce its tariffs on goods imported from South Africa under the SADC Protocol on Trade.

Focusing on preferences for imports by Zimbabwe from SADC partners other than South Africa, average tariffs are very low, at 1 percent, and 94.8 percent of lines are duty-free, which is not surprising since the SADC Protocol on Trade became a free trade area in 2008. Still, there are some sector differences, with agricultural products facing average tariffs of 4.7 percent and nonagricultural products facing average tariffs of 0.5 percent even though both types of products show very high shares of duty-free lines.

It should be noted that this discussion of preferential tariffs does not separately consider tariffs on either products in the sensitive list (Category C) or products excluded (Category E) from SADC preferences.[4] The original SADC tariff phase-down offers show that by 2008 8.9 percent of Zimbabwe's tariff lines were classified as sensitive and therefore not eligible for any preferences under the differentiated offer (to all SADC countries excluding South Africa), whereas for imports from South Africa, 27.4 percent of Zimbabwe's tariff lines remained classified as sensitive and thus not eligible for preferences.

These sensitive list tariffs were scheduled to be phased out for imports from all SADC countries excluding South Africa by January 2012. However, Zimbabwe applied for and received a derogation that remains in effect as of October 2013; therefore, the MFN tariff rate continues to apply to the tariff lines in the sensitive list.

Zimbabwe applies zero tariffs to imports from all the COMESA countries implementing the free trade area (and moving toward the customs union). Zimbabwe's average tariff on imports from COMESA members that are not implementing the free trade area (the Democratic Republic of Congo, Eritrea, Ethiopia, Swaziland, and Uganda) is 3.7 percent and about a third of HS 8-digit products can be imported duty-free. As with the MFN tariffs, under COMESA, protection is higher than average for foodstuffs (13.2 percent), footwear (8.1 percent), and textiles and clothing (5.5 percent); tariffs are the lowest for animal products (1.9 percent).

Trade under COMESA provides a lower rate of protection (higher preferences) compared with the bilateral agreement with South Africa. Although tariff rates, on average, are lower under SADC preferences, countries that are members of both COMESA and SADC (Malawi, Swaziland, and Zambia) mostly use COMESA preferences, mainly because the rules-of-origin requirement is more straightforward to meet under COMESA.

In summary, the tariff structure in Zimbabwe implicitly favors intraregional trade over trade with the world. Within the region, SADC partners other than South Africa and COMESA are given preference over South Africa under the bilateral agreement. In all regimes, agriculture receives more protection than manufactures, save for the quirk of relative protection vis-à-vis South Africa under its bilateral trade agreement. Finally, the highest protection under the MFN regime, but also under the preferential agreements, is granted to food products and transportation equipment, and for selected tariff lines in stone and glass, selected metal products, and footwear. Before returning to an analysis of the consequences of nominal protection for trade performance, it is important to review several NTBs.

Nontariff Measures Imposed in Zimbabwe

As of June 28, 2013, stakeholders in Zimbabwe had registered 68 nontariff measures (NTMs) under the Tripartite Monitoring Mechanism (box 2.1). Of these 68 complaints, 32 were related to NTBs prevailing within Zimbabwe, and 36 were complaints about other countries. Other countries (Botswana, the Arab Republic of Egypt, Malawi, South Africa, Swaziland, and Zambia) had raised 16 complaints against Zimbabwe.

As of the end of 2012, Zimbabwe has 19 outstanding NTM complaints based on the terminology used in the portal described in box 2.1. Most of these complaints relate to customs and transport and transit issues. In fact, during the first half of 2013 Zimbabwean traders registered six complaints on the Tripartite Non-Tariff Barriers website. One of the complaints related to transport issues

Box 2.1 Collective Regional Efforts to Curb Nontariff Measures: The Tripartite Monitoring Mechanism

The reported nontariff measures (NTMs) applied in Zimbabwe are based on the information available on the public website http://www.tradebarriers.org, a portal established by the Common Market for Eastern and Southern Africa (COMESA), the East African Community (EAC), and the Southern African Development Community—the Tripartite Monitoring Mechanism. Under this mechanism, stakeholders, including the Regional Economic Community secretariat, government departments and agencies, firms, private sector associations, or individuals, can report the barriers they encounter in cross-border trade within the Tripartite Community. The website provides instructions on how to submit a report online. The website went live in 2009 and by the end of June 2013 had formally registered 457 complaints and reported that 349 complaints had been resolved, leaving 108 outstanding. Of these 108 complaints, 100 had been outstanding longer than 60 days. The nontariff barriers (NTBs) are classified in accordance with the categories agreed to by the 2009 Multi-Agency Support Team. The team identified eight categories:

Category 1: Government participation in trade and restrictive practices
Category 2: Customs and administrative entry procedures
Category 3: Technical barriers to trade
Category 4: Sanitary and phytosanitary measures
Category 5: Specific limitation
Category 6: Charges on imports
Category 7: Other procedural problems
Category 8: Transport, clearing, and forwarding

Based on the terminology used in the website, a complaint remains "outstanding" if it has not been responded to (thus "resolved") by the challenged country. Thus, the "resolution" of a complaint does not necessarily translate into the removal of the NTMs or a reduction in trade costs in question; it only means that the country applying the trade restriction has responded with an explanation. However, the explanation does not have to result in any material change for the potential importer.

Two illustrative examples relating to Zimbabwe are given below:

- Complaint against banning of day old chicks: Zimbabwe reported that this ban was imposed to protect animals from diseases originating across borders (Complaint NTB-000-427, reported October 14, 2010, and resolved April 26, 2012).
- Complaint against banning of potatoes: Zimbabwe reported that this ban was imposed to protect plants from pests originating across borders (Complaint NTB-000-426, reported July 1, 2011, and resolved April 26, 2012).

Complaints registered by Zimbabwean importers on the Non-Tariff Barriers website between January and June 2013 include the following:

- Communication issues between Zimbabwe Revenue Authority head office and Kariba border post resulting in duty being wrongly levied and delay in clearance and reimbursement

box continues next page

Box 2.1 Collective Regional Efforts to Curb Nontariff Measures: The Tripartite Monitoring Mechanism *(continued)*

- Customs duties levied on goods exempt under the COMESA Simplified Trade Regime at Kariba
- Customs impounded goods at Kariba border post claiming false invoicing
- Closure of the old bridge at Beit Bridge adding to delays
- Arbitrary customs classification at Kariba; plaintiff complained that customs more than doubled the value of the goods
- The Federation of East and Southern African Road Transport Associations complained that the road authorities in Zimbabwe do not recognize foreign certificates of fitness, insisting on precise compliance with Zimbabwe regulations even when a vehicle is compliant in the country in which it is registered.

Source: Fernandes and Kirk 2013.

and the rest concerned customs. Customs valuation emerged as a serious problem. In addition, several burdensome procedures, permits, and certifications that impose costs on exporters impede exports (see chapter 4 for more details on these procedures).

The Pattern of Incentives: A Bias against Exports

Tariffs convey price messages to private producers, such as where to invest and which markets to serve. Because nonmineral export performance in Zimbabwe has been comparatively lackluster, analyzing the incentive effects of trade policies is worthwhile. The next sections do so, first from the point of view of one producer and then from the point of view of all producers.

Tariffs Change the Profits of One Producer[5]

Consider the profit incentives facing a single large producer and exporter of cooking oil in Zimbabwe. Its hypothetical costs and revenues are shown in table 2.4.[6] The total value of raw material inputs accounts for 60 percent of the total value of the ex-factory price of the cooking oil of 100, so the value added of the product at world market prices (without price distortions) is 40.[7]

Tariffs change this calculation. In particular, the effective rate of protection (ERP) quantifies the combined effect of tariffs or price distortions on outputs and inputs; it measures the proportion by which an activity's value added at domestic prices differs from the value added that would be realized if the prices of its products and inputs were not distorted. In the example presented here, three ERPs are considered: the one received in the domestic market, the one enjoyed in the regional (preferential) export market, and the one prevailing in the world market. These three ERPs are derived by respectively

Table 2.4 Example of Anti-Export Bias in Cooking Oil

Zimbabwe food processor	World market value	Sales destination: Domestic market	Regional market (SACU)	World market
NRP on inputs (%)	n.a.	26	26	26
Cost of inputs	60	75.6	75.6	75.6
NRP on output (%)	n.a.	83.4	20	0
Value of output	100	183.4	120	100
Value added	40	107.8	44.2	24.4
ERP (%)	n.a.	170	11	−40
Anti-export bias	n.a.	n.a.	2.43	4.5

Source: Fernandes and Kirk 2013.
Note: Fernandes and Kirk's (2013) calculations based on World Trade Organization tariff data and the 2011 South African supply table. ERP = effective rate of protection; n.a. = not applicable; NRP = nominal rate of protection; SACU = Southern African Customs Union.

applying domestic, regional (SADC, COMESA), and no tariffs to the domestic production structure.

By looking at the relative ERPs for each of these markets, it is possible to quantify the extent to which domestic producers are discouraged from producing for export, depending on the level of protection they enjoy in their various markets. As mentioned above, the analysis considers two alternative export markets: (1) exports to preferential markets in the region (SADC, COMESA) where exports enjoy some tariff protection, to the extent that the partner country extends a preference over the MFN rate in effect for imports into that market and (2) exports outside the region, assumed to be markets where Zimbabwe can export duty-free through preferences to developing and least developed countries (for example, those preferences it enjoys in the EU). For the purposes of calculating anti-export bias (AEB) and taking into account preference erosion in the Organisation for Economic Co-operation and Development countries, it is assumed that to export outside the region Zimbabwe has to sell at undistorted world prices (with no protection).

The AEB compares the average ERP for import-competing producers if they were producing solely for the domestic market with the average ERP that applies to exports in a given market.[8] Specifically, to assess the aggregate degree of protection within the regional market, AEB is calculated by comparing the ERP in the domestic market with the ERP if firms produced entirely for the regional market. To assess the aggregate degree of protection in the world market, AEB is calculated by comparing the ERP in the domestic market with the ERP if firms were selling all their output in the undistorted world market.[9] Where AEB is greater than 1, there is a bias against exporting in the relevant market: the level of effective protection enjoyed in the home market exceeds the level achieved by exports and thus discourages producers from exporting. This result implies an import-substitution regime and has negative implications for foreign exchange revenues, openness, and economic growth. A ratio of 1 indicates neutrality, and an AEB of less than 1 reflects a pro-export bias.

The cooking oil producer has different profit margins depending on which of the three markets it targets (table 2.4). The producer imports some of its intermediate inputs at zero duty and produces largely for the domestic market with an average tariff on the final product of 32.4 percent. Even with a zero tariff, inputs have to be transported to Zimbabwe and transport costs of 26 percent (based on World Bank 2013) act as protection on inputs. The final product (margarine, beans, or other food products) is also subject to the tariff surtax of 25 percentage points that is currently imposed in Zimbabwe). This cumulates to a tariff equivalent of 83.4 percent without considering the price-raising effects of fees connected with NTMs and other duties (for example, specific and formula duties) associated with the import of intermediate inputs.[10] Although a firm facing such costs would potentially thrive behind protective barriers in the domestic market, it would find its value added substantially reduced in regional and world markets. In the example in table 2.4 the AEB in the regional market and in world markets would be 2.4 and 4.5, respectively.[11] Said differently, selling in the domestic market is more than twice as profitable as selling in the regional market, and more than 4.5 times more profitable than selling in the world market.

Tariffs Change the Profit Incentive of All Producers

The consequences for one firm can be generalized to all Zimbabwean firms given that all firms' profit incentives are affected by tariffs (and NTBs), even if with varying degrees of price effects. Because different industries experience different rates of nominal protection on their inputs and outputs, ERPs vary across industries. The ERPs presented in table 2.5 for each industry are calculated under three different scenarios. The base scenario consists of production for sale in the domestic market, the second scenario consists of production for sale in the domestic market assuming a duty rebate on imported inputs, and the third scenario consists of production for export to the world market with no protection on the final product.

The three sets of ERPs are derived by respectively applying domestic, regional (SADC, COMESA), and no tariffs to the Zimbabwe domestic production structure. The results show the different degrees of effective protection afforded to import-competing sectors in Zimbabwe under these three different scenarios. Knitted fabrics, fabricated metal products, and furniture show the highest levels of effective protection. The large resource-based traditional exporters in the mining sector have marginally negative levels of effective protection in the domestic market. Under the scenario with rebates for duties on inputs, the level of effective protection increases across all sectors and is particularly high in knitted fabrics, footwear, fabricated metal products, and motor vehicles. Those sectors with high ERPs after rebates on imported inputs could potentially compete in regional markets with external tariff levels similar to those of Zimbabwe—this

Table 2.5 Sectoral Effective Rates of Protection and Anti-Export Bias

ISIC	Sector	Total sectoral exports (thousand US$)	Input coefficient world prices (percent)	Tariffs on inputs (percent)	Tariff on outputs (percent)	ERP domestic (percent)	ERP rebates on inputs (percent)	ERP world market (percent)	Anti-export bias in world market (percent)
1	Agriculture	899,684	0.550	15.0	19.9	25.9	44.2	−18.3	1.54
2	Forestry	58	0.374	14.9	10.0	7.0	16.0	−8.9	1.18
10	Mining of coal and lignite	6	0.331	15.4	5.0	−0.1	7.5	−7.6	1.08
13	Mining of metal ores	146,457	0.354	12.6	5.0	0.8	7.7	−6.9	1.08
14	Other mining and quarrying	203,092	0.417	15.1	5.8	−0.9	9.9	−10.8	1.11
15/16	Food beverages and tobacco	181,252	0.556	27.0	28.9	31.1	64.9	−33.8	1.98
17	Spinning, weaving, and finishing of textiles	23,222	0.742	14.2	16.0	21.2	62.1	−40.9	2.05
18	Knitted, crouched fabrics, wearing apparel, fur articles	2,688	0.667	17.0	39.1	83.5	117.5	−34.1	2.78
19	Leather footwear	10,777	0.709	22.7	33.9	61.2	116.6	−55.5	3.62
20	Sawmilling, planing of wood, cork, straw	8,147	0.631	16.1	21.9	31.8	59.3	−27.5	1.82
21	Paper	980	0.736	12.4	13.5	16.5	51.0	−34.5	1.78
22	Publishing, printing, recorded media	43	0.595	13.4	18.6	26.3	46.0	−19.7	1.57
23	Coke oven, petroleum refineries	17,939	0.775	5.8	9.2	21.0	41.0	−20.1	1.51
24	All chemicals	6,275	0.723	11.4	6.7	−5.7	24.0	−29.6	1.34
25	Rubber plastic	11,345	0.650	9.6	16.7	29.9	47.8	−17.9	1.58
26	Glass non-metallic minerals	2,394	0.621	12.5	20.3	33.0	53.4	−20.4	1.67
27	Iron steel non-ferrous metals	196,073	0.771	7.0	8.4	13.2	36.7	−23.5	1.48
28	Fabricated metal products	5,801	0.659	9.9	20.2	40.0	59.2	−19.2	1.73
29	Machinery and equipment	6,039	0.641	11.6	7.7	0.8	21.4	−20.7	1.27
31	Electrical machinery and apparatus	2,000	0.734	11.8	10.4	6.5	39.0	−32.5	1.58
32	Radio, television, communic. equipment and apparatus	589	0.626	16.5	23.8	36.0	63.7	−27.7	1.88
33	Medical, precision, optical instruments, watches, clocks	1,454	0.624	18.1	8.2	−8.3	21.8	−30.1	1.31
34	Motor vehicles, trailers, parts	1,440	0.746	13.9	17.1	26.3	67.2	−40.9	2.14
35	Other transport equipment	62	0.655	11.9	10.0	6.3	29.0	−22.7	1.38
36	Furniture manufacturing nec	6,840	0.639	13.5	27.5	52.3	76.3	−24	2.00

Source: Fernandes and Kirk 2013.

Note: ERP = effective rate of protection; ISIC = International Standard Industrial Classification; nec = not elsewhere classified. The input coefficient derived from the South African supply table is deflated to world prices using the Zimbabwe tariff on inputs for each sector. The tariffs on inputs and outputs reflect the 2012 Zimbabwe most favored nation tariffs.

is the case in many of the COMESA and SADC countries—subject to receiving the tariff preferences.

Although with considerable variation, the ERPs on exports to the world market are consistently negative across all sectors. This result illustrates, given actual tariff structures on inputs and outputs in Zimbabwe, the strong incentives to produce for the domestic (or regional) market rather than selling to the world market where Zimbabwe has to sell at unprotected output prices.[12] (See box 2.2 for more information on performance of manufacturing firms.)

Box 2.2 Through Another Lens: Trade Performance of Manufacturing Firms

The effects of these strong incentives to produce mainly for the domestic market and possibly the regional market can be seen through the comparative lens of manufacturing firms. Comparing Zimbabwean exporters with neighboring firms offers insight into the nature of firm dynamics underlying the decline in exports. Five characteristics are evident in the comparison (see Edwards and Kirk [2013] for more detail on these comparisons):

- *Only a small portion of manufacturing firms report any exports, well below comparator countries* (table B2.2.1). Only about 17 percent of manufacturing firms in Zimbabwe export

Table B2.2.1 Export Participation in Zimbabwe and Comparator Countries
Percentage of manufacturing firms exporting; weighted sample

	Total	*Small (fewer than 20 employees)*	*Medium (20–99 employees)*	*Large (100 or more employees)*	*Number of firms*
Botswana	15.5	8.6	17.9	24.2	85
Kenya	47.0	11.0	46.3	79.1	396
Malawi	19.1	2.7	10.8	61.7	71
Mozambique	5.7	1.2	9.4	49.0	336
South Africa	23.5	10.9	26.4	46.0	680
Tanzania	14.2	6.9	16.4	37.5	273
Zambia	31.7	13.8	25.4	70.4	304
Zimbabwe	16.8	4.0	16.7	43.0	376
Cross-country median	17.9	7.7	17.3	47.5	n.a.
Cross-country average	21.7	7.4	21.2	51.4	n.a.

Source: Edwards and Kirk 2013.
Note: Population weights used for each country. This table presents a firm-based analysis based on enterprise data sourced from the 2011 World Bank Enterprise Survey and the Competitiveness Survey of Zimbabwean firms: Botswana (2010), Kenya (2007), Malawi (2009), Mozambique (2007), South Africa (2007), Tanzania (2006), and Zambia (2007). The data for Zimbabwe are for 2011. A caveat regarding the data is required. The analysis draws on the population weights provided in each of the Enterprise Surveys. Although random sampling with stratification is applied in each country, the representativeness of the samples is dependent on the comprehensiveness of the firm registers. The economic crisis in Zimbabwe during the past decade will have had a substantial impact on entry and exit and the size of firms in Zimbabwe. This may have affected the comprehensiveness of the firm register. Zimbabwe is compared with the cross-country average or cross-country median. There are insufficient countries in the sample to test whether cross-country differences are statistically significant. n.a. = not applicable.

box continues next page

Box 2.2 Through Another Lens: Trade Performance of Manufacturing Firms *(continued)*

compared with an average of 22 percent for the other countries. The highest participation rates are found in Kenya, where 47 percent of manufacturing firms export. The lowest is in Mozambique, where only 5.7 percent of manufacturing firms export.

- *All Zimbabwean firms, regardless of size, export less than do firms in other countries.* The export participation rates in Zimbabwe are below the cross-country average and median in all firm size categories. The gap is largest for small firms. Only small and medium enterprises in Malawi and Mozambique have lower export participation rates than similar enterprises in Zimbabwe. When other factors are taken into account statistically—firm age, managerial experience, foreign ownership, and imported inputs—Zimbabwean firms are found to export less than the other seven countries (Edwards and Kirk 2013).
- *Large firms, as in most countries, are more likely to export than small and medium firms.* Some 43 percent of Zimbabwe's large manufacturing firms export in comparison with 4 percent of its small manufacturing firms (with fewer than 20 workers) and 17 percent of medium firms (20–99 employees).
- *Zimbabwean firms, on average, export a smaller-than-average share of output.* On average, Zimbabwean exporters export 24 percent of their output. This is low compared with the 30 percent average across the sample of neighboring countries. Only in South Africa, which has a large domestic market, do exporters sell a lower proportion of their output abroad.
- *Zimbabwean manufacturing exporters focus almost entirely on supply to the regional market.* More than 80 percent of manufacturing exporters sell to the SADC market where they obtain preferential access. The European Union follows, but less than 10 percent of manufacturing exporters sell into this market. The number of exporters selling to other markets is even lower.

These firm-level statistics tend to confirm what was evident in the aggregate trade statistics: manufacturing firms, responding to policy-altered incentives emanating from the pattern of trade barriers, make their main profits in the domestic market, though some large firms take advantage of the sheltered regional market to export.

Source: Edwards and Kirk 2013.

Does Anti-Export Bias Translate into Slow Growth of Exports?

If the incentives described above are translated into relative prices and then profit opportunities, a strong relationship between the incentives provided by the tariff system and export patterns should be observed. On the one hand, higher tariffs on outputs raise the incentive to produce locally, so they should be negatively correlated with exports; conversely, lower tariffs on imported inputs would be expected to foster exports. This outcome can be seen in an analysis of sectoral patterns of tariffs and trade.

Low Tariffs on Inputs Foster Exports

Fernandes and Kirk (2013) in their detailed economic study of tariff and trade patterns find an adverse effect of the level of protection on intermediate inputs on an MFN basis in the previous period on total sector exports in Zimbabwe, after controlling for year fixed effects. A decline in average MFN input tariffs of 10 percent is associated with an average increase in total sector exports of 19 percent (see table 2A.1).[13] Hence, it appears that facilitating the access of Zimbabwean producers to imported inputs more cheaply through a lowering of tariffs would benefit their exports substantially.

Input tariffs are particularly important for exporters. Sectors facing lower MFN tariffs on their intermediate inputs are shown to have higher exports to preferential partners as a whole (table 8 in Fernandes and Kirk 2013). Sectors facing lower MFN tariffs on their intermediate inputs also exhibit higher nonpreferential exports. The negative correlation between protection on intermediate inputs and sector exports to preferential partners is statistically significant for exports to all preferential partners, to SADC partners, and to South Africa. A decline in average MFN input tariffs of 10 percent is associated with an average increase in sector exports to SADC partners of 24 percent.

Exporters (in manufacturing) rely more heavily on imported intermediate inputs than do firms that only serve the domestic market. The share of imports in material inputs for manufacturing exporters averages 48 percent, distinctly more than the 28 percent for nonexporters (table 2.6). Access to low-cost intermediate inputs is essential to the competitiveness of Zimbabwean exporters. Any policy that would raise barriers or keep barriers high would adversely affect exports.

Preference Margins Shape Overall Trade Patterns

Edwards and Kirk (2013) show that preference margins—through which high MFN tariffs shield producers from outside competition but low preferential tariff rates give them a price advantage—have a strong and significant impact on the

Table 2.6 Mean Share of Imports in Material Inputs and Supplies
Percent

	Nonexporter	*Exporter*
Botswana	58.8	73.3
Kenya	19.6	48.3
Malawi	38.1	46.6
Mozambique	16.8	65.9
South Africa	10.8	28.3
Tanzania	22.6	37.6
Zambia	28.1	47.3
Zimbabwe	25.7	40.6

Source: Edwards and Kirk 2013.

destination of Zimbabwean exports. For each product, exports are, on average, higher to countries where the preference margins are relatively large. In deciding where to direct their exports, Zimbabwean firms target countries that provide a combination of low applied tariffs and high MFN barriers.

Reviewing the product composition of exports to each destination, the evidence in Edwards and Kirk's (2013) estimations shows that applied tariffs have a strong negative impact (controlling for preferences) on the product composition of exports to each destination. For a given export destination, the value of Zimbabwean exports tends to be higher in products that face low applied tariffs. This result is consistent with expectations regarding the impact of tariff barriers on exports.

It is no wonder that much of Zimbabwean trade goes to markets where preference margins are highest. Table 2.7 shows the preference margins based on applied rates and trade destination of Zimbabwe's exports for 2010–11.[14] Because of the SADC-COMESA-South Africa preferential regimes as well as unilateral preferences from the United States and the EU, the average applied tariffs facing Zimbabwean exporters is very low (1.79 percent). The MFN rate is substantially higher at 11.51 percent. The difference (9.72 percentage points) reflects the average preference margin granted on Zimbabwean exports.

Preference margins have a strong influence on Zimbabwe's trading patterns. With the exception of China, Zimbabwean firms face close to zero applied tariff rates on their exports to most of the country's dominant trading partners. The preference margin on exports to the United States is also

Table 2.7 MFN Rates and Applied Tariffs on Zimbabwean Exports, Average for 2010–11
Percent

	Applied	*MFN*	*Preference*	*Share of imports*
All countries, all goods	1.79	11.51	9.72	100.00
European Union	0.01	3.97	3.97	28.92
China	8.87	8.87	0	20.55
South Africa	0.04	9.76	9.72	17.91
Mozambique	0.87	10.20	9.33	5.68
Zambia	0	16.00	16.00	4.16
Japan	1.13	1.79	0.66	2.98
Hong Kong SAR, China	0	0	0	2.57
United States	3.53	4.68	1.16	2.19
Malawi	0	14.77	14.77	1.94
Botswana	0.14	13.37	13.23	1.88
Russian Federation	3.76	9.00	5.25	1.06
All countries, industrial goods	1.52	11.36	9.84	n.a.
All countries, agricultural goods	3.19	12.44	9.25	n.a.

Source: Edwards and Kirk 2013.
Note: MFN = most favored nation. Top export destinations based on the import data of reporter. The share of imports is based on UN Comtrade mirror data, not on exports reported by Zimbabwe. The geographical composition of exports reported by Zimbabwe differs vastly from the UN Comtrade mirror data. n.a. = not applicable.

low (1.16 percent), but the MFN rate is low too, resulting in applied rates of only 3.53 percent. The highest preference margins are granted on Zimbabwean exports to regional trading partners. Because Zimbabwe is a joint member of COMESA and SADC, Zimbabwean firms have duty-free access (subject to rules-of-origin requirements) to many Sub-Saharan African countries. These economies tend to have relatively high MFN rates (particularly on final goods), resulting in high preference margins for Zimbabwean exports.

South Africa accounts for the bulk of Zimbabwean exports to the Sub-Saharan African region. The average MFN tariff on products Zimbabwe exports to South Africa is 9.76 percent, but the average applied rate is only 0.04 percent.[15] Despite stringent rules of origin in some industries, Zimbabwean exports to South Africa benefit from a preference of up to 9.76 percentage points relative to firms in other countries not granted preferential access. Exports to other regional partners are substantially lower, although the average preference margins on the products exported to these economies are higher than in South Africa.

Trade Policies to Promote Growth

Trade policies in Zimbabwe generally discourage exports except when sheltered by preferential tariff agreements, especially in the region. This structure undermines the attainment of objectives in the government's NTP and Medium-Term Plan (MTP) in several ways. By creating incentives to sell at home rather than abroad, it weighs down overall expansion for the value added goods industries. (Of course, tariffs affect minerals minimally because there is no import competition.) By giving the greatest protection to low-technology activities that are also slow growing in the world market—footwear, textiles, agricultural products—the incentive system encourages private investment to flow into these industries instead of into higher–value added sectors. The incentive system channels those firms that do export into preferential markets. Because the regional markets have high levels of protection, domestic industries are shielded from international competition, lessening the incentive for firms to invest in the latest, cost-lowering technologies. Moreover, this structure indicates that growth of nonmining exports is highly dependent on the relatively small markets of the region and their relatively slow growth rates. On its face, these incentives contravene national trade objectives.

The sectoral analysis also suggests that the industries receiving the greatest protection are low-technology, low–value added industries, notably textiles, footwear, and furniture. If the objective of trade policy over the past decade was to stimulate growth in these industries, this measure indicates that it was unsuccessful. These industries have generally stagnated. And, although labor intensive, these industries are not those envisioned in the NTP to propel Zimbabwe into the 21st century on a higher growth trajectory.

Trade Policy Options

The Zimbabwean government has expressed a desire to enhance the growth and diversification of Zimbabwean exports. Policies to achieve these outcomes are spelled out in *National Trade Strategy (2012–2016)* (Ministry of Industry and Commerce, n.d.). Other policies have been recommended in various studies on Zimbabwean trade flows (Kaminski and Ng 2011; Davies, Kumar, and Shah 2012).

Reduce the Disincentive to Export

If the government wishes to encourage deeper integration, particularly of manufacturing firms, into the regional and global economy, policies that reduce the bias against exporting should be revamped. The current trade policy consisting of tariffs, NTMs, and regulations results in established import-competing firms receiving high levels of protection in the domestic market. High tariff rates and trade costs create incentives for illicit cross-border trade, which undermines the level of protection without changing the incentives at the margin.

Adopt Efficient and Lower Tariffs

Consideration should be given to adopting a major tariff reform that would bring Zimbabwe closer to regional practices. On the one hand, lowering maximum tariffs to 15 percent, removing the import surcharge, and reducing the disparity in tariffs within sectors would contribute to eliminating the anti-export bias, and would allow greater import competition to drive productivity gains. On the other hand, reducing the complexity of the tariff structure by replacing all specific and formula tariffs with their ad valorem equivalents, reducing the number of tariff bands that provide a wellspring for corruption, and zeroing-out "nuisance" tariffs below (say) 5 percent would reduce opportunities for corruption that act as a tax on trade. Sensitive products that the government wishes to restrict consumption and imports of, such as alcohol, cigarettes, fuel, and motor vehicles, could be addressed by increasing the excise duty rate.

Implement a Duty Drawback System

A critical reason that the anti-export bias is so high in Zimbabwe is that domestic producers are compelled to pay tariffs on their inputs and must bear inefficiency-imposed costs of transportation that other competitors in the global market do not. In effect, Zimbabwe is exporting its taxes embedded into the price of its would-be exports. A key recommendation therefore is to implement an efficient and extensive duty drawback system as is suggested in the NTP document.[16] Extension of the Preferred Economic Operator Rating status to more firms by ZIMRA will also help reduce border constraints for existing exporters, although reducing these barriers for all firms should be the primary objective.

Reduce Delays in Transportation and at the Border Crossing

Transportation is analyzed in detail in chapter 4, but the issue of delays merits emphasis here as well. Reductions in the delay and cost of accessing imported intermediate inputs and reductions in border delays and in transport costs associated with exporting are critical to reducing the cost disadvantages Zimbabwean firms experience. Remedies might include streamlining procedures at the border posts to allow for advance clearance and introducing the Authorized Economic Operator facility for precleared companies, eliminating licensing for all but the most sensitive products, developing an online trade information portal containing all required trade information, publishing data on cross-border delays, inviting dialogue with users and small businesses on trade facilitation, and establishing a process of subjecting all regulations to regulatory impact assessments.

Negotiate Improved Access in Foreign Markets

Zimbabwe has negotiated a wide range of regional and bilateral trade arrangements with regional trading partners (SADC, COMESA, Botswana, Namibia, Malawi, Mozambique, and South Africa). These arrangements have proved to be successful in enhancing Zimbabwean exports. Nevertheless, NTBs remain a constraint to the country's exports. In particular, the rules of origin that apply under the SADC free trade area constrain Zimbabwean firms' ability to gain access to the SADC (mainly South African) market. This constraint affects the clothing sector in particular because a double transformation rule applies (as opposed to the single transformation rule that applies to COMESA). Negotiating a more relaxed SADC rule of origin for clothing has already been prioritized by the Zimbabwean government in *Industrial Development Policy (2012–2016)* (Ministry of Industry and Commerce, n.d.).

An important arena in which Zimbabwean policy makers may shape access to regional markets is the Tripartite Free Trade Agreement negotiations currently under way. The Tripartite Free Trade Agreement negotiations between COMESA, the East African Community (EAC), and SADC pose a number of challenges to Zimbabwean policy makers. Zimbabwe already has preferential access to SADC, the COMESA Free Trade Area, and EAC members, so the scope for further gains through reductions in bilateral tariffs for Zimbabwe is limited. However, Zimbabwean firms may face increased competition in COMESA markets from South Africa and other SADC members under the Tripartite Free Trade Agreement. Zimbabwe's interests are therefore to ensure an alignment and relaxation of the stringent SADC rules of origin that would better enable it to export to the region, and to South Africa in particular. Enhancing access to markets through the regional infrastructure pillar of the SADC Regional Infrastructure Development Master Plan is also important for Zimbabwe given its centrality and connectivity with other countries in the southern African region.

Reestablishing stable international relations with foreign economies outside the region is necessary if Zimbabwe is to substantially expand exports. The Economic Partnership Agreement with the EU signed in 2012 constitutes a step in that direction because it provides new market access opportunities to Zimbabwean exporters in European markets.

Zimbabwe currently does not qualify for access to the United States under the African Growth and Opportunity Act (AGOA) (although its exports do benefit from tariff reductions under the General System of Preferences).[17] AGOA has significantly improved exports from African beneficiaries, particularly of clothing products from countries such as Lesotho that are eligible for duty-free or quota-free access for apparel made from fabric originating anywhere in the world (under a special rule for lesser developed AGOA countries) (Edwards and Lawrence 2010). Access to AGOA preferences is potentially an additional source of export growth and employment creation within Zimbabwean clothing firms.

Annex 2A

Table 2A.1 Effect of MFN Input Tariffs on Export Performance by Sector: Total and Preferential versus Nonpreferential

	Log total sector exports	*Log sector exports to PTA partners*	*Log sector exports to non-PTA partners*	*Log sector exports to SADC*	*Log sector exports to COMESA*	*Log sector exports to South Africa*
Log average MFN input tariffs lagged	−1.616	−2.038*	−0.848	−2.048*	−0.764	−2.060*
	(1.406)	(1.066)	(1.869)	(1.070)	(1.265)	(1.213)
Year fixed effects	Yes	Yes	Yes	Yes	Yes	Yes
Broad sector fixed effects	Yes	Yes	Yes	Yes	Yes	Yes
Observations	51	51	47	51	42	50
R^2	0.077	0.136	0.014	0.136	0.412	0.055

Source: Fernandes and Kirk 2013. Estimations based on World Trade Organization data, World Integrated Trade Solution data, and the 2011 South African supply table.
Note: COMESA = Common Market for Eastern and Southern Africa; MFN = most favored nation; PTA = preferential trading agreement; SADC = Southern African Development Community. Robust standard errors in parentheses. Ordinary least squares estimation is used. The sample period covers 2010–12.
Significance level: * = 10 percent.

Notes

1. See Government of Zimbabwe (2012).
2. Bulawayo 24 News, September 29, 2013, "Govt: 'There is no intention to completely ban imports'." http://bulawayo24.com/index-id-news-sc-national-byo-36695.html#sthash.f64u4awP.dpuf.
3. Full nominal protection is likely to be higher in textiles and clothing, footwear, foodstuffs, and hides and skins given the predominant presence of non–ad valorem duties on top of tariffs in these industries. See Fernandes and Kirk (2013) for additional technical details on these non–ad valorem differences.
4. Category E includes tariff lines in HS Chapter 93 (Armaments and Munitions) for all SADC countries. In addition, for Zimbabwe Category E also includes Jet/Specialized Fuels, Vehicles/Part, Rear View Mirrors, Used Clothing, Radioactive Products, Used Tires, and Precious Metals (2012 Audit of the Implementation of the SADC Protocol on Trade, USAID Trade Hub, http://www.satradehub.org/activities/enabling-environment/trade-liberalization/item/2012-audit-of-the-implementation-of-the-sadc-protocol-on-trade).

5. This example is taken from Fernandes and Kirk (2013). The authors' calculations are based on World Trade Organization tariff data and the 2011 South African supply table (Fernandes and Kirk 2013).
6. For the purpose of this calculation we assume inputs are purchased at world prices, as are nontraded goods such as electricity, water, and security.
7. Inputs accounting for 60 percent of the total value of production is a realistic assumption for this example given that the technical input coefficient for the food, beverages, and tobacco sector based on the 2011 South Africa supply table is 0.568 and that an interview with Olivine Industries, a manufacturing firm, revealed that their technical input coefficient for margarine was 81 percent.
8. Algebraically, the bias against exporting to regional (preferential) or world undistorted markets is expressed by AEBE = (ERPI + 1)/(ERPE + 1), where ERPI is the effective rate of protection when producing for the domestic market and ERPE is the effective rate of protection when selling to either regional or undistorted world export markets.
9. In the absence of a detailed firm-level survey with information on input usage, the analysis remains highly illustrative.
10. The value of 83.4 percent is the sum of import duties (32.4 percent), import surtax (25 percentage points), and transport cost (26 percent).
11. The AEB of producing to export to the regional [*world*] market is calculated as the ratio of (ERP in the domestic market + 1) to (ERP in the regional [*world*] market + 1).
12. The exception would be those markets in which Zimbabwe has preferential access (duty-free) but that impose tariffs on third-country suppliers.
13. Note that a decline in MFN input tariffs of 10 percent is a proportional change of 10 percent not a 10 percentage point change, so, for example, it means that a tariff would decline from a rate of 25 percent to a rate of 22.5 percent.
14. All data are sourced from the Trade Analysis and Information System. Some important caveats: The product may actually still be imported under MFN tariff rates. This is particularly relevant where the product does not meet the rules-of-origin requirements of the preferential trade agreement. The applied rate is therefore likely to be biased downward (toward zero). The average tariffs are affected by the product composition of exports, which in turn are affected by the tariff rates. For example, the tariff barriers on certain products may be prohibitively high, leading to an underestimate of the measure of protection.

    Not all Zimbabwean goods necessarily enter into the foreign countries under the preferential rate because rules-of-origin restrictions need to be met. The applied tariffs presented in table 2.7 assume that these rules-of-origin requirements are satisfied. This assumption does not appear to be highly restrictive. According to the firm interviews conducted, most manufactured exports from Zimbabwe to the region comply with the rules-of-origin requirements. Furthermore, transaction data for Zambia reveal that only 11 percent of imports from Zimbabwe entered under MFN rates in 2010. Most imports from Zimbabwe enter Zambia under the COMESA Free Trade Area (89 percent of trade).
15. The Southern African Customs Union has reduced most tariffs on imports from SADC to zero. The exceptions are on imports of various motor vehicle components. Access to the South African market by SADC exporters, however, is constrained by restrictive rules-of-origin requirements (Flatters and Stern 2007).

16. Various rebates are provided for by ZIMRA, but access is confined largely to mining-related projects or specific approved projects. These include (1) rebate of duty on chemicals for the mining industry, (2) rebate of duty on goods imported under a special mining lease, (3) suspension of duty on goods imported for specific mine development operations, and (4) rebate of duty on goods temporarily imported or to be incorporated in approved projects, and various others (see ZIMRA website http://www.zimra.co.zw/ for further information).
17. "The AGOA Act authorizes the President to designate countries as eligible to receive the benefits of AGOA if they are determined to have established, or are making continual progress toward establishing the following: market-based economies; the rule of law and political pluralism; elimination of barriers to U.S. trade and investment; protection of intellectual property; efforts to combat corruption; policies to reduce poverty, increasing availability of health care and educational opportunities; protection of human rights and worker rights; and elimination of certain child labor practices" (http://trade.gov/agoa/eligibility/index.asp).

References

Behar, A., and L. Edwards. 2011. *How Integrated Is SADC? Trends in Intra-regional and Extra-regional Trade Flows and Policy*. Washington, DC: World Bank.

Davies, Rob, Praveen Kumar, and Manju Kedia Shah. 2012. "Re-Manufacturing Zimbabwe: Constraints and Opportunities in a Dollarized Economy." Background paper for *Zimbabwe: From Economic Rebound to Sustained Growth*, World Bank, Washington, DC.

Edwards, Lawrence, and Robert Kirk. 2013. "The Opportunities and Constraints for Stronger Regional and Global Integration of Zimbabwe." Unpublished, World Bank, Washington, DC.

Edwards, L., and R. Z. Lawrence. 2010. "AGOA Rules: The Intended and Unintended Consequences of Special Fabric Provisions." Working Paper 16623, National Bureau of Economic Research, Cambridge, MA.

Fernandes, Ana, and Robert Kirk. 2013. "Creating Incentives for New Dynamism in Zimbabwe's Merchandise Exports: The Role of Trade and Industrial Policies." Unpublished, World Bank, Washington, DC.

Flatters, F., and M. Stern. 2007. "Trade and Trade Policy in South Africa: Recent Trends and Future Prospects." Development Network Africa.

Government of Zimbabwe. 2012. *Competition and Tariff Commission: Annual Report, 2012*.

Kaminski, B., and F. Ng. 2011. *Zimbabwe's Foreign Trade Performance during the Decade of Economic Turmoil: Will Exports Recover?* Washington, DC: World Bank.

Ministry of Industry and Commerce. n.d. *Industrial Development Policy (2012–2016)*. Harare, Zimbabwe.

———. n.d. *National Trade Strategy (2012–2016)*. Harare, Zimbabwe.

World Bank. 2013. *Doing Business 2013: Smarter Regulation for Small and Medium-Size Enterprises*. Washington, DC: World Bank.

CHAPTER 3

Revamping Incentives: Industrial Policy

Introduction

Much like trade policy instruments, industrial policies comprise regulations, taxes, and subsidies intended to promote objectives for selected industries. In Zimbabwe, industrial policy has been an active instrument of industrialization since the 1960s, and has been used to influence the structure of the country's economic activity. More recent industrial policy comprises industry-specific policies aimed at ownership structure and the Indigenization and Economic Empowerment (IEE) legislation. Industrial policies, particularly the indigenization process, have had different effects in the mining, agricultural, and manufacturing sectors, with nontrivial consequences for investment (domestic as well as foreign) and trade performance.

This chapter explores the impact of current industrial policy, particularly ownership requirements, in achieving the objectives of more rapid growth, job creation, poverty reduction, and greater participation of the historically disenfranchised indigenous population in a more inclusive growth process. The chapter begins with a focus on the effects of policy on foreign investment inflows, and then considers policies toward the three mainstay sectors of the economy—mining, agriculture, and manufacturing. A final section considers policy options that might help the government achieve its objectives of broad-based growth, job creation, and poverty reduction.

Foreign Investment in Zimbabwe

Current policies place significant limitations on foreign investment. At the global level, countries are liberalizing their regulatory frameworks to attract foreign investment and connect to global value chains. Of all policy changes undertaken worldwide in the past decade, three-quarters entailed greater liberalization and promotion rather than restrictions (figure 3.1). This continues a trend begun in the early 1990s when liberalizing measures outnumbered restrictions often by as

Figure 3.1 Most Countries Are Now Liberalizing Investment Policies

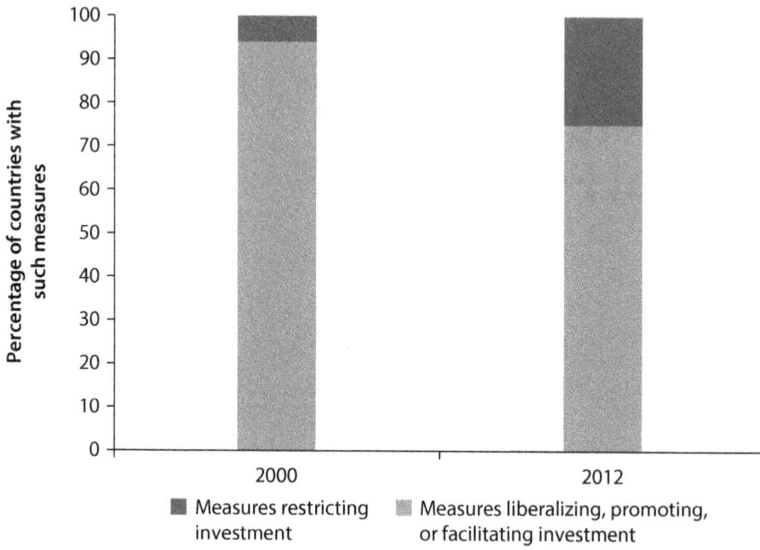

Source: UNCTAD 2012.

much as 9–1. Countries as diverse as Mexico, Peru, and China that once permitted only joint ventures have now moved to liberalize ownership restrictions either across the board or progressively in selected sectors.

One motivation for this liberalization is so that these countries can tap into global value chains (GVCs). The emergence of GVCs of production has created new opportunities for the integration of industries in developing countries. Production that once was primarily located near sources of major input supplies or near consumers in the final market is now commonly segmented across several countries in which the costs of local factors specific to that segment confer comparative advantage. One indication of the dynamism of value chains is the rapidly growing share of intermediate inputs in world trade. Another is that intrafirm trade within transnational companies now accounts for a substantial portion of world trade (OECD/WTO 2013).

GVCs have allowed developing countries to establish more-sophisticated industries in earlier stages of economic development as multinational companies choose to offshore fragments of the production value chain to countries where labor is cheaper or where other locational advantages confer a competitive cost advantage on the whole GVC (Baldwin 2011). Because this organization has reduced costs across the whole GVC, the second consequence of a world of GVC-dominated production is that countries that try to industrialize through the import-substitution policies prevalent before the 1990s are unlikely to ever reduce their costs to the point of being competitive on global markets. In general, the more technologically sophisticated the product (or production process), the greater the role of the brand name, and the greater the market share of the lead firm, the more difficult it is for new entrants to gain entry into the chain (or final market) without following the protocols of the lead firm.[1] Stated differently, GVCs make it more difficult for countries to become competitive in export markets by using domestic industrial policy to build competing production networks domestically; high border barriers will only result in high-cost local production and poor connectivity to the global market. This is a major reason countries have been trying to attract foreign investment via free trade zones and other policies, and leveraging it for greater exports and employment.

Zimbabwe Goes in the Other Direction

Zimbabwe has taken the opposite tack.[2] Zimbabwe formally put in place its Policy Framework on the Indigenization of the Economy in 1998. The policy was revised in October 2004 and adopted by the Cabinet as the Revised Policy Framework for the Indigenization of the Economy. The indigenization policy framework culminated in the enactment of the Indigenization and Economic Empowerment Act (IEEA), March 2008. The main objective of this act is "to endeavor to secure that at least 51 percent of the shares of every public company and any other business shall be owned by indigenous Zimbabweans" (IEEA Chapter 14:33). To facilitate implementation of the act, the government of Zimbabwe promulgated the Indigenization and Economic Empowerment (General) Regulations. The regulations provide that all businesses with a net asset value of US$500,000 or more located in Zimbabwe should formulate plans that would lead to 51 percent of the shares in the firm being transferred to indigenous Zimbabwean shareholders within five years of the date of operation of the regulations. Later, different implementation rules were specified for various sectors (table 3.1).

The IEEA defines indigenization as "a deliberate involvement of indigenous Zimbabweans in the economic activities of the country, to which hitherto they had no access, so as to ensure the equitable ownership of the nation's resources." It further defines an "indigenous Zimbabwean" as "any person who, before the 18th April, 1980, was disadvantaged by unfair discrimination on the grounds of

Table 3.1 Indigenization and Economic Empowerment: Asset Values and Time Frame for Implementation

Sector	*Minimum net asset value*	*Time Frame*
Mining	$1	No later than December 24, 2011
Manufacturing	$100,000	Yr. 1–26%, Yr. 2–36%, Yr. 3–46%, Yr. 4–51% beginning October 28, 2011
Finance	As per minimum capital prescribed by the RBZ	One year from July 2012
Other	$1–$10,000,000	One year from July 2012

Source: Zimbabwe Indigenization and Economic Empowerment Act: General Notices 114 and 459 of 2011 and 280 of 2012.
Note: RBZ = Reserve Bank of Zimbabwe. "Other" sectors include education and sports; arts, entertainment, and culture; engineering and construction; energy; services; telecommunications; and transport and motor industry. Minimum net asset value also varies across subsectors within these sectors.

his or her race, and any descendant of such person, and includes any company, association, syndicate or partnership of which indigenous Zimbabweans form the majority of the members or hold the controlling interest."

The IEE program also includes manufacturing, mining, and the financial sector. The announcement of the IEE program has been accompanied by diminished domestic investment and foreign direct investment (FDI) flows into Zimbabwe. At a global level, evidence suggests that significant ownership restrictions can adversely affect the performance of firms with a foreign stake by diluting incentives to transfer technology and improve management (box 3.1). There is also evidence that these restrictions could limit spillover benefits for domestic firms, which is especially relevant for Zimbabwe given that existing firms need to overcome the lack of investment throughout the past two decades.

Box 3.1 Foreign Ownership Restrictions: Do They Matter?

The New Economic Policy of 1971 was an ambitious socioeconomic restructuring, affirmative action program launched by the Malaysian government on behalf of the "bumiputra." Bumiputra is a Malaysian term that describes the Malay ethnic group and other indigenous peoples of Southeast Asia. The New Economic Policy strove to increase the bumiputra share of corporate equity so that it comprised at least 30 percent of the total. In fact, in many services sectors, from telecommunications to finance, the Malaysian government still allows only minority foreign ownership in new providers.

Kee (2005) examines the impact of these restrictions and finds that firms with foreign equity are more productive, except when constrained by foreign ownership regulations. In fact, only those firms that are not restricted to having 30 percent foreign ownership turn out to be more productive than an otherwise identical domestic firm. Those firms that have foreign ownership of 30 percent or less are significantly less productive than their domestic counterparts. Furthermore, the efficiency of unconstrained firms increases with the share of foreign equity. Firms that have majority foreign ownership are the most productive. These findings suggest that foreign equity restrictions hurt the productivity of firms in the services industries.

The study also investigates the effects of foreign presence on productivity of domestic firms, both because of increased competition and possible spillover benefits. Firm fixed effects are used to control for firm heterogeneity, and only the effects of the presence of foreign firms and new entrants in the industry on firm unobserved productivity is estimated, controlling for capital intensity and export share of the firms. The author finds that domestic firms tend to benefit from the presence of foreign firms. When restricting the sample to domestic firms that have no foreign investment in their equity, regression results suggest that domestic firms benefit significantly from the presence of foreign firms in the same industry. For the business-support services sector, a 1 percent increase in industry sales that originates from firms with foreign equity increases the productivity of domestic firms in the same

box continues next page

Box 3.1 Foreign Ownership Restrictions: Do They Matter? *(continued)*

industry by 3.3 percent. The author concludes that the result is not surprising because the presence of foreign firms in the industry may bring in foreign technology and know-how, from which domestic firms may learn through the networking of personnel and contacts. Similar effects have also been found in firm surveys conducted in Lithuania (Smarzynska 2002), the United Kingdom (Haskel, Hawkes, and Pereira 2003), and the United States (Keller and Yeaple 2003).

A study by Arnold, Mattoo, and Narciso (2008) suggests that spillover effects from improvements in the services sector could also be felt downstream in the manufacturing sector. This paper investigates the relationship between the productivity of African manufacturing firms and their access to services inputs. Using firm-level data from 10 Sub-Saharan African countries (not including Zimbabwe), the authors show a significant positive association between the performance of manufacturing firms in a region and indicators of the availability of services in the region. The paper provides support for the argument that reforming services industries contributes to enhancing the performance of downstream economic activities, and thus is an essential element of a strategy for promoting growth and reducing poverty. Similar results have been found for Chile, the Czech Republic, and India (Pavcnik 2002; Arnold, Mattoo, and Narciso 2008; Arnold, Javorcik, and Mattoo 2011; Arnold and others 2014).

Zimbabwe's IEE program not only establishes restrictions on foreign ownership but also actively aims to restrict ownership within the domestic economy (of nonindigenous domestic agents). Although originally aimed only at new firms or acquisition processes, the 2011 legislation, which updated the 1998 and 2004 laws, also included changes to the shareholding structures of existing firms. It also applies to both private and public firms. Lack of clarity about the program's financing has compounded existing uncertainty about protection of asset ownership, which rose to very high levels during the fast-track land reform and hyperinflation years in the early 2000s. This is reflected in the low overall level of investor confidence; the World Economic Forum's Global Competitiveness Index of 2013 places Zimbabwe at the bottom of different rankings of investor confidence (figure 3.2).

Uncertainty about property rights and concerns about asset protection remain distinguishing features of the Zimbabwean economy. As observed in figure 3.2, the country ranks nearly last on various measures of investor confidence. For that reason, outside of large-scale exploitation of known deposits in mining, Zimbabwe has not been able to attract foreign (or domestic) investors in sectors that could otherwise integrate Zimbabwe into global value chains—and accelerate export growth (figure 3.3, panel a). Its share of new FDI going to low-income countries in the past decade is less than a third its share during the 1990s (figure 3.3, panel b).

Figure 3.2 Investor Confidence Is Weakening

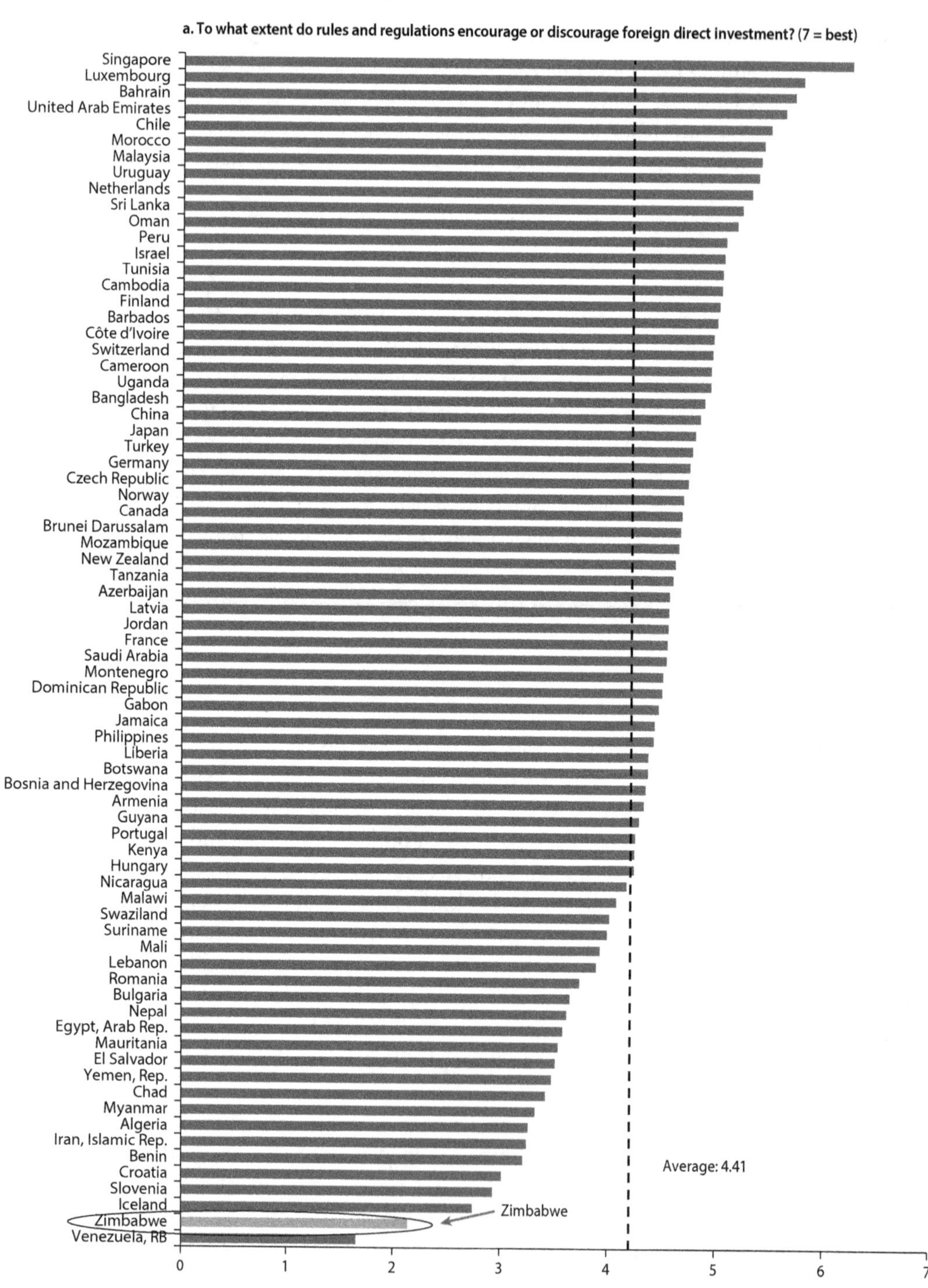

figure continues next page

Figure 3.2 Investor Confidence Is Weakening *(continued)*

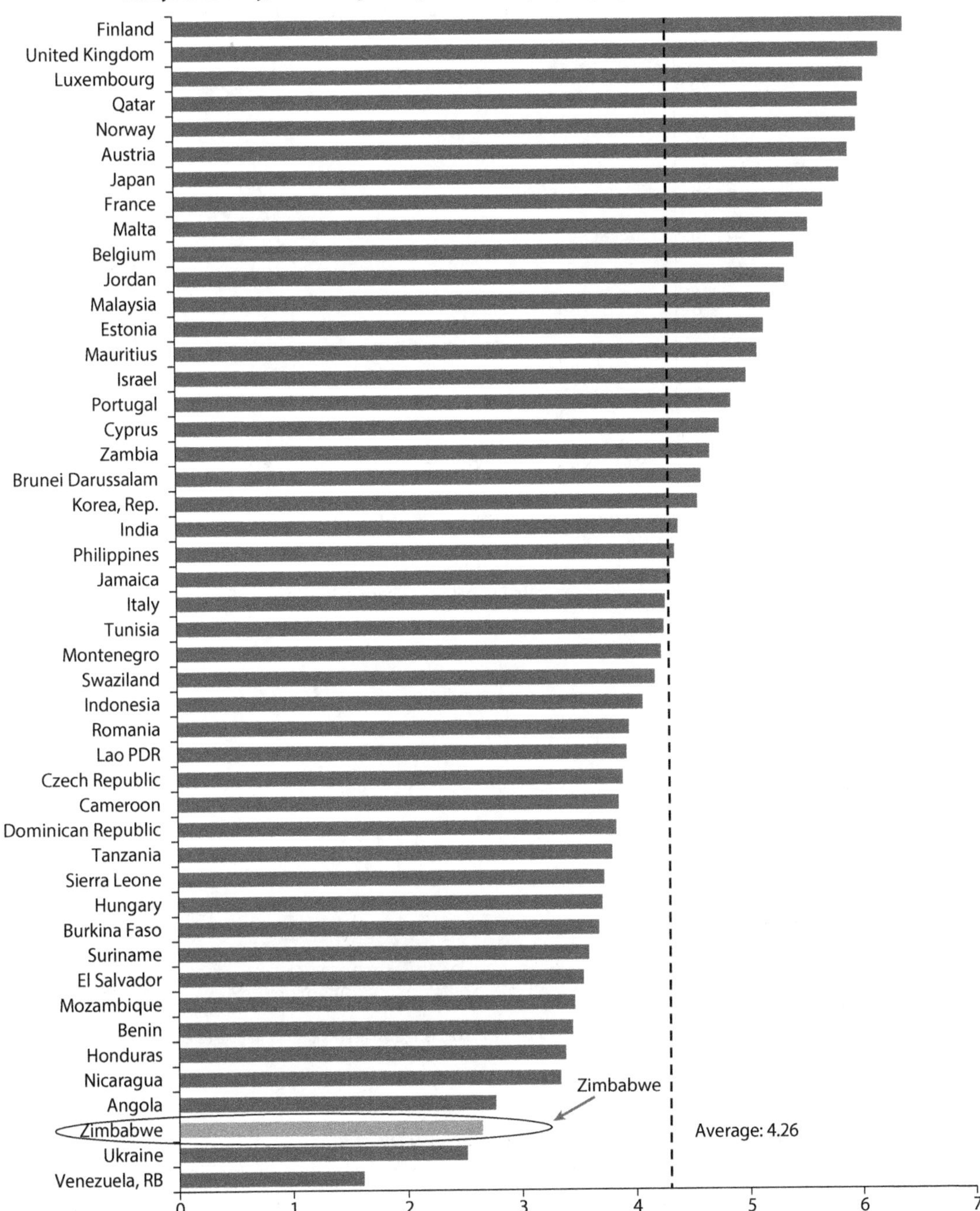

Source: World Economic Forum (WEF 2013).

Figure 3.3 Zimbabwe's Foreign Direct Investment Inflows, 1991–2011
Three-year rolling average

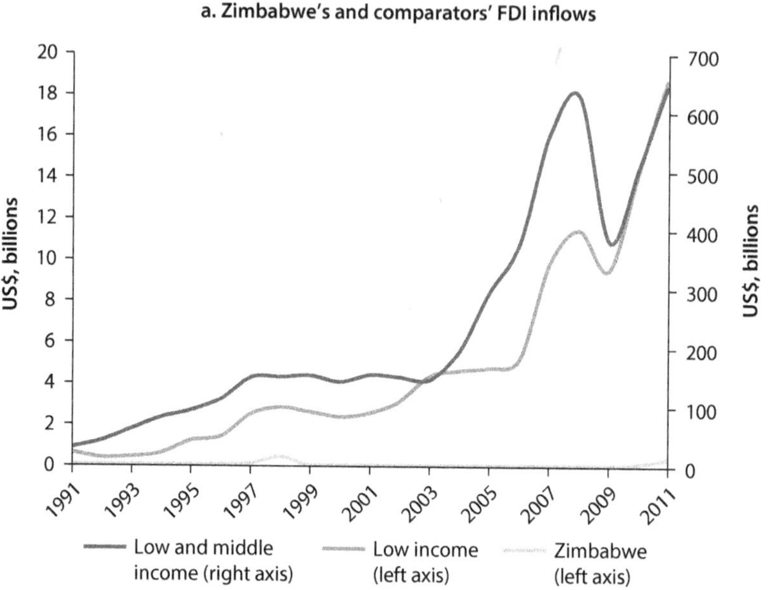

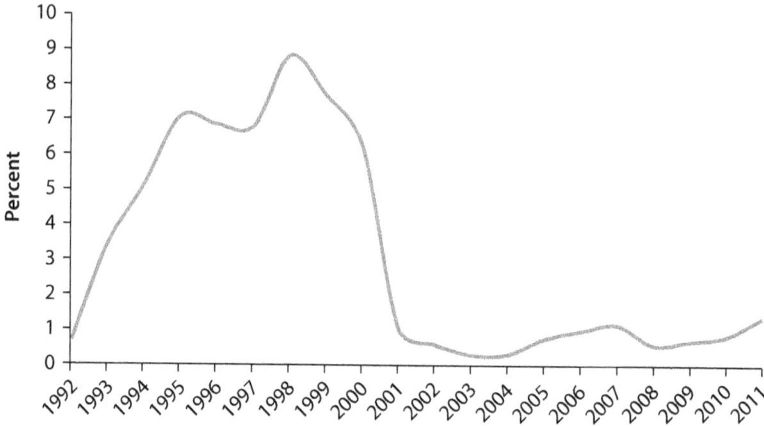

Source: World Bank, World Development Indicators, http://data.worldbank.org/data-catalog/world-development-indicators.
Note: FDI = foreign direct investment.

Missing Out on the Integration Driven by FDI

FDI brings to the host country access to global value chains' integration, management, technology, and much-needed capital investment, as well as connections to major world markets. Zambia, for example, has supported stronger flows of FDI, and that FDI growth is associated with expanding imports of machinery—a sign of investment (figure 3.4). In contrast, machinery imports in Zimbabwe have fluctuated around a declining trend, and so have FDI inflows. Investment levels

Figure 3.4 Zambia's versus Zimbabwe's Use of FDI, 1995–2011

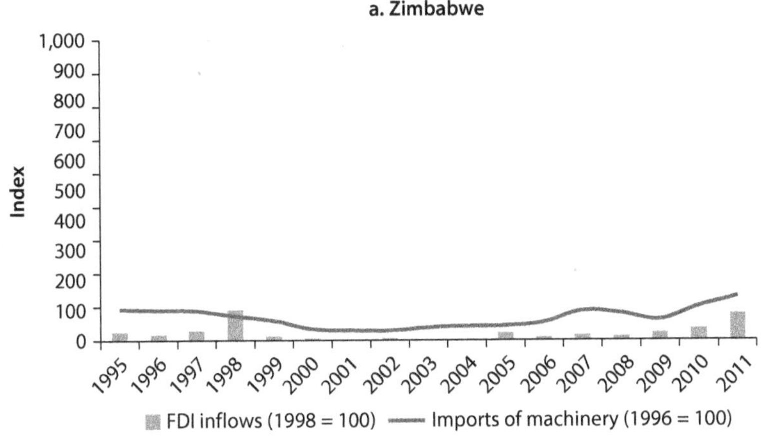

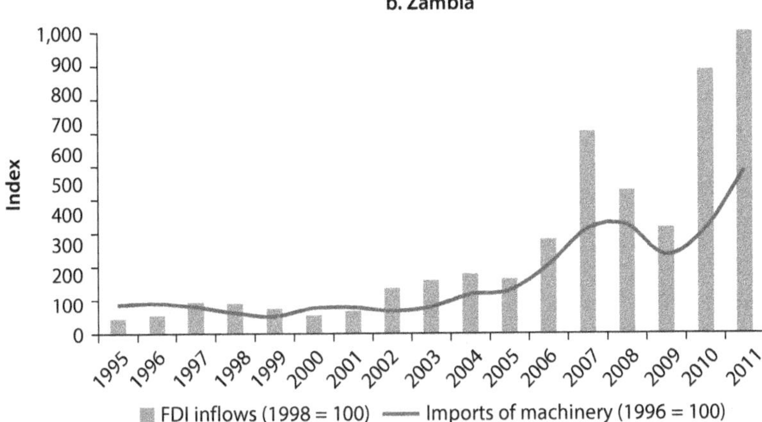

Sources: UN Comtrade at http://comtrade.un.org/; World Bank, World Development Indicators, at http://data.worldbank.org/data-catalog/world-development-indicators.
Note: FDI = foreign direct investment.

remain very low outside the large-scale mining sector. Seizing opportunities that could contribute to reversing the stunted growth of agricultural processing, and supporting the diversification effort in general, requires addressing the perceived unwelcoming policy environment toward FDI.

Industrial Policy: Mining

The mining sector has led the rebound observed in exports since 2010, and because the potential for recovery in the post–land reform agricultural sector remains stunted, the importance of the mining sector is steadily growing, even though investment remains below potential and is limited to large-scale known deposits. The value of mineral exports increased only about 30 percent between 2001 and 2009, but in 2010 mineral exports increased more than 150 percent, followed by another increase of nearly 30 percent in 2011 (figure 3.5). The share

Figure 3.5 Zimbabwe's Mineral Exports, 2001–11

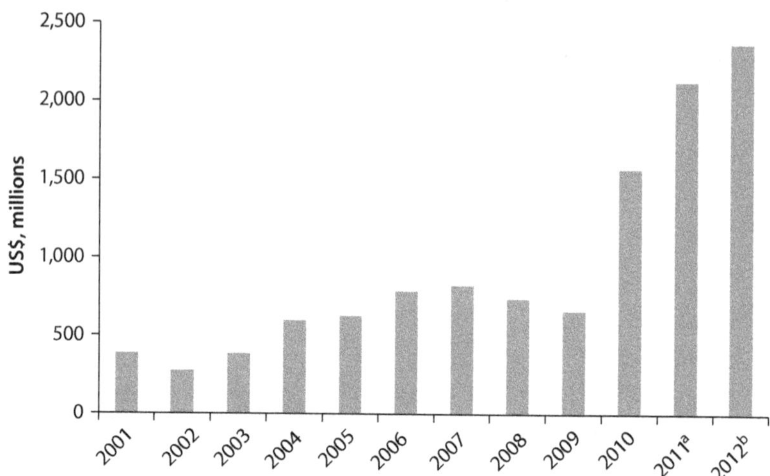

Source: Reserve Bank of Zimbabwe data at http://www.rbz.co.zw/.
a. Estimated.
b. Projections.

of mining in GDP rose from 10.2 percent in the 1990s to almost 17 percent in the period 2009–11.

The sector's export growth was largely due to resurgent mineral prices subsequent to the financial crisis of 2009. The recovery in prices coincided with substantial expansion in the production of platinum and diamonds and a partial recovery in the volume of production in gold. The mining sector boom has also been accompanied by a transformation within the sector itself: once dominated by small-scale gold production, in recent years large-scale operations in platinum and diamonds have surged.

The boom, however, understates the potential of existing mining projects, let alone the potential of development through new discoveries. Based on findings from a World Bank survey (McMahon and others 2012), investment of about US$5 billion is planned for existing mining projects through 2018. This amount is less than half the potential absorption of new investment by existing projects (US$12 billion).

Investments in transport infrastructure are essential for developing the bulk commodities of coal and iron ore, as is increasing access to lower-cost power.

Tax policy is also important. Despite the economic and political turmoil since late in the first decade of the 2000s, policy in Zimbabwe for the mining sector was generally less hospitable by international standards. Royalties have been increased substantially as have various fees associated with exploration and exploitation, and are now among the highest in the world (see table 3.2). Although most of these fees can be borne by an operating mine, exploration companies that have no income and that need to hold large areas will find these fees untenable. These fees will scare off what little investment in exploration there is.

Table 3.2 Changes in Royalties and License Fees

	Gold	*Diamonds*	*Platinum group metals (PGM)*	*Coal*
Old royalty (%)	4.50	10.0	5.0	n.a.
New royalty (%)	7.0	15.0	10.0	1.0
Old fees	n.a.	US$1 million and nil	Varies; less than US$50,000 in total	US$5,000
New fees	n.a.	US$1 million application fee for prospecting and US$5 million registration fee for a claim, which includes mining if feasible deposit	US$500,000 application fee and US$2.5 million registration fee	US$100,000 application fee and US$0.5 million registration fee
Ground rental	n.a.	From nil to US$3,000/ha	From nil to US$1,000/ha	From nil to US$1,000/ha

Source: Government of Zimbabwe 2012.
Note: ha = hectare; n.a. = not applicable.

The National Trade Policy raises the possibility of introducing export taxes on primary products to stimulate further value addition. However, experience shows that using export taxes as an incentive for encouraging investment in value addition or mineral-beneficiation projects is a high-risk strategy for which there are few successful examples. Private investors (domestic and international) are the best-informed sources for identifying potentially profitable mineral-beneficiation projects. An export tax is a negative incentive because it reduces the profitability of an existing economic activity on the assumption that this tax will encourage firms to invest in downstream production. There are no guarantees upfront that the downstream producer will be internationally competitive. A strategy for value addition and beneficiation would require that the constraints to realizing mineral beneficiation be correctly identified and addressed. Without this analysis, the introduction of export taxes might just reduce profitability and introduce unwanted distortions into extraction operations.

The IEE policies are having nonnegligible effects in suppressing investment in the mining sector and are freezing exploration. Except for investments in very lucrative known deposits, investment levels in other deposits appear to be largely below potential.

In the 2012–13 survey of mining companies undertaken by the Fraser Institute, Zimbabwe ranked among the least favorable destinations at 91st out of 96 jurisdictions, falling from the already low rank of 73rd in the previous year, probably because the survey took place after the announcement of the indigenization policy toward mining (Fraser Institute 2013). The IEEA has had substantial effects in stunting mining exploration outside known deposits and constraining capital inflows to smaller projects, especially less lucrative ones. Conversely, Zimbabwe ranked 11th of 96 jurisdictions on the "room for improvement" index, which considers where a country could be with its geological potential if it had a good policy environment. The 2012 Behre Dolbear (2013, 2) survey of best mining countries to invest in made a point of noting that it did not include Zimbabwe (or República Bolivariana de Venezuela) in the 25 countries surveyed "due to their inherently low ranking reflecting unfavorable policies and investment climate." A study related to development of the cadaster and obstacles to exploration in Zimbabwe explains

> The lack of large scale exploration activities implies that the unknown mineral resources of the country continue unexplored and consequently the true potential of the country will remain unrealized. During the last three decades, the evolution of exploration technology has been tremendous with development of powerful geophysical and geochemical tools, which are essential to discover hidden and blind deep deposits. This is very sophisticated and specialized technology that is deployed mainly by international mining companies. Without opening the door and attracting investment by these companies, it will not be possible to develop the mining sector proportionally to its geological potential. (Ortega 2010, 35)

Exploration licenses are a related industry regulation strategy. No large-scale exploration licenses have been issued since 2005, despite 319 applications. As a result, companies make small claims of 1 hectare, which can be granted by district mining commissioners for six-month periods—larger claims must be granted by the president. Ortega (2010) estimates that about 5,000 claims are being issued per year, which ties up land that should be allocated for exploration. Because they are unable to get longer-term claims covering large areas, companies get dozens or hundreds of small claims and block them together, but given their short duration, it is too risky for the companies to undertake serious exploration.

To increase exploration for and eventually discovery of new deposits, policies guaranteeing security of tenure for companies will be particularly important. Because most exploration is undertaken by junior companies, the ability to sell any discoveries to other companies appears central.

According to the Fraser Institute's survey undertaken in 2012, overall improvement of business conditions could dramatically increase investment plans and thus lead to more exploitation of the current potential of the sector. Should incentives be altered to create an investment-friendly mining policy, competitive taxes and fees, and an efficient transport and power infrastructure, increases in production and value added could be expected to more than double.

Industrial Policy: Agriculture

The fast-tracked land reform, implemented in the mid-2000s, redefined the market structure in agriculture, with a corresponding loss of capital accumulation, productivity, and vital economic linkages with both the domestic industry and international markets. Zimbabwe went from being a net exporter to a net importer of maize. The confluence of the return of the economy to macroeconomic stability (via dollarization), liberalization, and high international prices during the years after 2009 led to an increase in agricultural profitability and a rebound of production in the sector, with a strong supply response in the tobacco sector.

Agricultural sector exports have expanded since 2009 but at a slower pace than mining. Its contribution to export growth in the country has remained positive and stable in the period 2010–12. Tobacco and cotton have led the rebound in the sector, with cotton supported by high international prices. Maize and poultry exports have experienced growth; all other commodities, however, remain far from recovery levels. Because of the sector's high vulnerability to weather patterns and very low yields, the maize sector's performance remains dramatically below pre-2000 levels: in 2012 and 2013 the country had to strongly increase imports of maize from neighboring countries.

The recovery in the commercial farm sector has been held back by lack of strong demand due to broken downstream linkages with the manufacturing sector, and by unfulfilled recapitalization needs, given high interest rates, short maturities, and limited liquidity in the banking sector.

Investment policies will be critical. Enhancing land and labor productivity and increasing the output-to-capital ratio are critical elements of fostering medium- and longer-term agricultural growth. Irrigation equipment deteriorated sharply during the economic downturn, significantly reducing the areas under irrigation. Medium-term growth will require rehabilitation of irrigation schemes and their redesign to adapt to the new agricultural structure and different farm typologies.

Current expenditures on public programs are also important to addressing the different requirements of contract farming, including marketing support, extension and veterinary services, and input supply arrangements.

Finally, the lingering insecurities about land tenure must be addressed to provide the security to farmers necessary to rekindle private investment in agriculture, in particular investment in irrigation. Nearly one-fifth of beneficiaries of the land reform cite land conflicts or their lack of a title and fear of eviction as factors limiting their production and investment, and nearly a third of households surveyed in 2007–08 had not started to build solid houses because of perceived persistent tenure insecurity (Binswanger-Mkhize and Moyo 2012).

Industrial Policy: Manufacturing

The manufacturing sector has been stagnant since well before the crisis of the past decade. Its decline started in 1996. Its share of GDP fell from 21 percent in the 1990s to 15.4 percent during the recovery period.[3] Exports of manufactures recovered and close to doubled in value between 2009 and 2011. Much of this growth can be attributed to the increase in resource-based manufactures exports such as pig iron, spiegeleisen, sponge iron, and iron or steel granules and powders (Standard International Trade Classification group 671). Exports of other manufactures fell in absolute and in relative terms during the decade leading up to

Table 3.3 Obstacles to the Expansion of Capacity Utilization
Percentage of exporters

	Nonexporter	*Exporter*	*P-statistic*	*Significance*
Demand obstacles				
Lack of demand for its products	18	32	0.05	a
Uncertainty about future market prospects	33	51	0.04	a
Excessive abundance of cheap imports	61	47	0.12	
Supply and capacity obstacles				
Unavailability of inputs of production	**55**	**58**	0.74	
Obsolete machinery and equipment	**74**	**67**	0.39	
Lack of financing mechanisms	**83**	**83**	0.99	
Brain drain	20	27	0.35	
Failure in electricity supply	43	62	0.03	a

Source: World Bank Enterprise Survey 2012 at http://www.enterprisesurveys.org/.
Notes: Population weights used.
a. Denotes significant at 5 percent level.

2010, followed by a small recovery in 2011. Most firms operate at low levels of capacity utilization.[4]

The main supply obstacles include lack of finance, obsolete machinery and equipment, and the unavailability of inputs of production (table 3.3); also, impediments to increasing output are not the lack of foreign demand or knowledge about foreign markets but unavailability of inputs, obsolete machinery, and poor electricity supply. These responses find echoes in firm interviews conducted for this study that asked about obstacles to exporting. Firms most frequently cite "insufficient production capacity" and "lack of financing" to sell abroad. Putting these responses together with the fact that average capacity utilization hovers around 50 percent (well below regional averages) suggests that a major problem afflicting the sector is antiquated equipment, a reflection of a continuing lack of investment in modern productive facilities that would make firms internationally competitive.

Nonprice restrictions in foreign markets appear to be a greater barrier to export than foreign tariffs—about 38 percent of exporters emphasize nonprice restrictions as a constraint (table 3.4). The importance of these barriers is dependent on the product exported as well as the destination. The firm interviews, for example, identify various instances in which nontariff measures affect exports of particular products.

Restrictive trade policy in foreign markets was the dog that did not bark in this survey: firms did not see neighboring countries' tariffs and nontariff barriers as being a principal obstacle to exporting. Only 13 percent of current exporters find that trade policies in importing countries have led to a decline in their exports (table 3.5). Of the manufacturing firms that have discontinued exporting, only 5 percent cite foreign trade policies as the reason for their exit.[5]

Table 3.4 Obstacles to Export Growth in Zimbabwe
Percentage of exporters

	Do not know	Yes	No
Demand obstacles			
Lack of foreign demand for its products	2.38	19.1	78.6
Lack of knowledge of foreign markets	0	14.3	85.7
Nonprice restrictions on foreign markets	0	38.1	61.9
Supply, cost, and capacity obstacles			
High costs of transport	2.38	33.3	64.3
Red tape in customs	0	21.4	78.6
Insufficient production capacity to expand exports	0	59.5	40.5
Lack of financing mechanisms to sell abroad	0	69.1	31.0

Source: World Bank Enterprise Survey 2012 at http://www.enterprisesurveys.org/.
Note: A total of 42 firms that export directly are in the sample. There are no small firms in the sample that export directly.

Table 3.5 Reasons for Decline in Value of Exports or Having Stopped Exporting
Percentage of firms affected

	Previous exporter	Current exporter	P-statistic
Share of all firms	30	20	n.a.
Production declined	71	65	0.82
Lost orders because you could not supply products in time	64	50	0.58
Lost orders because your products could not compete on price	81	40	0.03
Lost orders because your products could not compete on quality	24	0	0.17
Lost orders because importers were worried about reliability of supply	55	75	0.41
Trade policies in importing countries	5	13	0.44

Source: World Bank's "Competitiveness Survey for Zimbabwe 2012" (World Bank 2012).
Note: Uses population weights. n.a. = not applicable.

Industrial policies have so far failed to make a dent in supporting recovery in the manufacturing sector given that they fail to address core bottlenecks undermining firms' performance:

- Firms' future performance hinges on recapitalization and investment in modern plants and machinery. Investment requires macroeconomic policies that increase domestic savings and expand access to long-term investment funds, including foreign capital flows. However, limited domestic saving, poor rates of return on investment, vulnerability in the banking sector, and continued uncertainty of property rights combine to keep real interest rates prohibitively high.

- At the same time, non–factory floor costs are substantially higher than in comparator countries (Davies, Kumar, and Shah 2012), with access to stable and affordable energy being among the key constraints.

In addition, policies restricting ownership have discouraged both domestic and foreign investors, with a particularly strong effect on sectors that present lower expectations of profitability. Current industrial policies are directly restricting opportunities to upgrade technologies and integrate into global value chains.

Industrial Policies: Options for Reform

As with trade policy, industrial policies have sought to promote a more inclusive growth path—one that empowers groups historically excluded from participating in rising incomes. Industrial policy objectives might be summarized as (1) rapid growth to create jobs and reduce poverty, (2) wealth redistribution and provision of assets to the indigenous population, and (3) wealth creation to generate a sustainable empowerment program for all Zimbabweans.

Policies aiming at wealth redistribution have actively undermined growth, with negative effects on job creation, wealth creation, and poverty reduction. Rates of poverty reduction and job creation are lagging and fall far short of those in well-performing economies. However, options for reinvigorating growth exist. Policy options in specific areas include the following:

Indigenization and Property Rights

Key to achieving all three of Zimbabwe's economic goals is reducing the property-rights uncertainty commonly associated with implementation of the indigenization program. Lack of clear criteria for the policy's implementation and exposure to regulatory takings of private businesses shroud expected returns to investment in a veil of uncertainty. The highest priority therefore is to clarify the rules and the scope of the program. Establishing clear and predictable rules of the game will go far toward reducing the strongly perceived uncertainty that hobbles investment. A second priority is to explore policy options that would achieve empowerment without undermining other national priorities, including growth, investment, and export potential.[6]

Tax Policy, Licensing, and Other Regulations

Tax and royalty policy as well as licensing can be adjusted and adapted to reflect the cost of the indigenization program, and the trade-off between ownership and tax return, so as to achieve all three industrial policy goals. The general objective ought to be to raise resources with neutral influences across industries and sectors so market signals allow Zimbabwe to tap into its considerable natural competitive advantages. Similarly, licensing ought to be reviewed so as to encourage competition and investment from whatever source.

Public Investment Policy

Each of the sectors has an acute need for greater public investment. Deficiencies in roads and rail transport and in electric power are common impediments to the expansion of growth in mining and manufacturing. Correcting these deficiencies requires mobilization of greater public savings, and an improvement in relations with international creditors to access untapped and relatively inexpensive international credit. Credit from these sources could open the doors to greater public investment in infrastructure, though the current inhospitable economy-wide incentives have to be reversed if these sources of growth are to be unleashed.

State-owned companies in electricity, rail, and air transport monopolize key segments of network services essential to exports from mining, agriculture, and manufacturing. As part of a program designed to promote greater investment infrastructure supporting these major export sectors, specific policies to reduce this monopoly power ought to be considered. (These constraints are discussed in greater detail in chapters 4 and 5.)

Rationalizing Industrial Policy

Dani Rodrik (2004), arguably the leading advocate of industrial policy, has suggested that a well-designed program of subsidies and incentives should have several key characteristics (box 3.2), including transparency, the provision of subsidies only to new activities, clear criteria for success, and sunset clauses. It is instructive that few if any of Zimbabwe's industrial policies seem to adhere to these guidelines.

Box 3.2 Ten Principles for a Smart Industrial Policy

1. Begin by focusing on removal of policy, institutional, and cost elements in the value chain that limit production and exports (for example, cost of doing business)
2. To enhance transparency, quantify current spending on industrial policy and present amounts in budget to parliament
3. Provide incentives and subsidies only to innovative activities
4. Objectives must be clear and include benchmarks and criteria for success and failure
5. Phase out subsidies progressively and automatically over about three to five years
6. Projects should entail private risk commensurate with public risks
7. Avoid raising barriers to entry and to competition, especially import competition
8. Agency administering industrial policy must have demonstrated competence, with clear political oversight and accountability
9. The Ministry of Industry and International Trade must maintain channels of communication with the private sector
10. Portfolio of industrial policy programs must be subjected to regular ex post external evaluation

Source: Adapted from Rodrik 2004.

Therefore, the government might undertake the following:

- *Conduct a brief evaluation of major incentive programs to determine if they correlate with best practice of smart industrial policy.* Particularly relevant are the principles describing transparency, subsidizing only new activities, providing clear objectives, sunset clauses, balanced risk, ensuring competition, and periodic evaluation.

- *Analyze the feasibility of adopting a uniform tax rate on all business activities to eliminate bias against particular sectors to move toward revenue neutrality.* The rationale for giving tax and other incentives to the manufacturing and agricultural sectors (particularly subsistence arable agriculture) is questionable in the context of diversification policy. It seems to be more justified by a perceived need to prop up failing sectors rather than to provide support to sectors with longer-term growth potential.

Notes

1. Not all GVCs are the same. Among other things, they differ in degree with respect to the extent of market competition within the chain, barriers to access to the final market, and the control exerted by the lead firm (over technology, product specifications, and branding). Gereffi, Humphrey, and Sturgeon (2005) distinguish five general types of GVCs, each with a different "governance" structure and role of firms:
   - *Market-driven* chains in which both buyers and suppliers have multiple sources of transactions, the price is fully market determined, and the cost of switching to new partners is low; an example is commodity markets.
   - *Modular* chains in which suppliers produce to the specification of the buyers using generic technology; an example is many apparel chains.
   - *Relational* value chains, in which interactions between buyers and sellers are mutually dependent, usually have sustained involvement over time, and are based on family or ethnic ties that tend to cement business relationships.
   - *Captive* chains in which the lead firm controls a highly differentiated product, the key technologies, product standards, or some combination thereof; suppliers have little incentive to move outside the production chain to work with the competitors. Leading electronic firms such as Apple and Samsung have these types of supplier relationships.
   - *Hierarchical* chains in which the buyer-supplier relationship is internal to the firm; auto companies have many suppliers that are internal to the firm; all intrafirm trade falls into this category.
2. This section is based on World Bank (2013).
3. This calculation excludes cotton lint, which falls under the manufacturing category.
4. Zimbabwean manufacturing firms only produced at 45.7 percent of their potential output in 2012. Low levels of capacity utilization are not isolated to a few manufacturing firms in Zimbabwe. Fewer than 1 in 10 Zimbabwean manufacturing firms produced at more than 75 percent of their productive capacity. In contrast, more than half of the manufacturing firms in the other African countries produced at capacity utilization levels of 75 percent or more (Edwards and Kirk 2013).

5. These results may seem to contradict the results in table 3.4 in which exporters (38 percent) declare nonprice restrictions on foreign markets to be an obstacle. However, these discrepancies arise from the different samples considered by the two tables. Table 3.4 addresses successful incumbent exporters that are growing whereas the question presented in table 3.5 is more directed toward exporters that are either shrinking or disappearing.
6. The use of specific policy instruments to promote economic empowerment of indigenous populations or to restrict foreign ownership is not unique to Zimbabwe. Other countries in Africa (Angola, Namibia, Nigeria, South Africa, Zambia), the Middle East and North Africa (Qatar, Saudi Arabia, the United Arab Emirates) and Asia (China, Malaysia) as well as Botswana (in its relation to De Beers) adopted policies that aimed to empower indigenous peoples. None of these jeopardized relations with foreign creditors, and virtually all encouraged foreign direct investment in clearly defined sectors with stable rules—and without provoking the uncertainty that seems to have been engendered in Zimbabwe. One element that may affect mining in particular is consequences stemming from any regulatory takings that violate bilateral investment treaties that Zimbabwe has signed with various countries. Countries as diverse as Argentina, the Czech Republic, Ecuador, and Indonesia have found themselves facing judgments amounting to billions of dollars in investment dispute arbitration panels. See Frischtak and Newfarmer (2013) for a summary of these cases. For a more detailed country case study, see Wells and Ahmed's (2007) study of Indonesia.

References

Arnold, J. M., B. Javorcik, M. Lipscomb, and A. Mattoo. 2014. "Services Reform and Manufacturing Performance: Evidence from India." *Economic Journal*. Published online ahead of print, doi: 10.1111/ecoj.12206.

Arnold, J. M., B. Javorcik, and A. Mattoo. 2011. "The Productivity Effects of Services Liberalization: Evidence from the Czech Republic." *Journal of International Economics* 85 (1): 136–46.

Arnold, J. M., A. Mattoo, and G. Narciso. 2008. "Services Inputs and Firm Productivity in Sub-Saharan Africa: Evidence from Firm-Level Data." *Journal of African Economies* 17 (4): 578–99.

Baldwin, R. 2011. "Trade and Industrialization after Globalization's 2nd Unbundling: How Building and Joining a Supply Chain Are Different and Why It Matters." Working Paper 17716, National Bureau of Economic Research, Cambridge, MA.

Behre Dolbear Group, Inc. 2013. "2013 Ranking of Countries for Mining Investment. Where 'Not to Invest'." Sydney, Australia.

Binswanger-Mkhize, H., and S. Moyo. 2012. "Zimbabwe: From Economic Rebound to Sustained Growth—Note II: Recovery and Growth of Zimbabwe Agriculture." Unpublished, World Bank, Washington, DC.

Davies, Rob, Praveen Kumar, and Manju Kedia Shah. 2012. "Re-manufacturing Zimbabwe: Constraints and Opportunities in a Dollarized Economy." Background paper for *Zimbabwe: From Economic Rebound to Sustained Growth*, World Bank, Washington, DC.

Edwards, Lawrence, and Robert Kirk. 2013. "The Opportunities and Constraints for Stronger Regional and Global Integration of Zimbabwe." Unpublished, World Bank, Washington, DC.

Fraser Institute. 2013. *Survey of Mining Companies 2012/2013*. Vancouver, Canada: Fraser Institute.

Frischtak, A., and R. Newfarmer. 2013. "International Investment Agreements: Investor Protections and Foreign Direct Investments." In *Handbook of Trade Policy for Development*, edited by A. Lukauska, R. M. Stern, and G. Zanini. Oxford, U.K.: Oxford Economic Press.

Gereffi, G., J. Humphrey, and T. Sturgeon. 2005. "The Governance of Global Value Chains." *Review of International Political Economy* 12 (1): 78–104.

Government of Zimbabwe. 2012. *Chamber of Mines Annual Report, 2012*. https://www.chamberofmineszimbabwe.co.zw/.

Haskel, J., D. Hawkes, and S. Pereira. 2003. "How Much Do Skills Raise Productivity? UK Evidence from Matched Plant, Worker and Workforce Data." Unpublished, CeRiBA, London.

Kee, H. 2005. "Firm Performance in the Services Sector." In *Malaysia: Firm Competitiveness, Investment Climate, and Growth*. Report 26841-MA. Washington, DC: World Bank.

Keller, W., and S. R. Yeaple. 2003. "Multinational Enterprises, International Trade, and Productivity Growth: Firm-Level Evidence from the United States." Working Paper 9504, National Bureau of Economic Research, Cambridge, MA.

McMahon, G., R. Hochreiter, R. Y. Kearney and B. Tracy. 2012. "Zimbabwe Current Potential for Mining Growth." In *Zimbabwe: From Economic Rebound to Sustained Growth: Growth Recovery Notes*. Washington, DC: World Bank.

OECD/WTO (Organisation for Economic Co-operation and Development/World Trade Organization). 2013. *Aid for Trade at a Glance 2013: Connecting to Value Chains*. OECD: Paris.

Ortega, Enrique. 2010. *Diagnostic Study on Modernization of the Mineral Licensing System in Zimbabwe*. Report prepared for the Ministry of Mines and Mining Development, Republic of Zimbabwe.

Pavcnik, N. 2002. "Trade Liberalization, Exit, and Productivity Improvements: Evidence from Chilean Plants." *Review of Economic Studies* 69 (1): 245–76.

Rodrik, Dani. 2004. *Industrial Policy for the Twenty-First Century*. Cambridge, MA: Harvard University.

Smarzynska, B. K. 2002. "The Composition of Foreign Direct Investment and Protection of Intellectual Property Rights: Evidence from Transition Economies." Policy Research Working Paper 2786, World Bank, Washington, DC.

UNCTAD (United Nations Conference on Trade and Development). 2012. *World Investment Report 2012: Towards a New Generation of Investment Policies*. Geneva, Switzerland: UNCTAD.

WEF (World Economic Forum). 2013. *The Global Competitiveness Report 2013–2014*. Geneva, Switzerland: World Economic Forum.

Wells, L. T., Jr., and R. Ahmed. 2007. *Making Foreign Investment Safe: Property Rights and National Sovereignty*. New York: Oxford University Press.

World Bank. 2012. "Competitiveness Survey for Zimbabwe, 2012." World Bank, Washington, DC.

World Bank. 2013. "Zimbabwe Recovery Note: Economic Empowerment." Unpublished, World Bank, Washington, DC.

CHAPTER 4

Enhancing Connectivity in Goods Markets

Introduction

Ease of connectivity to global and regional markets is a fundamental determinant of competitiveness, and landlocked countries are at a particular disadvantage in accessing foreign markets. High transportation costs, delays at borders or in transit through third countries, and poor logistical arrangements can drive up the costs of an export in foreign markets and price it out of the market. Zimbabwe is no exception. The costs of shipping a container laden with exports from Harare to Amsterdam are reportedly twice those from nearby Malawi (World Bank 2012).

The emergence of global value chains of production as a central feature of world trade has compounded potential disadvantages of being landlocked at the same time that it has created new opportunities. Speedy and low-cost transport services are key components of cost competitiveness in value chains. Time is money. Hummels and Schaur (2013) calculate that a one-day delay drives up costs by, on average, about 0.8 percent around the world. Similarly, Djankov, Freund, and Pham (2006), based on a study of 126 countries using a gravity model, find that each day in transit has the effect of reducing trade volumes by, on average, slightly more than 1 percent. The authors were able to capture the effects of administrative delays by using the proxy of number of signatures required to export or import. These administrative delays had the equivalent effect, they calculate, of adding 70 kilometers to the distance between the plant and the final market. Exporters of perishable products suffered the most because delays increase wastage. For exporters of these perishable agricultural products, every additional day of delay reduces exports by 6 percent, on average. Hoekman and Nicita (2011) estimate that efforts to raise average trade logistics of low-income countries to middle-income-country levels—as measured by the World Bank's Logistics Performance Index and Doing Business "cost of trading" indicator—would increase trade by 15 percent, double what would be achieved as a result of convergence to middle-income average levels of import tariffs.

This chapter reviews Zimbabwe's connectivity in goods markets. Cost-increasing impediments can occur at various parts of the value chain: transport costs, border crossings, and trade finance. The first section focuses on transport costs and evaluates road and rail transport systems with a view to identifying investment needs and policy impediments that increase costs. (Air transport, because of its importance to tourism, is analyzed as part of chapter 5's discussion of services.) The second section reviews ways to reduce costs by reducing policy-amendable transit times at borders and in trade-related public institutions, including customs and other border agencies. The third section examines the role played by constraints associated with trade finance. The final section presents general policy options that would reduce trading costs to improve Zimbabwe's competitiveness.

Transport and Transit Costs

The World Bank's Doing Business surveys have tracked the costs of importing and exporting annually since 2006. During this period the cost of importing a container more than doubled while the cost of exporting increased by 75 percent in Zimbabwe.[1] For imports, this constitutes a considerable surcharge in addition to tariffs. For exports, the high shipping costs may be thought of as equivalent to an export tax. Although firms in all countries have to pay transport costs to import and export their products, the incremental costs Zimbabwean firms have to pay relative to both their neighbors and other international competitors represents a significant disadvantage (figure 4.1).

The problems associated with transportation costs differ somewhat between roads and rails, but they share common stories: high costs, underinvestment and

Figure 4.1 Doing Business: Cost of Importing and Exporting a Container, 2013

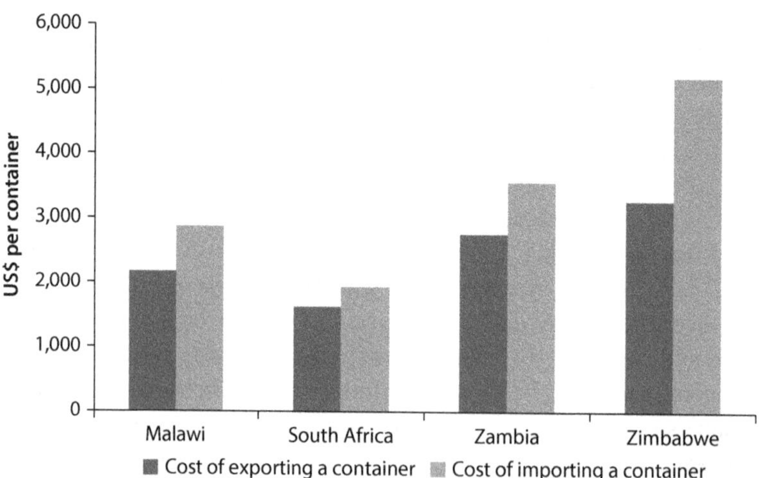

Source: World Bank 2012.
Note: Cost of importing and exporting a 20-foot container weighing 10 tons and valued at $20,000.

deteriorating infrastructure, and policy barriers to competition (especially state monopolies and restrictions on foreign competition) and to regional opportunities for collaboration and renewed efficiency.

Road Transport Services

High Transport Costs Undermine Competitiveness

The shipping costs faced by Zimbabwean firms are much higher than in neighboring countries. The costs of exporting a 20-foot container are about twice those of shipping from South Africa, and 18 and 50 percent higher than from Zambia and Malawi, respectively (figure 4.1). No less important, import costs are even larger multiples of those of these trading partners. Higher import costs saddle domestic industry and other activities with higher costs and put Zimbabwe at a significant competitive disadvantage in reaching foreign markets.

Trucking industry costs are also high. Because new trucks in Zimbabwe cost approximately 30 percent more than in South Africa, local trucking companies have imported second-hand trucks. However, many of them are left-hand drive (although imports of left-hand drive trucks were banned in November 2011) and are older vehicles with higher running costs. Diesel fuel, spare parts, licenses, and insurance are all more expensive in Zimbabwe relative to neighboring countries, which also results in higher operating costs. Transport companies also pay additional fees when transiting within Zimbabwe, including road toll fees, police fines (often imposed more to raise revenues than to deter petty offenses), and other solicited illegal payments.

Road Policies Limit Competition, Raising Prices

The lack of competitiveness in the transport sector is the result of several factors. An important one is the number of existing policy barriers to competition that drive up costs. These barriers include the following:

- *Vehicle equipment standards.* The Southern African Development Community (SADC) and the Common Market for Eastern and Southern Africa (COMESA) have different limits on vehicle equipment and dimensions. Mozambique and Tanzania do not allow the use of seven-axle interlinks, which poses a major challenge to Zimbabwean trucks using the Beira Corridor. The operators are either forced to use configurations specifically designed for this route (which is expensive) or have to use longer routes to the sea.

- *Cabotage and third-country rules.* The bilateral transport agreements signed in southern Africa do not allow cabotage (allowing foreign trucks to carry freight between domestic locations), and they also apply the "third-country rule" (not allowing foreign-registered trucks to pick up freight en route in the transit country unless it is homeward bound). These regulations are aimed at protecting domestic transport companies, particularly the smaller operators, from foreign competition, but they have the effect of reducing truck capacity utilization (because of empty hauls) and increasing transport prices. Transporters carry minerals and agricultural products to South Africa and return with consumer goods; allowing trucks to pick up internal cargo or to carry third-country cargo could increase competition, allow trucks to better balance loads, and reduce prices.

- *Limits on foreign ownership and competition*. Road shipping services is one of the sectors expressly reserved for investment by domestic investors under the Investment Regulations of 1993. As a matter of policy, the Zimbabwe Investment Authority limits foreign ownership to 35 percent in these reserved sectors. Moreover, foreign investment is possible only through joint ventures with local individuals or firms (though the Minister of Industry and International Trade may grant exceptions). License criteria differ between domestic and foreign investors in that the equity restrictions under the Indigenization and Empowerment Act (IEEA) and the Investment Regulations of 1993 take the form of conditions that include the number of employees who are nationals. These licenses are valid for three years. There is no requirement to provide a licensing decision within a specific time frame. Approval of the Reserve Bank of Zimbabwe is required for repatriation of earnings, and repatriation is subject to availability of foreign currency.

Zimbabwe has the most restrictive environment for foreign competition in road transport in all of southern Africa. One measure is the World Bank's Services Trade Restrictiveness Index (STRI), which shows that Zimbabwe has tight restrictions on foreign investment in road transport. Zimbabwe has an STRI of more than twice the SADC and Sub-Saharan African average (figure 4.2).

In general, SADC and COMESA have emphasized harmonization of technical standards. Donors have supported improvements in customs and the installation of one-stop border crossings. But it is also important to liberalize trade in road transport services. Liberalization would involve eliminating restrictions on the movement of, and carriage of freight and passengers on, vehicles regardless of where they are registered and who owns them (box 4.1). It also involves eliminating restrictions on foreign investment in transport services. In particular, the development of multimodal transport may need substantial external capital and expertise.

Road Infrastructure

In addition to the competition issues presented above, infrastructure is also a problem. Poorly maintained roads pitted with potholes increase wear and tear on trucks and slow transport times, thus driving up costs. During Zimbabwe's economic crisis of 1999–2008, maintenance and rehabilitation suffered. Of the country's total road network of nearly 90,000 kilometers, the proportion in fair to good condition had declined from 73 percent in 1995 to only 60 percent in 2011 (AfDB 2011). The World Bank and other donors have called for substantial increases in investment in road maintenance. However, the 2012 road budget of US$17.7 million would make only a small down payment on the US$2.7 billion

Figure 4.2 Services Trade Restrictiveness Index for Road Transport Services (2008; Zimbabwe 2013)

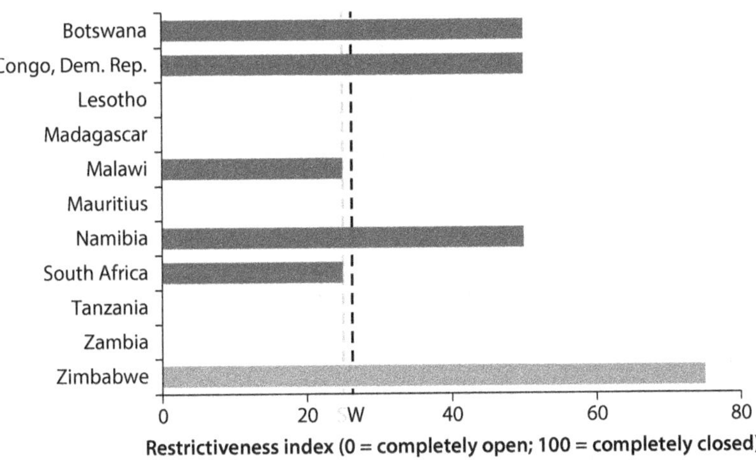

Source: Mattoo and Waris 2013.
Note: S = average of the Southern African Development Community; W = average of the 103 countries for which data were available. Data not available for Lesotho, Madagascar, Mauritius, Tanzania, and Zambia.

Box 4.1 The Soft Power of Competition in Road Transport

Teravaninthorn and Raballand (2008) show that trucking deregulation in Rwanda after the civil war led to a decline in nominal prices by 30 percent, and the domestic trucking fleet expanded instead of shrinking. By contrast, countries like Malawi, where domestic truckers were protected by restrictive entry regulations, ended up essentially penalizing farmers. The authors also highlight the deleterious effects of cartels and regulations through "freight bureaus" on Central African corridors where freight rates per ton-kilometer were about 80 percent more and truck-utilization rates 40 percent less than on East African corridors. Throughout West Africa, they find that bilateral agreements, queuing systems, and quotas stifled competition. Even on the most competitive trucking corridors of East Africa, anticompetitive regulations abounded, with, for example, Kenya prohibiting international transit trucks on the Mombasa-Kigali corridor from taking domestic freight on the return trip, forcing them to drive empty for 1,700 kilometers. Their conclusion was that introducing competition in trucking was essential to reap the benefits of investment in road and border infrastructure.

that the African Development Bank (AfDB 2011) estimates would be needed to fully rehabilitate the road system. Masiiwa and Giersing (2012, 37) write

> The current budget allocation means that it will take more than 112 years to rehabilitate all the roads as envisaged by the government, an impossible task because the rate of road damage will always be higher than that of rehabilitation.

They go on to suggest that priorities should include repairing regional corridors, urban roads, and paved primary roads that are in poor and fair condition.

Rail Transport

High Implicit Costs Derail Traffic

Even though it is generally cheaper to ship goods by rail than by road in Zimbabwe—some US$0.03–US$0.05 per ton-kilometer compared with US$0.07–US$0.12 by road—and more environmentally sound, only 10 percent of goods traffic in Zimbabwe is shipped by rail.[2] And that share has been falling precipitously for the past two decades. In 1990, rail freight amounted to 14.3 million tons. As of 2009 it accounted for less than 3 million tons (figure 4.3). Rail services, which in 2000 were already operating at only about 50 percent of capacity, dipped to less than 20 percent utilization, and have since bounced back with the recovery but only to their mid-2000s utilization rates.

Worn Out Tracks and Broken Equipment

The secular elements of these declines reflect a combination of systematic underinvestment in maintenance of tracks, locomotives, and rail cars and increased competition from road transport. The state enterprise operating the rail system, the National Railways of Zimbabwe (NRZ), has suffered steady attrition of its most skilled staff. In addition, the worsening economic situation adversely

Figure 4.3 Declining Rail Usage, 2000–09

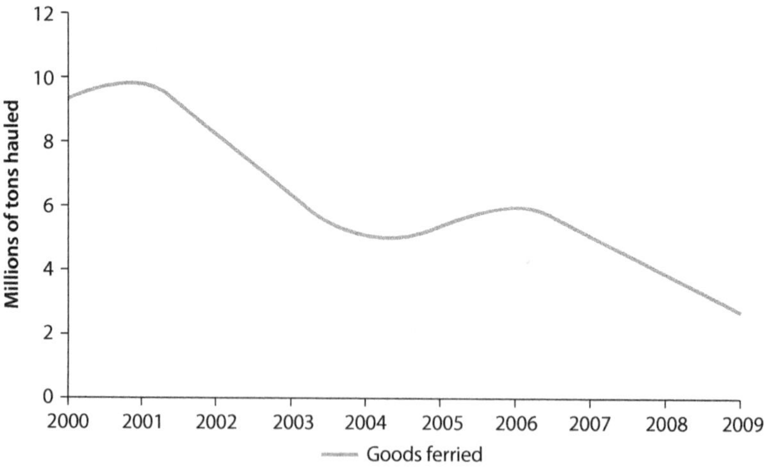

Source: Masiiwa and Giersing 2012.

affected export traffic. The rail track infrastructure and signaling systems have deteriorated because of a lack of regular maintenance, and the traction and rolling stock have deteriorated. By 2007–09, only half of the wagons, one-third of the locomotives, and more than half of the coaches were in operation (AfDB 2011). As a consequence, labor productivity, as measured by traffic units per employee, was only 75 percent that of neighboring Zambia, slightly more than 50 percent of that Botswana and Mozambique, and barely 12 percent that of South Africa in 2000–05 (Bullock 2009).

Because much of the rail infrastructure was built in the 1950s, it is well beyond the normal 40-year life span of track and would warrant additional investment in any case. However, because maintenance has been insufficient, especially in recent years, many of the segments need full rehabilitation. The rails are worn out in some areas; sleepers and ballast need replacement; and the signal systems are not functioning because of vandalism, theft, and lack of funds for maintenance. A manual system is used for signaling, which is only feasible because of the decline in traffic volumes, exposing the system to accidents associated with human error. The problems of vandalism and theft are so severe that the entire Harare-Dabuka route (313 kilometers) has been stripped of overhead copper cables, grounding the use of electrical trains (Masiiwa and Giersing 2012). The African Development Bank (AfDB 2011) estimates that the government would need to spend some US$1.15 billion over 10 years to remove speed restrictions, repair electrification, upgrade signaling and telecommunications, and rehabilitate track.

And because virtually no new addition to the rail system has occurred for two generations, enhancing Zimbabwean competitiveness requires adding new links. For example, the absence of a direct link between Harare and Lusaka in Zambia means that trains using the Beira Corridor have to go through Bulawayo, Victoria Falls, and Livingstone, driving costs up some 41 percent (Masiiwa and Giersing 2012).

Regulations and Policy Barriers Limit Competition and Private Investment

The difficulties associated with underinvestment stem from government controls. Price controls on freight and passenger traffic have depressed revenues and left the network with insufficient funds to cover the costs of maintenance and to undertake new, much-needed investment. Moreover, government requirements limit flexibility in opening and closing lines, and the railroad is saddled with uncompensated public service obligations. As a consequence of these policies, even with below-market prices, the degraded state of the network has reduced average speeds and the overall quality of service, and has meant that the system has lost market share to road traffic.

Policy barriers prevent competition and new foreign entry. Railway transport is one of the sectors expressly reserved for investment by domestic investors under the Investment Regulations of 1993. NRZ has a de facto monopoly on railway services but is free to enter into agreements with other entities to grant rights or concessions for transport services or other operations. As a matter of policy, the Zimbabwe Investment Authority limits foreign ownership to 35 percent in railway transport. Moreover, foreign investment is possible only through joint ventures with local individuals or firms. The composition of the board of directors must reflect the requirement, set out in the IEEA, that in any company the controlling interest should be in the hands of indigenous Zimbabweans. License criteria differ between domestic and foreign providers in that the equity restrictions imposed by the IEEA and the Investment Regulations take the form of license conditions. The investment license would state the number of national employees as a license condition. There is no fixed number or percentage but the employment of foreign staff is generally subject to a labor market test.

The NRZ board has the capacity to grant concessions for rail transport services by third parties. It has done so once for Beitbridge-Bulawayo Railway, a joint venture with a South African consortium in which NRZ holds a 15 percent stake. For repatriation of earnings, approval of the Reserve Bank of Zimbabwe (RBZ) is required and subject to availability of foreign currency. These rules make Zimbabwe the most restricted market in the region, save only for the Democratic Republic of Congo. As one measure, Zimbabwe's score on the STRI for rail services is nearly twice the SADC average and one-third greater than the average for the whole world (figure 4.4).

In view of the challenges in the rail sector, the government is working toward the review of the regulatory framework governing railway transport. The government also has a policy for concessioning of sections of the track to allow private sector participation and should extend this policy beyond the

Figure 4.4 Services Trade Restrictiveness Index on Rail Transport Services (2008; Zimbabwe 2013)

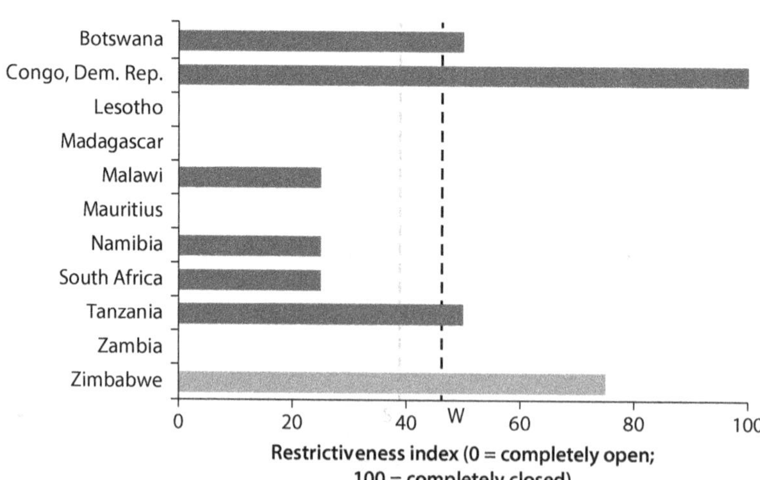

Source: Mattoo and Waris 2013.
Note: S = average of the Southern African Development Community; W = average of 103 countries for which data were available. Data not available for Lesotho, Madagascar, Mauritius, and Zambia.

Beitbridge-Bulawayo Railway. The government needs to act before the assets of the railway network deteriorate to the point that it is no longer possible to attract a concessionaire, as occurred in air transport.

Regional Obligations and Integration Opportunities

Zimbabwe is strategically located along the main transport corridors of the SADC region and is critical to the region's economic development and growth agenda. The SADC Protocol on Transport, Communications, and Meteorology, to which Zimbabwe is a signatory, specifies that member states should facilitate the provision of a seamless, efficient, cost-effective, safe, and environmentally friendly railway service that is responsive to market needs and provides access to major centers of population and economic activity. To attain this objective, member states have agreed to develop a harmonized regional policy in respect of the economic and institutional restructuring of the railways in a phased and coordinated manner. This process includes consideration of the following: according autonomy to railways to enable them to achieve full commercialization by, among others, streamlining railway organizations, reforming management, upgrading essential railway labor, and improving labor productivity; increasing private sector involvement in railway investment with a view to improving railway work and service standards and lowering the unit cost of services; enhancing operational synergy among railway service providers in the region; promoting an integrated transport system that supports fair competition between railway service providers on the one hand and the providers of other transport services on the other hand; and expansion and strengthening of government capacity to develop supportive regulatory and investor-friendly legislation, and to monitor compliance with such policy and legislation. There is a strong case for ratifying and implementing the SADC Protocol.

Trade Facilitation: Crossing Borders Efficiently

Import and Export Procedures

To be internationally competitive, domestic producers must be able to easily access imports at competitive prices. Complex procedures, permits, import duties, surcharges, and other charges all serve to increase the cost of inputs, which reduces the ability of the domestic firm to compete effectively in export markets. In addition to obtaining inputs at internationally competitive prices, producers wish to be able to procure inputs at short notice (to increase flexibility and reduce inventory costs) and with a reasonable degree of certainty about the length of the delivery time. The 2013 World Bank Doing Business report indicates that the average time to import in the Organisation for Economic Co-operation and Development countries is 10 days, Sub-Saharan Africa averages 37 days, and Zimbabwe's two landlocked neighbors Malawi and Zambia weigh in at 22 and 56 days, respectively. Importing into Zimbabwe takes 73 days, 17 days longer than in Zambia and almost double the Sub-Saharan African average (World Bank 2012).

The documents required for commercial imports and exports are numerous (http://www.zimra.co.zw):

- Bill of Entry (Form 21)
- Suppliers' invoices
- Export or transit bill of entry
- Bill of lading (if applicable)
- Value declaration forms
- Consignment notes (or bill of lading)
- Freight statements
- Cargo manifests
- Insurance statement
- Certificate of Origin (if using preference)
- Port charges invoices (if applicable)
- Original permits
- Licenses, duty-free certificate, rebate letters, value rulings (if applicable)
- Agent or importers worksheet
- Customs Declaration (CD1) Exchange Control Form

The administrative costs involved in exporting from Zimbabwe are significantly higher than those of comparator countries in the region. These costs apply to any commercial transaction regardless of size. To export using either the SADC or COMESA preference, the trader is required to have a Certificate of Origin form, a Customs Declaration (CD1) Exchange Control Form (required for any transaction exceeding $5,000), and a Bill of Entry. The total cost of these three documents was estimated by ZimTrade in 2012 to be $105. Subsequent to a lobbying effort, the cost of obtaining SADC/COMESA/EUR1 documents was reduced to $1 (the Ministry of Industry and Commerce had been requesting a fee of $20 per document). Following this reduction, the total cost facing Zimbabwean exporters is now approximately $80 per transaction. This may be compared with zero for South Africa, $12 for Zambia, and $62 for Malawi. There are also cumbersome compliance requirements surrounding the use of the CD1 Form, which increase costs for Zimbabwean firms.

Once the CD1 Form has been issued and the Bill of Entry presented to the Zimbabwe Revenue Authority (ZIMRA), the goods have to be shipped within 10 days. If there is a delay beyond the 10 days the RBZ levies a US$500 fine. The CD1 Form is acquitted when the funds are received by the commercial bank. The RBZ requires all CD1 Forms to be acquitted within 90 days. According to representatives from the private sector interviewed for this report, there is no automated exchange of information between the commercial bank and the RBZ regarding acquittal. One major exporter said they had to write numerous letters every month requesting that the CD1 be acquitted. Without acquittals, the exporter is not able to obtain refunds on the value added tax (VAT) levied on any inputs.

Border Management and Delays at the Border

Border posts are manned not only by customs officials but also by officials of numerous government agencies. The "Strategy and Action Plan for Integrated Border Management in Zimbabwe, December 2012" lists eight different agencies, each with its own representation at 12 different borders (including Harare International Airport), including the Environmental Management Agency, the Ministry of Health and Child Welfare, the Ministry of Transport Vehicle Inspection Department, the Plant Quarantine Service, the Department of Veterinary Services, the Zimbabwe Revenue Authority, and the Zimbabwe Republic Police (Zimbabwe Revenue Authority 2012). The existing legal framework does not provide for coordination among the multiple agencies with responsibility for different elements of border management. Agencies are not empowered to share data and cooperate with each other. There are currently overlapping responsibilities and some tasks are duplicated, which results in unnecessary border checks and inspections (see table 4A.1).

The negative consequences of these overlaps are noted in the congestion observed in Beitbridge, one of the main border posts in Zimbabwe. For example, global positioning system data from companies and from TradeMark Southern Africa show that it takes much longer for trucks to enter Zimbabwe than to enter South Africa (figure 4.5). Northbound trucks take more than twice as long as southbound, which suggests the delay is primarily on the Zimbabwe side of the border. In any one month, the data are based on more than 900 observations and reveal a high rate standard deviation. Going into South Africa, the average border crossing time during the period observed was 13.5 hours. But heading north the comparable figure was double during the same period.

Most of the eight agencies on the Zimbabwean side of the border inspect all imported shipments. ZIMRA reports that it is applying a risk-management system using three channels, with only 20 percent of shipments with correct documentation being subject to checking and inspection. ZIMRA is not operating an Authorized Economic Operator facility. None of the other agencies practice risk assessment, and it is not unusual for the same documents to be inspected multiple times. Environmental Management, Plant Quarantine, Veterinary Services, Vehicle Inspection, and others all levy fees in the range of \$5–\$15 per transaction. The multiplicity of agencies along with unpredictable staff shortages results in frequent delays. There are also complaints by ZIMRA that some of the customs agents compound the delays by completing the required paperwork incorrectly. This could be addressed by establishing standard qualification and screening criteria for customs brokers, establishing a code of practice, and setting up a formal mechanism for dialogue between the border agencies.

The flat-rate fees levied for specific services (testing and approvals) are regressive and serve to crowd out small businesses from trading and create incentives for small traders to avoid using formal channels. Indeed, there is evidence of the widespread use of the small informal cross-border trade category. Many small transport businesses, referred to as "runners," ship goods to order from South Africa in three-ton trucks (small bakkies) loaded with goods up to the personal

Figure 4.5 Beitbridge Average Border Crossing Time

a. Southbound: Zimbabwe to South Africa

b. Northbound: South Africa to Zimbabwe

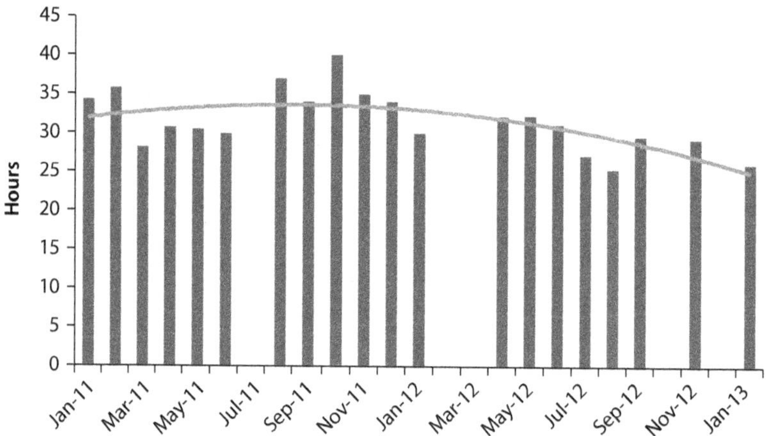

Source: Derived from Global Track GPS data provided by TradeMark Southern Africa (http://www.trademarksa.org).

limit of US$2,000 (if there are three persons accompanying the truck, duty-free imports of US$6,000 can be carried). Interviews with private firms confirmed that runners were widely used for obtaining inputs from South Africa. A runner will charge 25 percent of the invoice value for delivering the goods to Harare, generally within seven days of the order being placed.

Although the government of Zimbabwe has shown its commitment to introducing a coordinated approach—in December 2012, it finalized a draft strategy and action plan for Integrated Border Management (IBM) based on the SADC guidelines[3]—more work and enhanced cooperation is needed on this front. As observed with the border crossings experienced at Malaba, reforms to modify incentives and simplify selected clearance procedures result in dramatic decreases in border crossing times (Fitzmaurice and Hartmann 2013). Similarly, the development of a joint border post, in parallel with the enhanced cooperation mentioned above, can also lead to substantial decreases in border crossing times, as evidenced with the experience in Chirundu.[4]

Trade Finance

Trade finance is a constraint but does not seem to be the most binding constraint to exporters. Although Zimbabwean authorities and several private operators indicate that the lack of trade finance has been a major impediment to trade expansion in Zimbabwe since dollarization, the evolution of foreign trade and private sector credit since dollarization and closer discussions with exporters may not support this argument. In fact, relative to GDP, the value of exports has dramatically increased since 2009, and at the same time total credit outstanding has grown significantly faster than exports, overall trade, or GDP, averaging about 115 percent annually during 2009–12. During that same period, outstanding credit to the private sector has more than tripled (figure 4.6).

The RBZ data indicate that the combined stock of preshipment and postshipment credit averaged about 2 percent of outstanding credit to the private sector during 2009–12, but was sharply lower (0.35 percent) at end-2012. It grew from US$17.0 million at the end of 2009 to US$63.5 at the end of 2011, but declined to US$28.0 million at the end of the following year, and exhibited substantial quarterly variation during this period (figure 4.7).

Nonetheless, the strong growth of exports and imports since 2009, despite the small amount of bank-intermediated trade finance, could be an indication that financing has not been a major constraint on trade expansion. In fact, viewed against the background of the multitude of difficulties that exporters faced in trying to resume operations and reestablish their market relationships after dollarization, it is unlikely that excess demand for trade finance could have played a major role in inhibiting export growth during 2009–13. Although the available data do not allow a more robust analysis of the existence of excess demand for trade finance, discussions with market participants support this supposition.

The growth of exports has been dominated by a few large exporters in mining and agriculture. Therefore, although trade finance is a constraint, it has not been uniform for all companies across all sectors. In fact, bank-intermediated trade finance has been available almost uniquely for major exporters, especially those in the tobacco, cotton, sugar, fuel, and mineral sectors, but not for other firms.[5] In 2010, the bulk of trade finance (pre- and postshipment financing) funded agriculture (47 percent), especially tobacco and cotton, followed by mining (about 34 percent), especially gold and chrome (figure 4.8).

Manufacturing received only a small portion of trade financing. It could be argued, therefore, that trade finance could have been a more significant constraint for exporters not tied to global or regional value chains (like tobacco and cotton) and for small and medium exporters, mostly in manufacturing.[6] However, the main impediment to the export activities of these firms has been their inability to expand production and remain competitive, in part because of a lack of access to medium- and long-term finance rather than trade finance.

Figure 4.6 External Trade and Credit, 2008–12

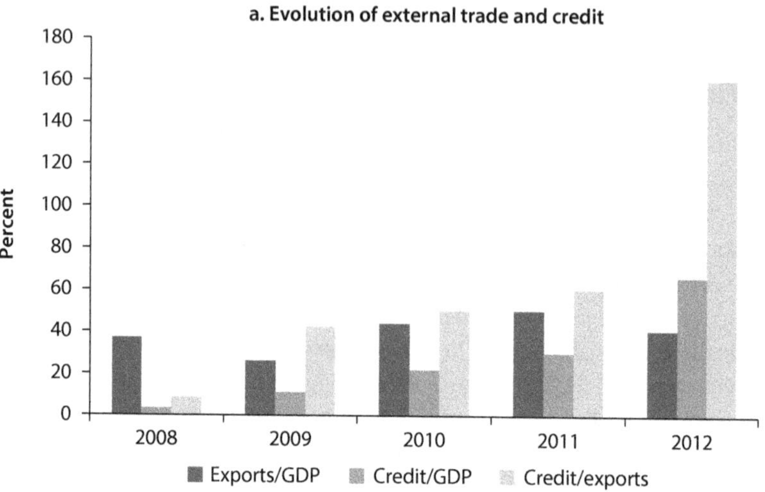

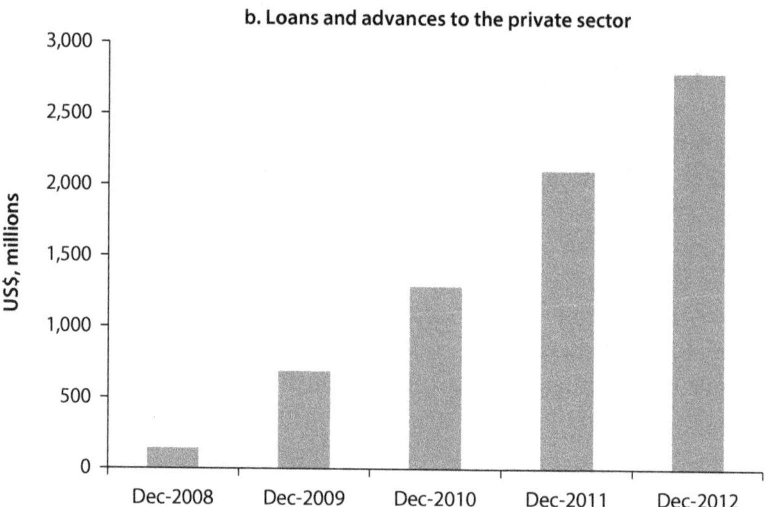

Source: Hove, Mawadza, and Vaez-Zadeh 2013.

Policy Options to Improve Connectivity

Improving connectivity by reducing transport costs and delays within the existing challenging environment and against a background of firms experiencing difficulties competing with imports from both the region and globally requires a coherent approach to reforming the policies, regulations, and institutions that could serve to reduce the cost of obtaining inputs, whether from overseas or sourced domestically. Some of the measures that follow involve minimal costs and can be done with relative alacrity—for example, lowering policy barriers to increase entry and competition in state monopolized sectors—while others

Figure 4.7 Zimbabwe: Pre- and Postshipment Credit Outstanding

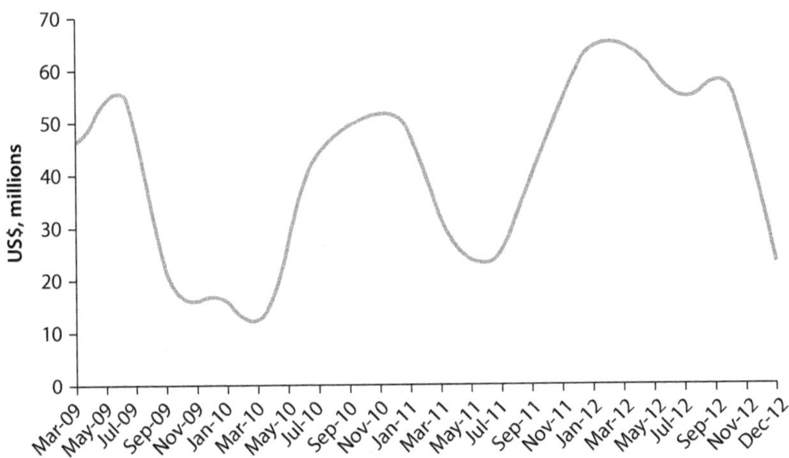

Source: Hove, Mawadza, and Vaez-Zadeh 2013.

Figure 4.8 Zimbabwe: Sectoral Distribution of Pre- and Postshipment Financing, 2010
Percent

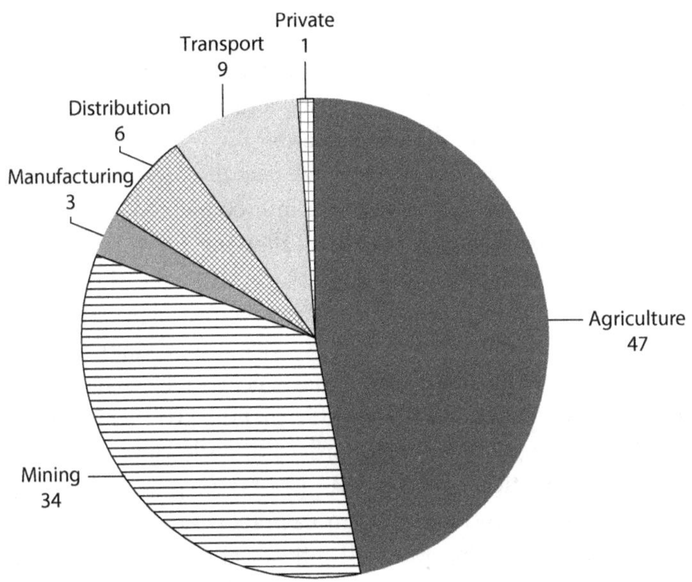

Source: Reserve Bank of Zimbabwe data at http://www.rbz.co.zw/.

require more sustained efforts. Policy options ranging from the quick and costless to the more long term include the following:

Revise the operation of state monopolies and introduce measures that increase competition and attract capital. For the rail system, revamping the board of directors and management of the rails system to make it an independent corporation with independent decision making designed to achieve specific profit and investment targets would mark an important beginning. Clear policies regarding (1) third-party operations and determination of track access charges, (2) contracts for public service obligations, and (3) parity between the road and rail services with respect to financing arrangements for maintenance of the infrastructure are needed to enhance the effectiveness and efficiency of rail transport. Similarly, concessioning additional rail lines to private operators would help.

Implement regional protocols in road transport and work to make them more conducive to competition. It is important that Zimbabwe (and its regional partners) expeditiously implement all regional transport protocol provisions, including those of the SADC Protocol on Transport, Communication, and Meteorology. Doing so would strengthen the regional integrated approach to transport management, thereby facilitating the provision of seamless regional traffic. Meanwhile, the bilateral agreement between Zimbabwe and South Africa restricts the transport of bilateral trade to carriers. Zimbabwe has also signed bilateral road-transport agreements (BRTAs) with Botswana, the Democratic Republic of Congo, Malawi, Mozambique, Namibia, South Africa, Tanzania, and Zambia. Cabotage is prohibited in accordance with the "third-country rule" enshrined in the BRTAs, unless authorized by the competent authority. These rules most adversely affect the landlocked countries, and Zimbabwe should seek to reduce their restrictiveness. Zimbabwe is also committed to a range of road-sector activities designed to promote regional integration in accordance with the SADC Protocol. These include harmonization of road signs, harmonization of drivers' licenses, provision of one-stop border posts, and upgrading of trunk roads to comply with SADC technical design standards.

Regional cooperation in the rail system could lead to efficiencies and new competition. In principle, Zimbabwe's railways are interconnected with other national networks along the North-South Corridor, allowing for through traffic across South Africa, Tanzania, Zambia, and Zimbabwe. But even though the rails are physically connected and of compatible gauge, reciprocal access rights between operators that would allow through train service are lacking, and there are no arrangements for servicing other operators' locomotives that may experience technical difficulties (Pushak and Briceño-Garmendia 2011). Locomotives therefore need to be exchanged at national borders, often leading to extensive delays due to shortages in traction capacity. EIU (2008) suggests that in neighboring Zambia, the operator Rail Systems of Zambia practices discriminatory pricing for rail freight, which is distorting rail traffic flows along the entire North-South Corridor, including those experienced by the NRZ. Reforms at home would strengthen Zimbabwe's hand in negotiating the deeper integration of railway markets in which it has a large stake.

Reducing delivery times and transport costs is essential. This effort might include streamlining procedures at the border posts to allow for advance clearance and introducing the Authorized Economic Operator facility for precleared companies, eliminating licensing for all but the most sensitive products, developing an online trade information portal containing all required trade information, publishing data on cross-border delays, inviting dialogue with users and small businesses on trade facilitation, and establishing a process of subjecting all regulations to regulatory impact assessments. These measures would allow all border agencies, Zimbabwe's in particular, to reduce forms and save multiple agencies from having to check the same goods, collect fees, and require identical information to be completed multiple times. Establishing more one-stop border posts could also reduce the long delays common at borders. Because of its importance to Zimbabwe, these efforts should focus on reducing delays in the North-South Corridor with South Africa as well as in the links with the east coast to facilitate trade with China and the European Union.

Increasing investment in infrastructure is critical. Rehabilitating infrastructure is imperative to reduce the high transport costs in Zimbabwe. New road and rail links also need to be constructed to cope with the rising trade business. Various studies have proposed specific priorities for roads, rails, and air facilities. These studies should be evaluated and, in a capital-scarce environment, ranked by estimated social rates of return. This ranking may require sophisticated techniques of capital budgeting and project planning in the public sector.

Attract foreign direct investment for infrastructure. It seems unlikely that domestic resources will be sufficient to promote adequate investment, so moving forward with efforts to attract foreign capital into infrastructure on a competitive basis would be helpful. Doing so requires attention to the overall investment climate (especially for projects with long gestation periods) and a well-developed regulatory framework. Given recent history and the needed policy changes, these efforts will take some time to show results. A high priority is to eliminate restrictions on foreign ownership in the sector.

Annex 4A

Table 4A.1 Government Agencies Involved in Cross-Border Approvals

	EMA	*Immigration*	*MOHCW*	*MOT-VID*	*PQS*	*VET*	*ZIMRA*	*ZRP*
Border Post								
Beitbridge	Y	Y	Y	Y	Y	Y	Y	Y
Chirundu	Y	Y	Y	Y	Y	Y	Y	Y
Victoria Falls	Y	Y	N	Y	Y	Y	Y	Y
Kariba	Y	Y	Y	Y	Y	Y	Y	Y
Kazungula	Y	Y	N	Y	N	Y	Y	Y
Plumtree	Y	Y	Y	Y	Y	Y	Y	Y
Nyamapanda	Y	Y	N	Y	Y	Y	Y	Y
Forbes	Y	Y	Y	Y	Y	Y	Y	Y
Harare Airport	Y	Y	Y	Y	Y	Y	Y	Y
Nkomo Airport	Y	Y	Y	Y	Y	Y	Y	Y
Victoria Falls Airport	Y	Y	Y	Y	Y	Y	Y	Y

Source: Zimbabwe Revenue Authority 2012.
Note: EMA = Environmental Management Agency; MOHCW = Ministry of Health and Child Welfare; MOT-VID = Ministry of Transport Vehicle Inspection Department; PQS = Plant Quarantine Service; VET = Department of Veterinary Services; ZIMRA = Zimbabwe Revenue Authority; and ZRP = Zimbabwe Republic Police.

Notes

1. Doing Business figures are based on a standard 20-foot container that weighs 20 tons, is valued at $10,000, and does not require any special handling or refrigeration to and from Zimbabwe. Because the particularities of the containers involved in actual trade transactions could differ considerably from the standard considered, we use the Doing Business estimate as a general reference on the evolution of transport costs. In fact, consistent with the evidence presented in the Doing Business estimates, the considerable increase in transport costs has also been acknowledged in interviews with exporters in the country.
2. Goods transported by rail in Zimbabwe include coal, fertilizer, chrome ore, ferro alloys, granite, raw sugar, maize, and wheat. Mining products account for about 40 percent of freight, agriculture about 35 percent, and manufactures about 15 percent (Masiiwa and Giersing 2012).
3. The Integrated Border Management strategy is being coordinated and overseen by the Ministry of Regional Integration and International Cooperation. The National Integrated Border Management Steering Committee comprises all the public agencies involved in cross-border trade and representatives from the private sector. The draft strategy plan notes how the Ministry of Industry, ZIMRA, and the Ministry of Finance all publish new regulations and government orders and recognizes that these occur without effective coordination and dialogue between the different agencies at the border.
4. A one-stop border crossing was initiated at Chirundu on the Zimbabwe-Zambia border in December 2009. This border post was heavily congested—total border crossing times in 2007 were recorded as being more than 35 hours northbound and approximately 15 hours southbound. Customs accounted for about 60 percent of this time, largely because there were no preclearance arrangements, but there were also long waiting times for payment of duties in the northbound direction, while different axle load limits in the two countries meant that inspection of trucks had to be carried out at weighbridges on both sides of the border. The two governments set up a one-stop border post that expedited movement through a common control zone; improved efficiencies through office locations and work flow procedures; and provided equipment to undertake preclearance of persons, vehicles, and goods. The effort paid off: clearance times for buses and autos were reported to have been reduced by one-half; commercial trucks that used to take five days to clear are now routinely cleared in less than 24 hours, and those in the fast lane are cleared in less than 5 hours.
5. These larger export firms have been the main clients of major banks (because these banks have tried to limit their exposure by lending to these types of firms only) and their export activities have not been hampered by a lack of export financing. Some of these firms have access to foreign borrowing as well. Direct foreign borrowing by firms is subject to RBZ approval.
6. Davies, Kumar, and Shah (2012) find that firm size is highly correlated with the likelihood of obtaining credit, and firms in the food and light manufacturing sectors are more likely to get supplier credit than are firms in other sectors. The government schemes Zimbabwe Economic and Trade Revival Fund (ZETREF) and Distressed and Marginalized Areas Fund (DIMAF) provide financing to smaller firms through banks, but disbursement rates have been low at only 38.5 percent and 30.5 percent for ZETREF and DIMAF, respectively.

References

AfDB (African Development Bank). 2011. *Infrastructure and Growth in Zimbabwe*. Tunis: African Development Bank.

Bullock, R. 2009. "Off Track: Sub-Saharan African Railways." Background Paper 17 for *Africa Infrastructure Country Diagnostic*, World Bank, Washington, DC.

Davies, Rob, Praveen Kumar, and Manju Kedia Shah. 2012. "Re-Manufacturing Zimbabwe: Constraints and Opportunities in a Dollarized Economy." Background paper for *Zimbabwe: From Economic Rebound to Sustained Growth*, World Bank, Washington, DC.

Djankov, Simeon, Caroline Freund, and Cong S. Pham. 2006. "Trading on Time." Policy Research Working Paper 3909, World Bank, Washington, DC.

EIU (Economist Intelligence Unit). 2008. *Zimbabwe Economic and Political Outlook: Country Report Zimbabwe*. London: Economist Intelligence Unit.

Fitzmaurice, M., and O. Hartmann. 2013. "Border Crossing Monitoring along the Northern Corridor." Africa Transport Policy Program Working Paper 96, World Bank, Washington, DC.

Hoekman, B., and A. Nicita. 2011. "Trade Policy, Trade Costs, and Developing Country Trade." *World Development* 39 (12): 2069–79.

Hove, Seedwell, Crispen Mawadza, and Reza Vaez-Zadeh. 2013. "Zimbabwe—Trade Finance as an Instrument of Trade Openness: Issues and Challenges in a Dollarized Economy." Unpublished, World Bank, Washington, DC.

Hummels, D., and G. Schaur. 2013. "Time as a Trade Barrier." *American Economic Review* 103 (7): 2935–59.

Masiiwa, M., and B. Giersing. 2012. "Trade and Transport Facilitation Assessment in Zimbabwe." World Bank, Washington, DC.

Mattoo, Aaditya, and Eshrat Waris. 2013. "Zimbabwe: Empowerment through Services Trade Reform." Unpublished, World Bank, Washington, DC.

Pushak, N., and C. M. Briceño-Garmendia. 2011. *Zimbabwe's Infrastructure: A Continental Perspective*. Washington, DC: World Bank.

Teravaninthorn, S., and G. Raballand. 2008. *Transport Prices and Cost in Africa: A Review of the Main International Corridors*. Washington, DC: World Bank.

World Bank. 2012. *Doing Business 2013: Smarter Regulations for Small and Medium-Size Enterprises*. Washington, DC: World Bank.

Zimbabwe Revenue Authority. 2012. "Draft Strategy and Action Plan for Integrated Border Management in Zimbabwe." Zimbabwe Revenue Authority, Harare.

CHAPTER 5

Enhancing Connectivity through Services Trade Reform

Introduction

Connectivity, both domestically and with other countries, is a key determinant of competitiveness. The capacity to communicate rapidly and at low cost, to move goods across borders inexpensively, and to tap into the global flow of ideas and knowledge is critical to rapid productivity growth and rising incomes. Connectivity in the age of the Internet provides entrepreneurs with access to the latest market information and technologies, and allows students access to the global trove of knowledge, a foundation for building human capital. Lowering connectivity costs opens the door to greater participation in global and regional value chains.

Connectivity is also a source of empowerment. Whether it is the small business discovering a new way to increase efficiency; a smallholder farmer using a cell phone to receive weather forecasts that shape decisions about when to plant, fertilize, and harvest; or a young girl exposed to new values that encourage her to gain an education, people can use information to invest and raise their standards of living.

These benefits hinge critically on efficient and modern services. On the one hand, services such as telecommunications and finance as well as air and land transport (the latter discussed in chapter 4) are inputs into production. On the other hand, services can be a source of export earnings, such as with tourism and business process outsourcing (BPO). Several studies have shown that efficient services are associated with more rapid economic growth (Hoekman and Mattoo 2012; Mattoo, Rathindran, and Subramanian 2006). The potential for trade in services in Zimbabwe is enormous, yet by several measures Zimbabwe is missing out on opportunities.

This chapter asks why. It first reviews Zimbabwean experience with services and services trade generally, and then delves into the main remaining challenges in five services sectors critical to exports: telecommunications, air transport, finance, tourism, and BPO.

Services in the Zimbabwean Economy

Services—and services trade—matter for Zimbabwe. The country derives about half of its output and one-fifth of its export revenues from services. More important, services include key sectors such as communications, transport, finance, distribution, health, education, and tourism.[1] Services "trade" is, by its very definition, far-reaching. It encompasses cross-border trade in road and air transport, which are lifelines for a landlocked country like Zimbabwe, as well as information technology–enabled (IT-enabled) BPO services, an opportunity that Zimbabwe risks missing; consumption by foreigners of tourism services, one of Zimbabwe's biggest export earners; foreign direct investment (FDI) in banking, communications, and distribution, which are key backbone sectors for the economy; and temporary migration of accountants, doctors, and teachers, in which Zimbabwe has a two-way stake. It is evident, therefore, that services are critical to Zimbabwe's overall economic performance and the well-being of its people, and that the constraints placed on services sector development by small markets and limited endowments could be alleviated by greater regional and global integration.

In practice, however, Zimbabwe has so far derived only limited benefits from services trade. It has underperformed in its services exports and in widening access to services for its firms, farms, and households. Through the 1980s and early 1990s, Zimbabwe's tourism earnings were slightly greater than Tanzania's; however, by 2011 they were one-tenth as high (figure 5.1, panel a). Exports of BPO, from which its educated, English-speaking population could have benefited as neighboring countries have, are virtually nonexistent (figure 5.1, panel b). From finance and accounting to telecommunications and international transport, access to services remains low and highly unequal—being available at affordable prices primarily to the affluent in urban areas and to larger firms.

The poor state of services access and exports is attributable to contrasting and imperfect policy choices at key stages in the country's post-independence history. In the early 1980s, the government moved aggressively, but unevenly, on the elimination of barriers to entry, sluggishly on the development of regulations to deal with market failure, and only notionally on the implementation of access-widening policies. The result is that both access and exports have been undermined by the persistence of barriers to competition, the weakness and inappropriateness of regulation, and the absence of meaningful access policies in virtually all sectors.

Despite these impediments, services are a mainstay of the Zimbabwean economy. The services sector is the largest contributor to Zimbabwe's GDP. Services accounted for 53 percent of GDP in 2012 (table 5.1). Within services, transport and communications, and distribution, hotels, and restaurants accounted for almost half of the sector's contribution in 2012. However, other sectors are showing great potential. For example, finance and construction grew in importance between 2009 and 2012. Similarly, Zimbabwe's high literacy level—the highest in the region—makes education a subsector with a potentially important role in the economy. This is even more important considering that this

Figure 5.1 Services Export Opportunities in Zimbabwe and in Other African Countries, 2000–12

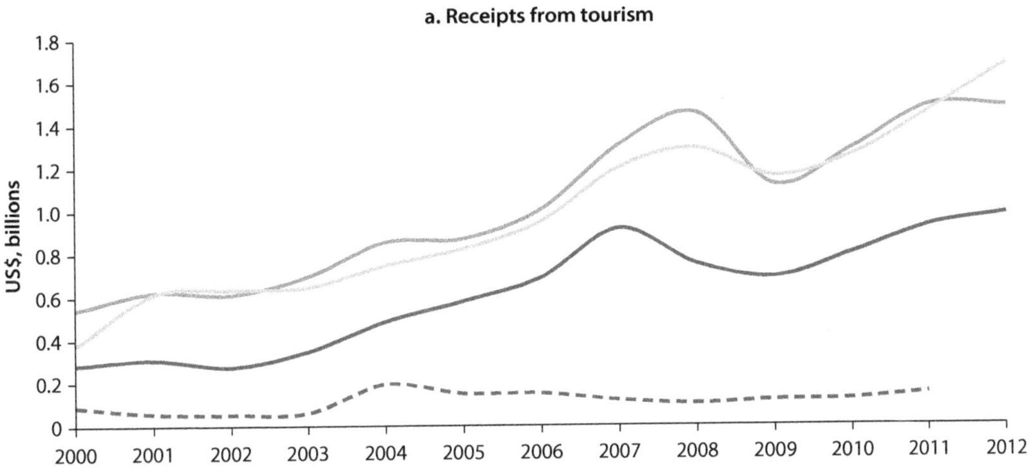

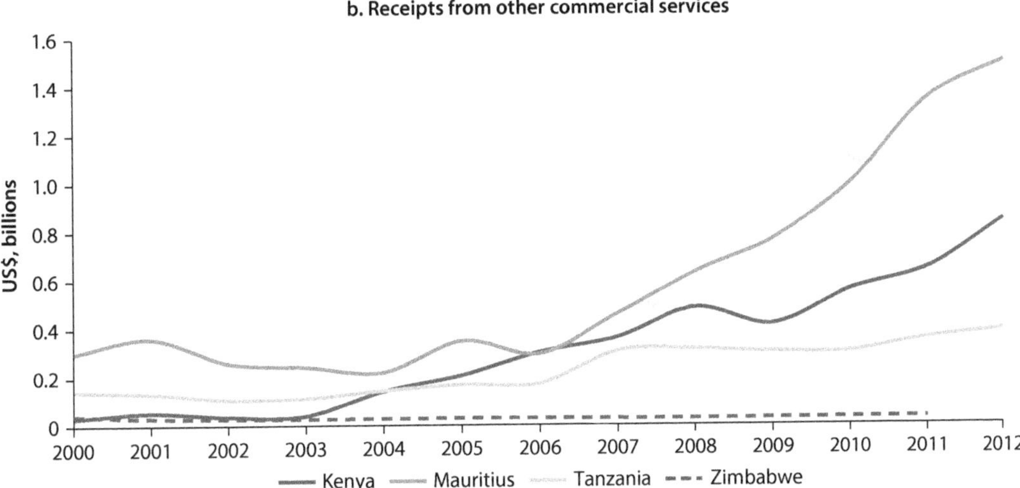

Source: Mattoo and Waris 2013.
Note: In balance of payments statistics, it is the subcategory "other business services" that most closely corresponds to exports of business process outsourcing. Unfortunately, not all countries report data for this subcategory, so the data presented here are for the higher-level category "other commercial services" of which "other business services" is a part.

subsector's contribution to GDP is also showing rapid growth: from a base of 3 percent in 2009, it doubled by 2012.

Trade in services is well below its potential, however. Trade in services lags growth in merchandise trade. Like many developing countries, Zimbabwe is a net importer of services (figure 5.2, panel a). Travel related to tourism is the main services export, while transportation is the main import (figure 5.2, panels b and c). Exports of IT-enabled BPO—a category well exploited by other developing countries—are insignificant in Zimbabwe. Although imports have recovered from previous years' levels, exports still lag behind. Even though travel export

Table 5.1 Sectoral Distribution of GDP, 2009–12
Percent

Sector	*2009*	*2010*	*2011*	*2012*
Agiculture, hunting and fishing, and forestry	13	12	11	11
Mining and quarrying	7	8	9	9
Manufacturing	13	12	12	12
Services	52	52	52	53
Electricity and water	3	4	3	3
Construction	2	2	3	3
Finance and insurance	7	7	7	8
Real estate	1	1	2	2
Distribution, hotels, and restaurants	15	14	13	13
Transport and communications	13	12	11	11
Public administration	2	3	3	3
Education	3	3	5	6
Health	1	1	1	1
Domestic services	0	0	0	0
Other services	4	4	4	3
Less financial international services indirectly measured	(0)	(0)	(0)	(0)
GDP at factor cost	84	84	84	84
Taxes	16	16	17	16
Total	100	100	101	100

Source: Zimbabwe National Statistics Agency, http://www.zimstat.co.zw/.

Figure 5.2 Services Exports and Imports, 1980–2010

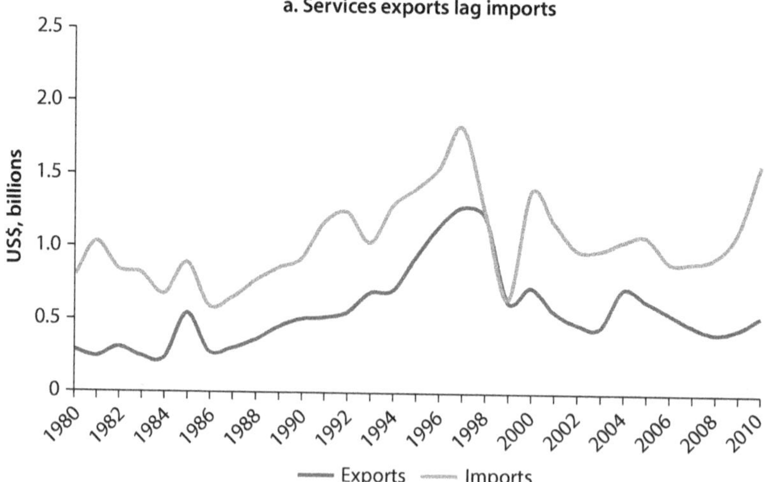

figure continues next page

Figure 5.2 Services Exports and Imports, 1980–2010 *(continued)*

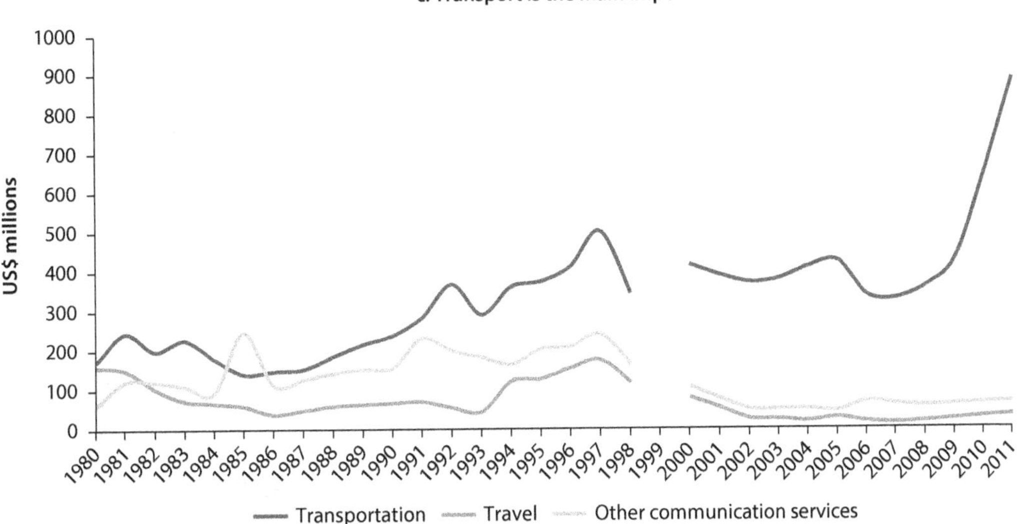

Source: Mattoo and Waris 2013.
Note: Data missing for transportation, travel, and other communication services for 1999.

earnings have recovered from the collapse of the past decade, they still languish at only half their levels at the end of the 1990s.

Why has Zimbabwe not seized the opportunities arising from trade in services? One potential reason is that Zimbabwe has a very restrictive set of policies toward services. In particular, competition in services is highly restricted. Whether at a regional or global level, Zimbabwe has one of the highest levels of restrictions in services (figure 5.3).

Figure 5.3 Services Trade Restrictiveness Index

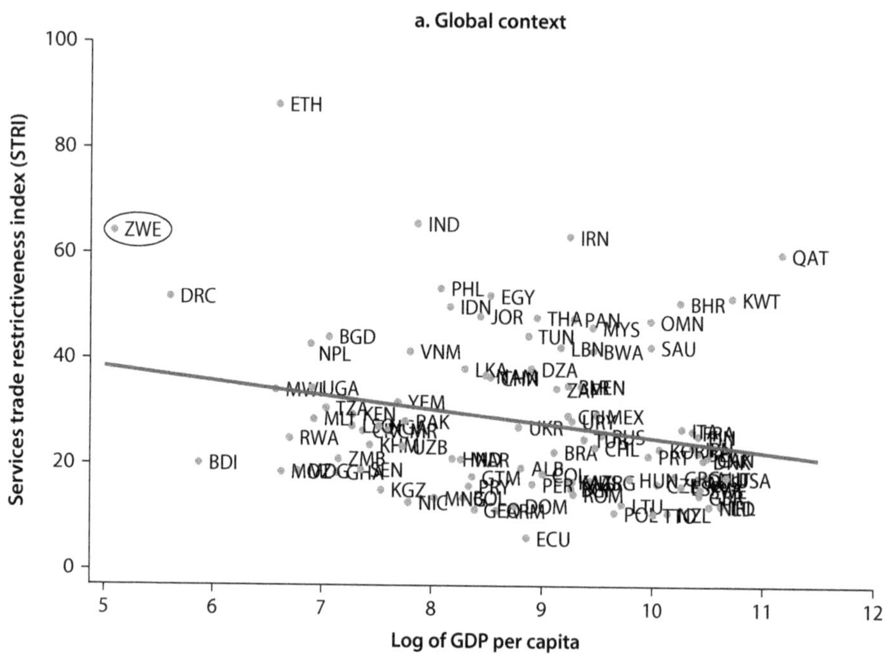

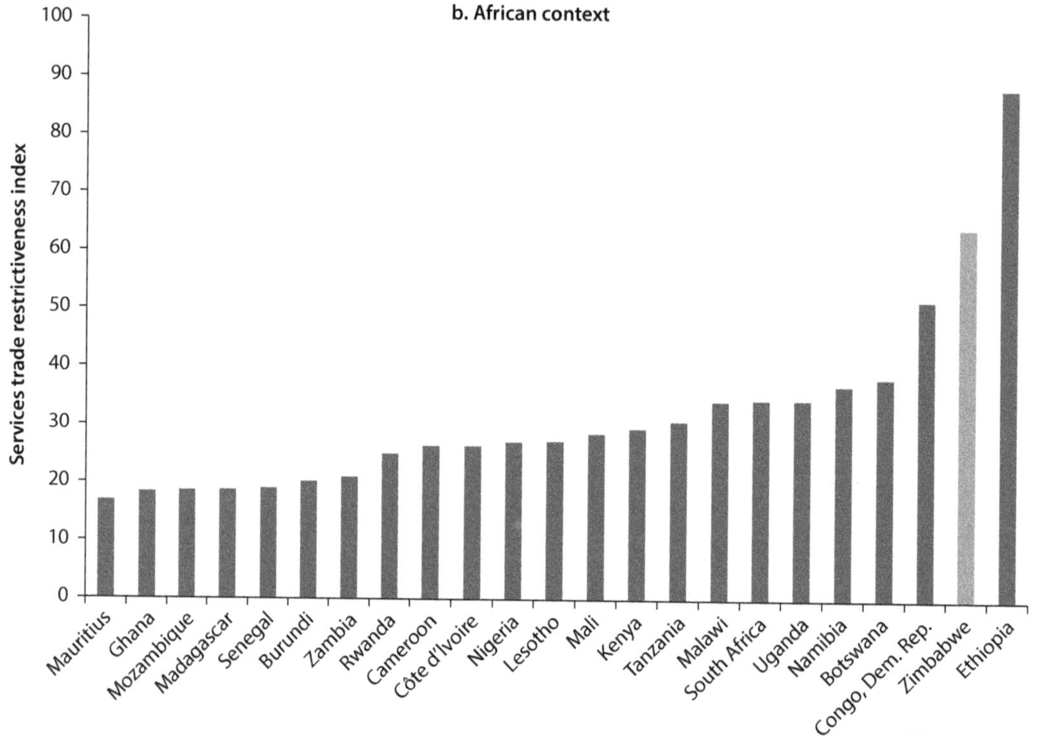

Source: Borchert, Gootiiz, and Mattoo 2012.

Note: In panel a, purchasing-power-parity 2007 GDP per capita in constant 2005 international U.S. dollars.

Three elements that diverge from the global trends observed in other countries make Zimbabwe's services policy highly restrictive. First, the number of services providers in sectors such as telecommunications and air transport is tightly restricted. Second, indigenization requirements (as discussed in chapter 3) limit the potential scope for foreign ownership to bring more competition and technology into the sector. Third, cross-border imports of services in banking and insurance require a demonstration of domestic unavailability.

In addition to explicit restrictions in each sector, another factor detrimental to the development of the services sector is the high degree of regulatory and policy discretion in the implementation of policies. One example is the allocation of new licenses, which remains highly opaque and discretionary across sectors. These policy impediments are common to varying degrees to four critical sectors—telecommunications, finance, tourism, and BPO.

Telecommunications

Lack of competition has hampered growth in the telecommunications subsector, especially in the fixed-line segment. Mobile services are more competitive, although prices are very high. TelOne runs a state monopoly on fixed-line services. As a result, consumers pay high fees and receive poor-quality services. Fixed-line penetration is low (3 percent), and given TelOne's bad financial situation it is unlikely that either line expansion or creation of a national backbone will take place.[2] As of 2011, most of the fixed lines (83 percent) were located in urban areas, while only 17 percent were in rural areas.

The situation in mobile services is slightly different. There are three cellular services operators, two privately owned—Econet and Telecel—and the state-owned NetOne. Econet is by far the largest of the three companies, holding about 70 percent of the market.[3] Each operator has its own network and is responsible for national and international traffic for its network, resulting in a fragmented wholesale market.[4] Operators continue to use very expensive satellite links for international communications, but that is beginning to change.

Mobile penetration has dramatically increased from 13 percent in 2008 to 68 percent in 2011. However, prices are still high even by regional standards (Safdar 2013). The average price of a mobile call in Zimbabwe was US$0.24 per minute in 2011 (figure 5.4, panel a). This price is roughly 500 percent higher than in comparator countries across the region.

Similarly, although there have been some reductions, prices for mobile broadband are still high in Zimbabwe in comparison with regional standards. For example, whereas mobile broadband (via 3G) is charged at US$0.08–US$0.17 per megabyte (MB) in Zimbabwe, in South Africa the price is US$0.03–US$0.04 per MB and US$0.015 per MB in Kenya (figure 5.4, panel b).

Overlapping regulatory authorities stifle performance. Regulation of the sector is divided between two agencies: the Postal and Telecommunications Authority (POTRAZ), which is accountable to the Minister of Transport and Communications, and the Broadcasting Authority of Zimbabwe (BAZ) and the Media and

Figure 5.4 Zimbabweans Pay More to Call or Surf the Web

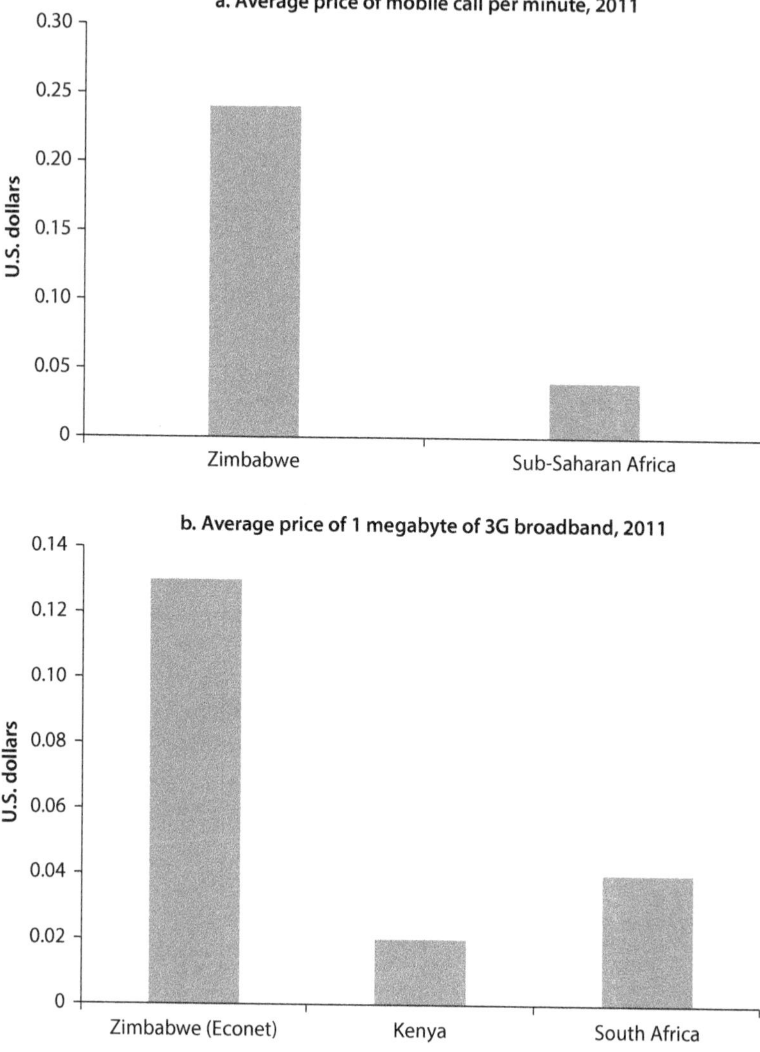

Source: Safdar 2013.

Information Commission (MIC), which report to the Minister of Media, Information, and Publicity. Although these regulatory institutions are meant to be independent, the government has powers to intervene in a range of matters, including connection fees, tariffs, and connectivity targets for licensees. Functions between the agencies regulating the sector overlap and are duplicated, and according to the World Trade Organization (WTO 2011), the fragmented nature of their arrangements impedes efficient development and harmonization of efforts.

Policies in the telecommunications sector are restrictive. The Indigenization and Economic Empowerment Act (IEEA) imposes strict limits on ownership and entry. The Postal and Telecommunications Act stipulates that for a license to be issued, the controlling interest is to be held by Zimbabwean citizens ordinarily resident in Zimbabwe. Foreign-controlled firms are in general disqualified from holding any telecommunications license because the controlling interest has to rest in Zimbabwean citizens. The ensuing maximum foreign ownership of 49 percent coincides with the general requirement of the IEEA of 2008. There are provisions, though, for a higher foreign ownership share on a temporary basis, provided that the license terms include a sunset clause such that a controlling interest will eventually vest in Zimbabwean citizens.

Other restrictive policies follow:

- Approval of the Reserve Bank of Zimbabwe is required for repatriation of earnings and is subject to availability of foreign currency, though these regulations were relaxed in 2009.[5]
- Although incumbent operators can continue to route international calls via Voice over Internet Protocol (VoIP), any new operator can route its VoIP calls only through TelOne, the state-owned monopoly and sole provider of international interconnection capacity.
- Interconnection agreements and prices are not publicly available. Operators are not required to publish their Reference Interconnection Offer.
- Licenses are allocated at the discretion of the regulatory body for 20 years for fixed-line operators and 15 years for mobile operators. It may take up to 180 days to receive a license.

One bright spot is that international connectivity, although poor, is improving. Much of Zimbabwe's international connectivity has been through satellite. In 2010, international bandwidth was 0.03 kilobits per second (kbps) per person compared with 0.11 kbps per person in Sub-Saharan Africa and 1.64 kbps per person in developing countries. Fortunately, vigorous activities are under way—including by Powertel, a subsidiary of the Zimbabwe Electricity Authority—to build out national fiber networks to obtain cross-border connectivity to undersea fiber cable. The recent spate of fiber optic backbone development by a number of private and public entities may help reduce the cost of services and improve connectivity.

Limited progress on utilizing the Universal Access Fund (UAF) has occurred in Zimbabwe.[6] POTRAZ began 8 projects using UAF, and is aiming for 24 development projects during 2012. The pool of funds under UAF is not known, though POTRAZ is reported to have collected roughly US$10 million to US$20 million. Safdar (2013) notes that more work is thus needed to refocus the UAF on the priority needs of Zimbabwe's telecom sector, to overcome procurement challenges, and to effectively design and disburse funds to achieve universal service.

Regional cooperation offers further opportunities. Zimbabwe is one of 23 countries that are participating in the installation of a seabed fiber optic cable between Mtunzini, near Durban in South Africa, and Sudan on the east coast of Africa. The project, known as the Eastern Africa Submarine Cable System, is being promoted by the New Partnership for Africa's Development E-Africa Programme with support from international funding agencies. From Sudan, connections will be made to the Middle East and Europe. Access to this cable by countries on the east coast of Africa, including Zimbabwe, will significantly improve their regional and international connectivity, with reduced reliance on expensive satellite links (Safdar 2013).

Air Transport

Zimbabwe has six airports of entry and dozens of domestic airports with designed capacity to carry 3.8 million passengers a year. However, both passenger and freight traffic declined progressively during the decade-long economic slide to 2009. International passenger arrivals decreased from a peak of about 1.277 million in 1999 to 701,000 in 2009. Freight traffic decreased from 36,015 metric tonnes in 2001 to 20,161 metric tonnes in 2009.

According to Masiiwa and Giersing (2012), during 1997–07, more than 20 scheduled airlines discontinued services in Zimbabwe, including major carriers such as Air France (1997), KLM (1998), Lufthansa (2000), Swissair (2000), and British Airways (2007). Today, a dozen airlines, mainly based in other countries of the region, operate services to and from Zimbabwe under bilateral air service agreements.[7] In addition to the economic downturn, high landing costs and the poor investment climate have deterred traffic.

The country's flagship airline, Air Zimbabwe, which operated flights throughout Africa and a few destinations in Europe and Asia, ceased international operations in February 2012. Its fleet was old and plagued by high maintenance costs and fuel consumption. Five of its eight aircraft had been in use for more than 15 years. The airline was experiencing financial difficulties (EIU 2008), and concerns about the safety of its aging fleet added to its woes. The difficulties increased sharply during the first decade of the 2000s, when the government maintained price controls on air tickets despite the country's rampant inflation. The airline's debt had risen from US$140 million to US$188 million, mostly to the government. In December 2011, it withdrew from flights to London and Johannesburg after one of its aircraft was seized at Gatwick Airport because of an outstanding US$1.2 million debt to a U.S. parts supplier.

The government is reported to have put up new capital of US$8.5 million, which has allowed Air Zimbabwe to service some debt and acquire leases for new aircraft. It was negotiating with London's Gatwick about reinitiating Harare-London service, possibly as early as November 2013 (but had not happened as of November 2014). It is also reported to be entering into partnerships with other operators, including AirFrance-KLM for maintenance and other operational support. The government faces a stark choice: to continue to operate a weak, subsidized state-owned carrier, or to withdraw from the market and leave it to private operators. In June 2013 the Transport Ministry confirmed that Air Zimbabwe had reregistered with the International Air Transport Association following its suspension in 2012 for failing to pass their safety audits, which must be carried out every two years.[8]

Masiiwa and Giersing (2012) contend that the civil aviation infrastructure (especially air traffic control and safety equipment) in Zimbabwe needs rehabilitation and more regular maintenance. The capability for aircraft communication to and from the ground also needs to be upgraded. Weather installations are inadequate, and broadband infrastructure is not available at most airports.

The progressive erosion of the air links, together with the dilapidated state of aviation equipment and facilities, makes it difficult for exporters dependent on air transport to export. Air transport plays a crucial role in the transportation of fresh produce like vegetables, fruits, and cut flowers to offshore markets, key among them being Europe and the United States. But the declining number of airlines serving Zimbabwe, combined with the operational challenges being faced by Air Zimbabwe, has resulted in a dramatic slump in the fresh-produce export business. From a peak of more than US$125 million in 2000, the export value of horticultural products declined to less than US$40 million in 2010, a clear indication that air transport services have to improve to boost horticultural production and exports. Still, since 2010, tourist arrivals have started to improve, which provides better prospects for business in the near future.

Although the underfinanced air transport state monopoly has arguably been the most important policy barrier to air traffic expansion, the restrictions the government imposes on new entry have also undermined competition and service competitiveness (figure 5.5). Zimbabwe ratified and incorporated in domestic legislation, through the Aviation Act (Chapter 13:16), the Standards

Figure 5.5 Services Trade Restrictiveness Index in Air Transport Services (2008; Zimbabwe 2013)

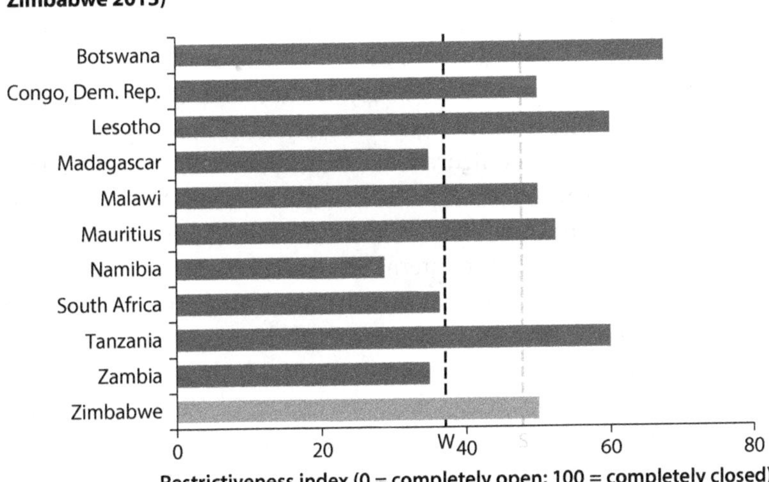

Source: Mattoo and Waris 2013.
Note: S = average of Southern African Development Community; W = average of all 103 countries for which data were available.

and Recommended Practices of the Convention on International Civil Aviation (Chicago Convention), which governs rules of airspace, aircraft registration and safety, and rights of the signatories in relation to air travel. It has also signed and ratified the Yamoussoukro Decision, which means that it is legally bound to the liberalization of scheduled intra-Africa air transport services to the fifth freedom.[9] Entry is also restricted because of the terms of the IEEA, which permits a maximum of 49 percent foreign ownership of a domestic private or public entity. Licenses are required to operate, and the license is available for five years, and although it can be renewed, the process is not automatic. There are restrictions on repatriation of earnings, which must be approved by the Reserve Bank of Zimbabwe (RBZ) and is subject to the availability of foreign currency.

The Air Liberalization Index constructed by the World Trade Organization (WTO) Secretariat (WTO 2006) weighs different provisions of air agreements in consultation with a group of experts on the aviation industry with the view to capturing the relative importance of each provision in liberalizing the sector. The index ranges between 0 and 50; 0 is associated with the most restrictive agreement and 50 denotes the most liberal agreement. The most liberal agreement that Zimbabwe has is with Namibia, with a score of 27. The country's agreements with Australia, Botswana, China, and the United Kingdom are relatively restrictive. The average score for 12 agreements is 7.8 (see table 5A.1 for more details on Zimbabwe's bilateral air services agreements [BASAs]). Not all BASAs are publicly available (for example, the agreement with South Africa is not), and not all details of the agreements are publicly available.

Foreign air transport companies apply to the Civil Aviation Authority of Zimbabwe for landing permission and rights to serve Zimbabwe. These rights are based on BASAs. According to WTO (2011), Zimbabwe has concluded several BASAs, and signed memoranda of understanding are being used to update and specify the details of the BASAs. None of the agreements has so far been deposited with the International Civil Aviation Organization. The carriage of passengers, goods, and mail via a third country is referred to as the "exercising of fifth freedom traffic rights." Zimbabwe's policy is that "this is only allowed on a case-by-case basis and where such rights are granted, reciprocity applies" (WTO 2011, 114). As is evident from figure 5.5, most countries in the region have relatively restrictive policies.

Zimbabwe is a contracting state of the Convention on International Civil Aviation, and as such, part of the International Civil Aviation Organization and the African Civil Aviation Commission. It has no liberal air service agreements such as an open skies agreement with any state. It has started to renegotiate and review existing air transport agreements in line with the key principles of the Yamoussoukro Decision. In 2009, the government of Zimbabwe resolved to implement an open skies policy. According to the Short Term Emergency Recovery Programme, the government hoped to introduce more liberal and less protective air transport policies, and offer competitive incentives to attract foreign airlines in accordance with the open skies policy. The extent to which these policies have been implemented is not clear.

Figure 5.6 International Comparison of Access to Air Transport Services and GDP per Capita, 2011

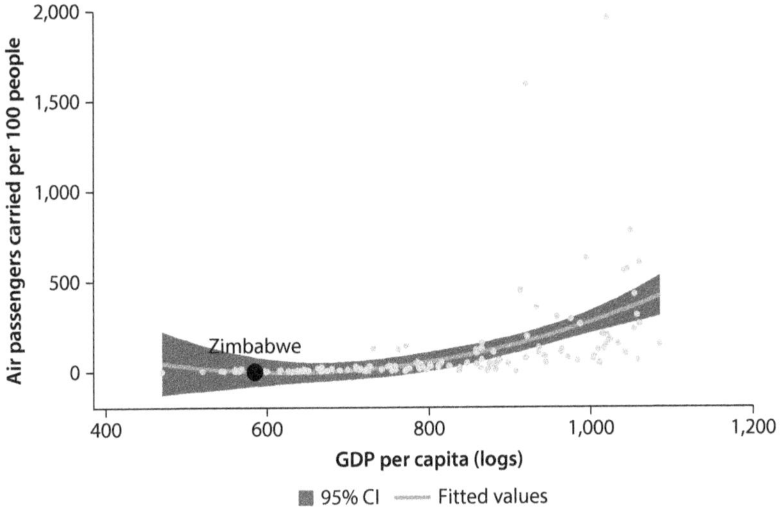

Source: Mattoo and Waris 2013.
Note: CI = confidence interval.

The number of passengers carried per 100 inhabitants is low but in line with countries that have a similar per capita income (figure 5.6). The civil aviation infrastructure, especially air safety and communications, is in need of rehabilitation. In these circumstances it may be worth considering, as AfDB (2011) advises, some form of private participation in airport operations, perhaps through a concession arrangement. The separation of the regulatory function for civil aviation and the creation of an organization such as the Airport Services Company of Zimbabwe that would be responsible for the commercial aspects of airport operations would enhance prospects for attracting potential investors.

During the past three decades, much of the world has moved from a strictly regulated air transport industry (as measured by traffic rights) to a more liberalized one. In principle, civil aviation in Africa has also embarked on a process of deregulation, thanks to the 1988 Yamoussoukro Declaration and 1999 Yamoussoukro Decision. Zimbabwe is a signatory to this agreement and is therefore committed to the liberalization of the international civil aviation regime in Africa. The main objective of the decision was the gradual liberalization of scheduled and nonscheduled intra-African air services, abolishing limits on the capacity and frequency of international air services within Africa, liberalizing fares, and universally granting traffic rights up to the "fifth freedom of the air." Even though the decision was a pan-African agreement to which most African states are bound, the parties decided that it should be implemented by separate regional economic organizations. In general, there has been very limited implementation of this agreement in southern Africa (Schlumberger 2010).

Finance

Finance is one of the most important service sectors in a growing economy. By providing incentives to save and intermediating those savings into efficient investment, a dynamic and secure financial sector can power growth. It is also crucial to trade growth through trade financing.

Since dollarization in 2009, investment in Zimbabwe has recovered but has been confined mainly to publicly financed infrastructure rehabilitation and foreign finance (mainly in mining and tobacco). Despite the recovery, investment remains at levels lower than predicted by Zimbabwe's level of financial development and institutional quality (figure 5.7).

Foreign sources of capital have become increasingly scarce, and banks rely heavily on domestic savings. With memories of hyperinflation and exchange controls still vivid, the role of the financial system has remained broadly confined to the management of payments, with most deposits being short term. The persistent vulnerability of banking institutions and cases of mismanagement that led to bank failures have sent low-level shock waves through the banking sector, contributing to a slower recovery of confidence, which has further constrained the availability of funds for investment.

The policy framework for the financial sector has placed Zimbabwe at the bottom of the list, as the most restrictive in the SADC region (figure 5.8).

Tourism

The tourism sector has experienced an unsteady path to recovery. Tourism is an important services export that has only gradually recovered from declines at the turn of the century.[10] After rising to 2.3 million tourists annually in the early 2000s, a 31 percent fall in visitors to Zimbabwe followed in 2005 (figure 5.9). After an unsteady recovery in 2006 and 2007, the sector faced another major decline in 2008. Tourist arrivals dropped from 2.5 million in 2007 to 1.8 million in 2008.

Tourism has great potential and could be fundamental to the growth objectives of the country. Zimbabwe is well endowed with attractions, including the Victoria Falls on the Zambezi River, which are shared with Zambia. In addition, Zimbabwe has one of Africa's best safari locations and is home to Great Zimbabwe, Hwange National Park, Gonarezhou National Park, Lake Kariba, Mana Pools, and the Eastern Highlands, most of which are UNESCO (United Nations Educational, Scientific, and Cultural Organization) World Heritage sites. Moreover, the sector has links with other industries and makes a significant contribution to GDP, employment, investment, and export earnings.

According to the World Economic Forum's Travel and Tourism Competitiveness Index (Blanke and Chiesa 2013), Zimbabwe ranks in the top quartile of the

Figure 5.7 Investment Levels in Zimbabwe and Other Developing Economies

a. Gross fixed investment rate and financial development (developing economies, 2010, and Zimbabwe, 2008–11)

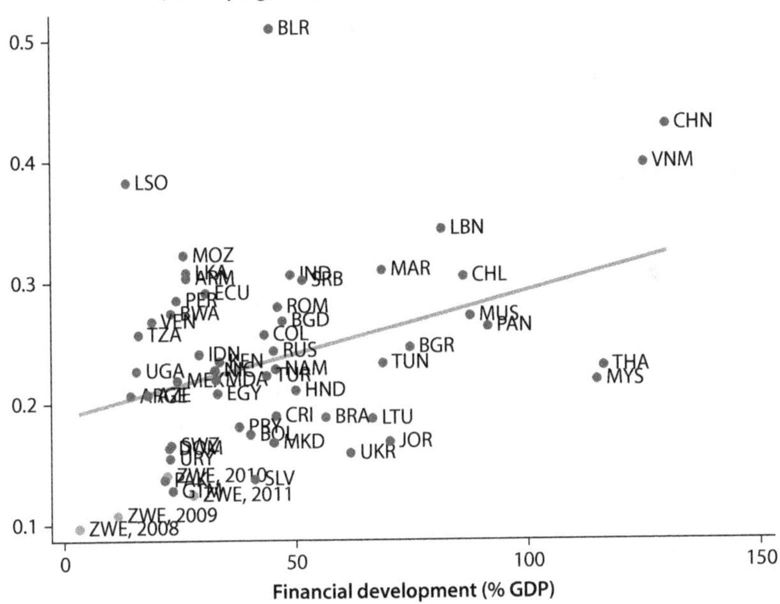

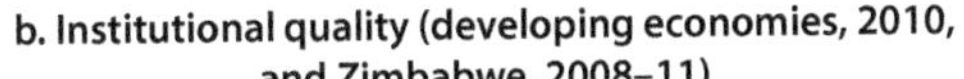
b. Institutional quality (developing economies, 2010, and Zimbabwe, 2008–11)

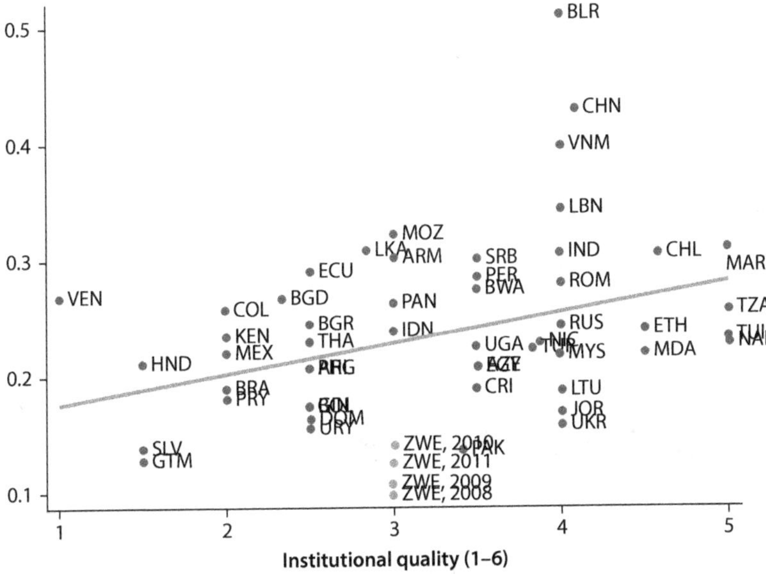

Source: Lim and Pommerenke 2012.

Figure 5.8 Services Trade Restrictiveness Index: Financial Services, 2008

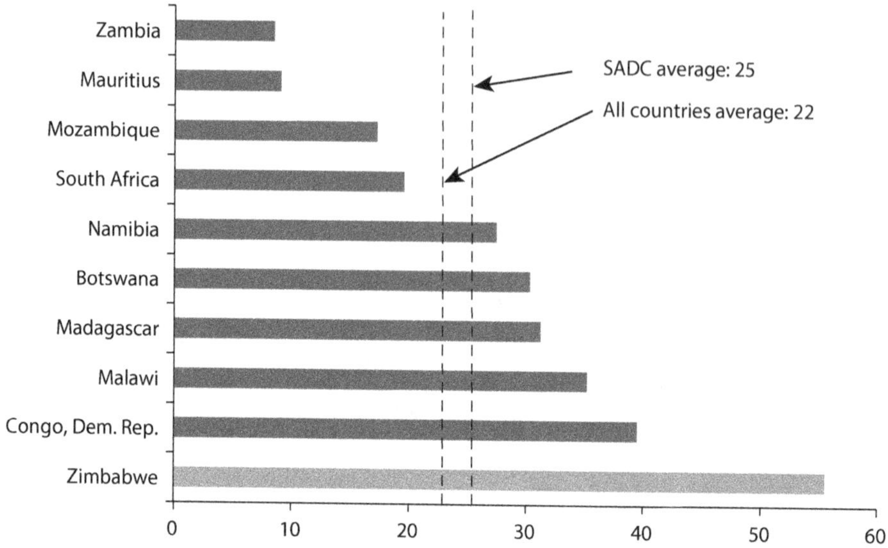

Zambia
Mauritius
Mozambique
South Africa
Namibia
Botswana
Madagascar
Malawi
Congo, Dem. Rep.
Zimbabwe
SADC average: 25
All countries average: 22
0
10
20
30
40
50
60
Restrictiveness index (0 = completely open; 100 = completely closed)

Source: Borchert, Gootiiz, and Mattoo 2012.
Note: SADC = Southern African Development Community.

Figure 5.9 Tourist Arrivals in Zimbabwe and Major Events, 1990–2012

Million arrivals
3.0
2.5
2.0
1.5
1.0
0.5
0
1990
1991
1992
1993
1994
1995
1996
1997
1998
1999
2000
2001
2002
2003
2004
2005
2006
2007
2008
2009
2010
2011
2012

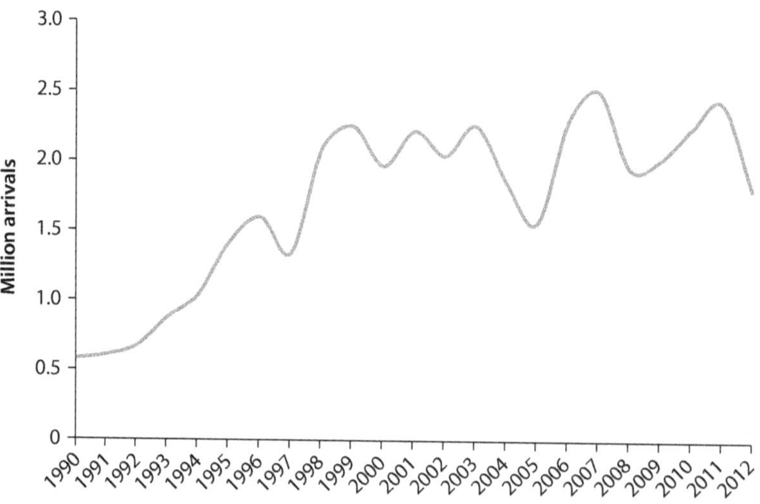

Source: Mattoo and Waris 2013.

133 countries included in the survey as measured by the attractiveness of its natural resources. For example, it is ranked 25th in number of World Heritage natural sites (table 5.2).

However, an unfavorable business environment stifles the sector's growth, and the policy environment limits the potential arising from the natural environment. Zimbabwe ranks 138th out of the 140 countries surveyed with regard to the

Table 5.2 Zimbabwe's Ranking in the Travel and Tourism Competitiveness Index

Series	*Rank Zimbabwe*[a]	*Score Zimbabwe*	*Best performer*	*Score of best performer*
Natural resources	22	4.9[b]	Brazil	6.2
Number of World Heritage natural sites	25	2.0	Australia	16.0
Quality of the natural environment	47	5.0[b]	Austria	6.7
Total known species	39	886	Brazil	3,188
Terrestrial biome protection (0–17 percent)	19	17	Zambia	17.0

Source: Data from Blanke and Chiesa 2013.
a. Total rank of 140 economies.
b. Scores are normalized on a 1–7 scale (1 lowest, 7 highest).

domestic policy environment (the regulatory framework) for tourism. It ranks 116th for the business environment and infrastructure support for tourism and travel, and 127th for air transport infrastructure (Blanke and Chiesa 2013).

The WTO (2011) observes that the main challenges and constraints in the sector include negative publicity; poor state of roads; poor maintenance of infrastructure, and water and electricity shortages; few direct flights to and from source markets; and shortages and high cost of utilities, all of which render tourism uncompetitive regionally. The sector has also been weakened by the departure of many experienced workers to South Africa in the years leading up to the 2010 World Cup. This "brain drain" combined with limited vocational and technical training capacity has handicapped the sector, limiting its ability to compete effectively with other African destinations.

In addition, other uncompetitive services also contribute to the hobbling of tourism development. Efficient telecommunications and air transport are particularly important to the development of the tourist industry. The Air Zimbabwe state monopoly has kept internal prices high and reduced frequency and dependability of flights. As explained above, recent efforts to revitalize its activities with foreign participation may improve its service. Nonetheless, prices and service are still less advantageous than in neighboring markets.

Business Process Outsourcing

Given Zimbabwe's existing resources, the development of BPO services has enormous potential.[11] Although BPO or more generally IT-based services, exports have grown significantly in many developing countries—including some in southern Africa, such as Kenya and Mauritius—in Zimbabwe this services industry remains a virtual infant.[12] The call center industry in Zimbabwe is close to nonexistent.

This situation is puzzling given the combination of resources available in the country.[13] For instance, Zimbabwe has one of Africa's highest literacy rates at more than 90 percent, and the population is believed to be better educated than the African average, although the exodus of teachers to other countries may have hurt this status. Declining government expenditure on education and weaknesses in educational infrastructure have added to the challenges of producing high-quality university graduates. Nevertheless, it has been estimated that of the recent population of university graduates, 44,000 are ready to be hired in the IT-based services industry, which includes all four subsectors in figure 5.10, panel a, and another 60,000 can be hired after training, out of an available population of 151,000 university graduates from recent years.

English is spoken throughout the country, and skills are better suited for data services or voice services in the lower-technology segments of the IT-based services, given that a large number of university graduates in Zimbabwe specialize in general disciplines rather than technical disciplines. Of the talent pool that is ready to be hired or trainable, roughly 70 percent can be recruited in data services and another 18 percent in voice services (figure 5.10, panel b).

With regard to infrastructure, recent investments in fiber backbone networks may improve the situation significantly in telecommunications. Also, the fact that Zimbabwe allows VoIP makes phone connectivity easier and cheaper.

Although measuring the effectiveness of enabling institutions is difficult, the environment for doing business provides a broad indication. Zimbabwe's rankings in 2012 and 2013 on the World Bank's Doing Business Indicators do not offer great encouragement to potential investors (figure 5.11). In 2013, Zimbabwe ranked even lower in the overall Ease of Doing Business. It also worsened its position in areas such as insolvency resolution, taxpaying, investor protection, getting credit, and registering property. Also, compared with other countries—either neighbors or developed—in BPO, Zimbabwe fares unfavorably on almost all accounts, except for the enforcement of

Figure 5.10 Assessment of Zimbabwe's Talent Pool

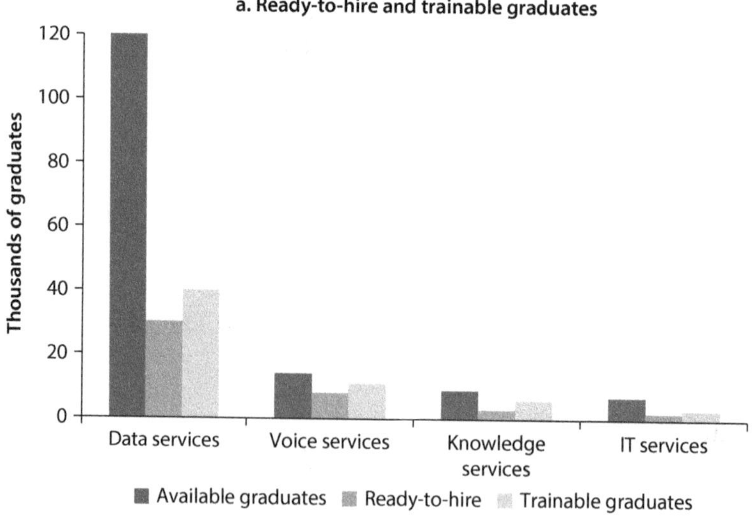

figure continues next page

Figure 5.10 Assessment of Zimbabwe's Talent Pool *(continued)*

b. Ready-to-hire graduates (out of 44,000)

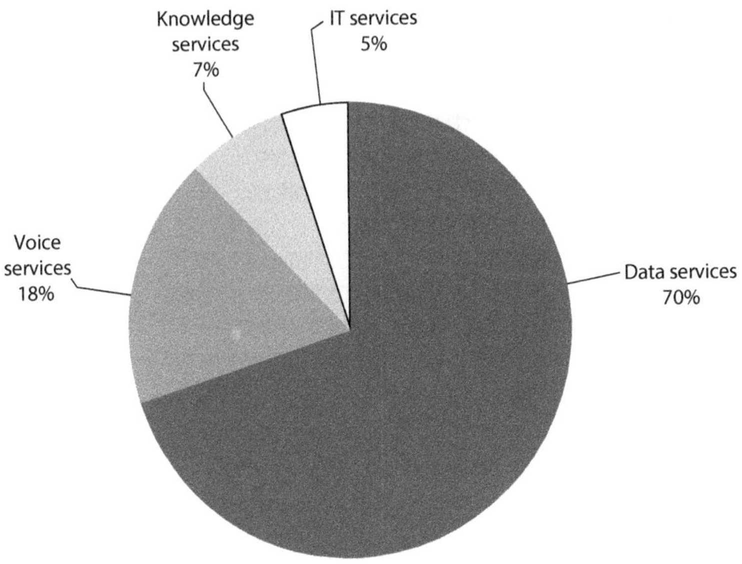

c. Trainable graduates (out of 60,000)

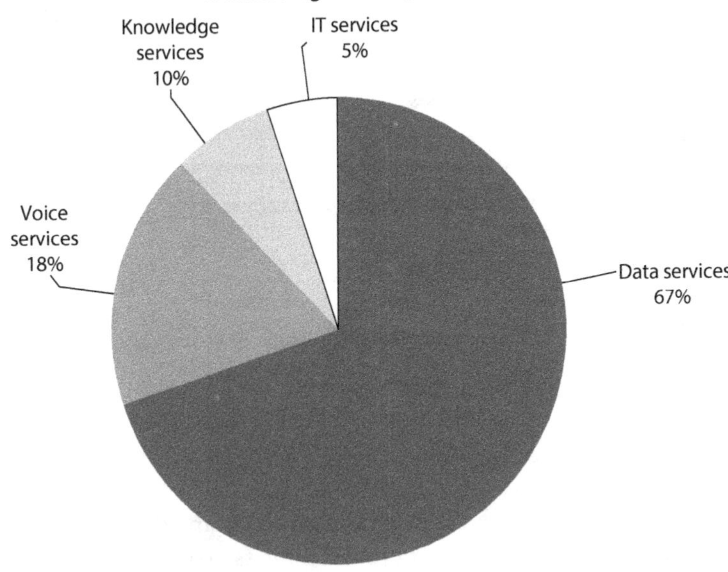

Source: Safdar 2012.
Note: IT = information technology.

contracts (Kenya and India score lower), starting a business (only India scores lower), and getting electricity (only Kenya scores lower).

Despite these negative indicators, there is still hope. The government has eased procedures for starting a business, reduced registration fees, improved procedures for company and tax registration, reduced corporate tax rates from

Figure 5.11 Doing Business in Zimbabwe

a. Doing business ranking in Zimbabwe (2012 vs. 2013)

Resolving insolvency
Enforcing contracts
Trading across borders
Paying taxes
Protecting investors
Getting credit
Registering property
Getting electricity
Dealing with construction permits
Starting a business
Ease of doing business rank
0 50 100 150 200
2012 2013

b. Doing business ranking 2013: Zimbabwe vs. comparators

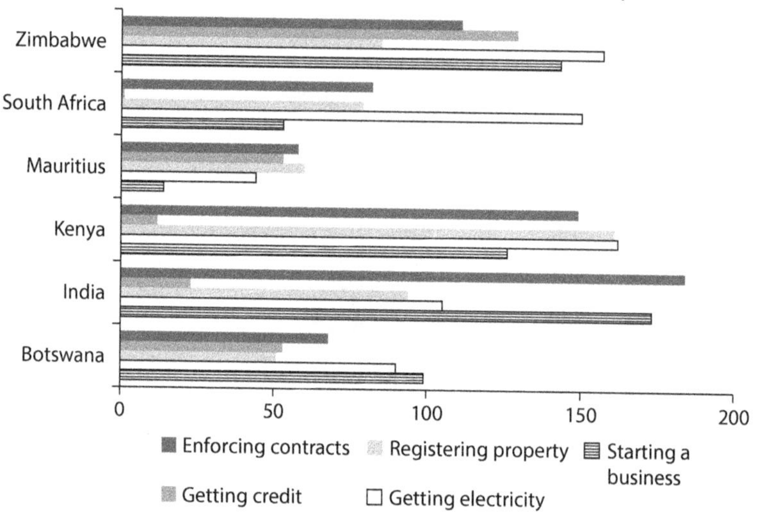

Sources: World Bank 2012, 2013.
Note: In restrictiveness index, 0 = completely open and 100 = completely closed.

30 percent to 25 percent, lowered capital gains taxes from 20 percent to 5 percent, and simplified the process for corporate income tax payments (Mattoo and Waris 2013). Given all these considerations, there may be potential to develop IT-based services in Zimbabwe, particularly in data and voice services.

Policy Options

Zimbabwe, a landlocked country, is entering a 21st century global economy in which some of the most dynamic trading opportunities are in parts and tasks—that is, in intermediate goods and services—as part of global and regional value chains. Services trade reform could help Zimbabwe redefine its comparative advantage and transcend the handicap of landlockedness by unleashing a connectivity revolution driven by telecommunications, finance, and air and land transport services, and a skills revolution driven by institutions of higher education. Services reform in one sector often benefits productivity and paves the way for exports in another. A modern low-cost telecommunications system opens the way for competitive advances in BPO. A modern competitive air transport system enhances the attractiveness of Zimbabwean tourism.

A necessary first step is to eliminate impediments to investment and competition in telecommunications and air transport. At the same time, the government needs to actively promote higher and especially technical education to produce the skills needed for the domestic economy as well as to enhance earnings from tourism and to develop exports of IT-enabled services. Deeper regional and international cooperation would magnify the benefits of domestic reforms in each of these areas.

The IEEA and ownership restrictions have inhibited foreign investment in services as well as in other sectors. Less FDI has meant even less competition and has diluted discipline in the functioning of services firms. Less FDI also means more-limited inflows of capital, technology, and management skills, which hurts both domestic availability of services and export possibilities. As a consequence, Zimbabwean consumers are getting either poorer quality, less diverse, more expensive services or more limited access to services, and in some cases all of the above. An often repeated maxim of Deng Xiaoping, widely credited with China's economic revolution, is that "It doesn't matter whether a cat is yellow or black, as long as it catches mice." Similarly, the ownership of services providers matters little as long as they deliver services and create employment opportunities.

Experience from a wide variety of countries has shown that enhancing connectivity through services requires three types of reform (Mattoo and Stern 2008):

- Ensuring competition between services providers by eliminating impediments to entry for all providers, domestic and foreign alike
- Improving domestic regulation so that it is both effective and appropriate
- Strengthening incentives for services providers to create vital infrastructure and to serve the poor and remote

These reform objectives play through the sectors in different ways.

In *telecommunications*, Zimbabwe stands to reap the development benefits of international integration by overcoming the handicap of being landlocked. This it can do by unleashing a connectivity revolution in services based on fiber optic broadband, to boost the diffusion of knowledge and to facilitate exports of IT-enabled services. Pushing for deeper regional cooperation on infrastructure (for example, building on existing cooperation such as the Eastern Africa Submarine Cable System) is crucial. Moreover, the regulatory framework could be improved through greater autonomy for the regulator and a more coherent distribution of responsibilities between regulatory agencies. In particular, a clearer interconnection policy could help foster more efficient interconnection between operators, and a policy toward infrastructure sharing can help avoid duplication of infrastructure and help direct investment toward underserved areas. Finally, the UAF needs to be focused more closely on the priority needs of the sector, and the procurement and disbursement challenges that have plagued such funds in other countries need to be overcome.

In *air transport*, it is crucial to push for open skies to increase competition in Zimbabwe and the region. Zimbabwe clearly has a high stake in more effective integration of the markets for air transport. It should support full implementation of continent-wide liberalization up to and including fifth freedom rights as set out in the Yamoussoukro Decision. Given the slow progress at the continental level, it could focus negotiation efforts regionally, on liberalization initiatives in the Common Market for Eastern and Southern Africa and the Southern African Development Community. In parallel, it could negotiate bilateral air service agreements that have conditions similar to the Yamoussoukro Decision. It could also use various international forums to eliminate protectionist arrangements between third countries, upon whose routes Zimbabwe relies. Finally, as discussed in chapter 4, it is important to revise the operation of the state monopoly and introduce measures that enhance competition in the sector. Such measures could include tightening of the hard budget constraint with any subsidies being incorporated into national budgets, and encouraging the hiving off of money-losing activities that can be performed by the private sector.

In *finance*, the focus on consolidating macroeconomic stability is critical for protecting the gains in the sector since dollarization. One key aspect of this, as noted in chapter 1, is normalizing relationships with creditors such that they reopen Zimbabwe's access to international capital markets. Another key aspect is to take steps to avoid expanding the public sector borrowing requirement for state operations so as to avoid crowding out private investment. There is also merit in supporting financial stability by relieving the banking and financial sector from the additional stress of the IEEA ownership requirements.

However, higher foreign participation by itself is not a magic bullet for improved access as has been shown by Zimbabwe's own experience as well as that of other countries. In Zambia, for example, foreign banks accounted for more than two-thirds of total assets, loans, and deposits, but credit to the private sector was only 8 percent of GDP—lower than in most other Sub-Saharan African countries—and at one point only about 5,000 people accounted for 90 percent of loans in a country of 10 million (Mattoo and Payton 2007). To be successful, opening to FDI has to be accompanied by sound regulations under a stable macroeconomic policy.

Enhancing access to finance, trade finance in particular, requires a number of measures with benefits that will not be immediately observable. However, it is necessary to begin the process. The reform program implicates the three main stakeholders. Exporters should put in place accounting and management procedures that would improve their creditworthiness. The authorities' main tasks include risk mitigation through appropriate macroeconomic policies and creation of a sound business environment, animating the interbank and money market, proper supervision of the banking system, and fostering needed institutions such as credit bureaus and Export Credit Agencies. The banking institutions should develop procedures for proper risk assessment, engage in innovating new instruments, and improve confidence in the banking system though publicity campaigns to reassure the public about the risks and inform them about their services.

Tourism, a sector already on the rebound, could be further promoted by accelerating current government measures for marketing improvement, image enhancement and rebranding, upgrading and diversification of the tourism product, and streamlined customs and immigration formalities, including through the introduction of the UNIVISA for tourists. Specialized institutions are needed to train and upgrade personnel engaged in the tourism industry and direct financial support and marketing support, chiefly to smaller resorts and small and medium tourism enterprises. The government plans to work with the private sector and international partners.

In the development of *BPO* activities, Zimbabwe has been handicapped by a massive brain drain of IT talent to industrial countries, such as the United Kingdom and the United States, and to neighboring South Africa.[14] An improved domestic environment could lure some of this talent back, even as entrepreneurs, as has happened in other countries, and is needed to prevent further emigration of skills from Zimbabwe.

Annex 5A

Table 5A.1 Zimbabwe's Bilateral Air Services Agreements with Selected Countries

Signatory	*ALI ST*	*Distance from Zimbabwe (kilometers)*	*Traffic (passengers)*
United Kingdom	8	8,293	100,000–500,000
China	4	10,898	10,000–50,000
Botswana	19	936	10,000–50,000
Australia	19	11,469	10,000–50,000
Tanzania	0	1,515	1,000–10,000
Germany	7	8,061	1,000–10,000
Namibia	27	1,548	1,000–10,000
Malawi	6	522	1,000–10,000
Mozambique	0	919	1,000–10,000
Netherlands	4	8,211	1,000–10,000
Russian Federation	0	8,214	0–1,000
Romania	0	6,947	0–1,000

Source: WTO Quantitative Air Services Agreements Review (http://www.wto.org/english/tratop_e/serv_e/transport_e/transport_air_e.htm).
Note: ALI ST = Air Liberalization Index, Standard, 2011 (0 = completely closed; 50 = completely open).

Notes

1. There is growing evidence that enhanced efficiency in key services boosts overall economic performance (Hoekman and Mattoo 2012). Better financial services would contribute to an efficient transformation of savings into investment, the deployment of resources to where they have the highest returns, and better risk sharing in the economy. Improved telecommunications would facilitate business connections and the diffusion of knowledge. More efficient transport would lead to efficient distribution of goods within the country and with other countries. More developed business services such as accounting and legal services would reduce transaction costs, which some believe are the biggest obstacle to growth. Enhanced education and health services would help build the stock of human capital, a key ingredient in long-term growth performance.
2. This company inherited a large foreign currency debt when the government separated post from telecommunications as part of a restructuring process that took place in 2001.
3. As in the fixed-line segment, it has been difficult for NetOne to raise capital to invest. In the case of Telecel, the indigenization requirement has affected investment in the company. Although there is more than one competitor, the degree of effective competition may be limited in reality. Safdar (2013) argues that the relatively high prices of mobile services, and the dominant position of Econet, suggest that competition is not yet fully effective even in that segment.
4. NetOne is licensed to operate international gateway services but is not carrying out these operations. Econet Wireless has its own international gateway.
5. Exchange Control (General) Order, 1996, and Reserve Bank of Zimbabwe Exchange Control Directive ECD1/2009.
6. The UAF was created by the government with the ultimate goal of increasing teledensity in rural and other underserved areas. To achieve this objective, the Regulatory Authority sets connectivity targets for fixed and mobile licenses. The general targets for teledensity are at least 10 fixed-line telephones per 100 citizens in urban areas, and 3 per 100 citizens in rural areas.
7. Along with Air Zimbabwe, these include Kenya Airways, Air Malawi, Botswana Airline, South African Airways, South African Airlink, Comair (which is a franchise partner with British Airways), Air Namibia, Fly Kumba, Zambezi Airline, Ethiopian Airlines, and Angola Airlines.
8. *Zimbabwe Daily News*, June 23, 2013, "Iata Lifts AirZim Suspension," http://www.dailynews.co.zw/articles/2013/06/23/iata-lifts-airzim-suspension.
9. "Fifth freedom traffic right" is the right of an Eligible Airline of one State Party to carry passengers, freight, and mail between two State Parties other than the State Party in which it is licensed.
10. Tourism in Zimbabwe is regulated by the Tourism Act of 1996. The act provides for licensing of persons who provide tourism and tourism-related services, a Tourism Authority, and a Tourism Fund. The Tourism Authority in Zimbabwe is responsible for promoting tourism, registration and grading of tourist facilities, and investigations and recommendations to the minister on matters affecting tourism. Provision of tourism and tourism-related services requires a license; to be designated as a tourist facility any place or facility must be graded and registered. It is not clear whether the licenses are burdensome, as, for example, in Zambia.

11. This section relies on Safdar (2012).
12. Zimbabwe in 2011 inaugurated a local industry association for outsourcing. The association is composed of professionals from the local industry and from South Africa. The association would help give more visibility to the benefits and needs of the industry before government officials and private investors.
13. According to Goswami, Mattoo, and Sáez (2012), to understand the basis for developing a comparative advantage in these services, it is convenient to think in terms of three factors: endowments, especially of skilled labor; infrastructure, especially telecommunications and electricity services; and the broader institutional environment.
14. An estimated 3–4 million Zimbabweans lived abroad by 2008, with an estimated 1.25 million of these in South Africa (Crush and Tevera 2010).

References

AfDB (African Development Bank). 2011. *Infrastructure and Growth in Zimbabwe*. Tunis, Tunisia: African Development Bank.

Blanke, J., and T. Chiesa, eds. 2013. *The Travel & Tourism Competitiveness Report 2013*. Geneva, Switzerland: World Economic Forum.

Borchert, I., B. Gootiiz, and A. Mattoo. 2012. "Guide to the Services Trade Restrictions Database." Policy Research Working Paper 6108, World Bank, Washington, DC.

Crush, J., and D. Tevera, eds. 2010. *Zimbabwe's Exodus: Crisis, Migration, Survival*. Cape Town: Southern African Migration Project; Ottawa: IDRC.

EIU (Economist Intelligence Unit). 2008. "Zimbabwe Economic and Political Outlook: Country Report Zimbabwe." EIU, London.

Goswami, Arti Grover, Aaditya Mattoo, and Sebastián Sáez. 2012. *Exporting Services: A Developing Country Perspective*. Washington, DC: World Bank.

Hoekman, B., and A. Mattoo. 2012. "Services Trade and Growth." *International Journal of Services Technology and Management* 17 (2/3/4): 232–50.

Lim, J., and K. Pommerenke. 2012. "Zimbabwe: Financing Investment in the Aftermath of Hyperinflation." Unpublished, World Bank, Washington, DC.

Masiiwa, M., and B. Giersing. 2012. "Trade and Transport Facilitation Assessment in Zimbabwe." World Bank, Washington, DC.

Mattoo, A., and L. Payton, eds. 2007. *Services Trade and Development: The Experience of Zambia*. Washington, DC: World Bank.

Mattoo, A., R. Rathindran, and A. Subramanian. 2006. "Measuring Services Trade Liberalization and Its Impact on Economic Growth: An Illustration." *Journal of Economic Integration* 21 (1): 64–98.

Mattoo, A., and R. M. Stern. 2008. "Overview." In *Handbook of International Trade in Services*, edited by A. Mattoo, R. M. Stern, and G. Zanini. Oxford, U.K.: Oxford University Press.

Mattoo, A., and E. Waris. 2013. "Zimbabwe: Empowerment through Services Trade Reform." Unpublished, World Bank, Washington, DC.

Safdar, Z. 2012. "Assessment of Zimbabwe's Opportunities in the Global Outsourcing and Off-Shoring Market." Unpublished, World Bank, Washington, DC.

———. 2013. "Telecommunication Sector Draft." Unpublished draft, World Bank, Washington, DC.

Schlumberger, C. 2010. *Open Skies for Africa: Implementing the Yamoussoukro Decision*. Washington, DC: World Bank.

World Bank. 2012. *Doing Business 2012*. Washington, DC: World Bank.

———. 2013. *Doing Business 2013*. Washington, DC: World Bank.

WTO (World Trade Organization). 2006. "Second Review of the Air Transport Annex: Developments in the Air Transport Sector (Part II). Quantitative Air Service Agreements Review (QUASAR) (Volumes I and II): Note by the Secretariat." Document S/C/W/270, WTO, Geneva.

———. 2011. "Trade Policy Review: Zimbabwe." WT/TPR/G/252, WTO, Geneva.

Environmental Benefits Statement

The World Bank Group is committed to reducing its environmental footprint. In support of this commitment, the Publishing and Knowledge Division leverages electronic publishing options and print-on-demand technology, which is located in regional hubs worldwide. Together, these initiatives enable print runs to be lowered and shipping distances decreased, resulting in reduced paper consumption, chemical use, greenhouse gas emissions, and waste.

The Publishing and Knowledge Division follows the recommended standards for paper use set by the Green Press Initiative. Whenever possible, books are printed on 50 percent to 100 percent postconsumer recycled paper, and at least 50 percent of the fiber in our book paper is either unbleached or bleached using Totally Chlorine Free (TCF), Processed Chlorine Free (PCF), or Enhanced Elemental Chlorine Free (EECF) processes.

More information about the Bank's environmental philosophy can be found at http://crinfo.worldbank.org/wbcrinfo/node/4.

www.ingramcontent.com/pod-product-compliance
Lightning Source LLC
Chambersburg PA
CBHW082356270326
41935CB00013B/1648

* 9 7 8 1 4 6 4 8 0 4 4 6 5 *